INTRODUCTION TO TEXTILES

INTRODUCTION TO TEXTILES

KANWAR VARINDER PAL SINGH
Department of Textile Technology,
National Institute of Technology,
(Deemed University)
JALANDHAR

KALYANI PUBLISHERS
LUDHIANA - NEW DELHI - NOIDA (U.P.)
HYDERABAD - CHENNAI - KOLKATA - CUTTACK

KALYANI PUBLISHERS

Head Office
BI-1292, Rajinder Nagar, **Ludhiana**-141 008

Administrative Office
4779, Ansari Road,
24, Daryaganj, **New Delhi**-110 002

Works
B-16, Sector 8, **Noida** (U.P.)

Branches
1, Mahalakshmi Street,
T. Nagar, **Chennai**-600 017

110/111, Bharatia Towers Badambadi
Cuttack-753 009 (Orissa)

3-5-1108, Narayanaguda, **Hyderabad**-500 029 (A.P.)

10/2B, Ramanath Mazumdar Street,
Kolkata-700 009

P-30293 03

First Edition,2004

Reprinted, 2019

Laser Graphics :
(TEXTILE-INTRODUCTION)
Pyramid Enterprises
215-Sangam Complex, Milap Chowk,
Jalandhar-144001. Ph.: 0181-2401913

ISBN 81-272-1766-2

PRINTED IN INDIA
At Kalyani Printings B-15, Sector 8, NOIDA (U.P.)
and Published by Mrs. Usha Raj Kumar for
Kalyani Publishers, New Delhi-110 002

PREFACE

This book is an attempt to introduce the students with the field of Textiles. It provides the elementary knowledge of different types of natural & man-made fibres and its properties.

The book has discussed the different types of yarns including fancy yarns commonly used in the textile & garment industry.

Different methods of fibre indeitification are also discussed.

The different methods of yarn formation both convetional & non-conventional are discussed along with the process of conversion of fibre to fabric.

Therefore, this book provides the conceptual image of conversion of fiber into fabric & will be helpful to the students dealing with textile, fashion & garment technology courses.

Date **KANWAR VARINDER PAL SINGH**

CONTENTS

1 INTRODUCTION TO TEXTILES

Textiles have such an important bearing on our daily lives that everyone needs to know something about them. From earliest times, people have used textiles of various types for covering, warmth, personal adornment, and even to display personal wealth. Today, textiles are still used for these purposes and everyone is an ultimate consumer. You use textiles in some form even if you are not the direct purchaser. Included among consumers are merchandisers of many types, from the wholesale textile manufacturer and merchant to the sales force in any retail store. Many industries, such as the automobile industry, are important consumers of textiles in various forms. Some other consumers are homemakers, dressmakers, interior decorators, and retail-store customers, as well-as students who are studying for these and various other occupations and professions in which a knowledge of textiles is of major importance.

The merchant, particularly, and all those engaged in the purchase and/or sale of goods must be thoroughly familiar with the merchandise they are handling if they wish to be successful. Only thorough knowledge will prevent the mistakes that are too often made in buying and selling.

A study of textiles will show, for example, why certain fabrics are more durable and therefore more serviceable for specific purposes. It will explain why certain fabrics make cool wearing apparel as well as give an impression of coolness when used as decoration. The matter of cleanliness and maintenance must also be estimated before purchasing, when that is an important factor.

Complete knowledge of textiles will facilitate an intelligent appraisal of standards and brands of merchandise and will develop the ability to distinguish quality in fabrics and, in turn, to appreciate the proper uses for the different qualities. As a result, both the consumer merchant and consumer customer will know how to buy and what to buy, and sales people will know how to render good service to those consumers who have not had the advantage of a formal course in textiles.

Great strides have been made in the textile industry, and have markedly influenced our general economic growth. The prosperity and growth of related industries, such as petroleum and chemistry, and dependent industries, such as retail apparel stores, have produced broader employment opportunities. New fiber blends have been created to combine many of these qualities into new types of yarns with new trademarks There are also new names for the fabrics made of these new fibers and yarns. New finishes have been developed to add new and interesting characteristics to fibers, yarns, and fabrics.

This welter of creativity and the myriad of trademarks present a challenge to the consumer who is sometimes knowledgeable but frequently confused. Yet one need not be. Without being overly technical, this information can be easily understood and consequently very useful to the consumer in business and personal life. All of this information call be adopted for such utilitarian benefits as economy, durability, serviceability, and comfort, as well as for such aesthetic values as hand (or feel), texture, design, and color.

In the study of textiles, the students' initial interest will become all absorbing interest when they discover the natural fascination of fabrics and their cultural associations, particularly when factual study is supplemented by actual handling of the textile materials. The subject will seem worthwhile as they become familiar with illustrative specimens and fabrics and begin to handle and learn to compare the raw materials of which fabrics are made as well as the finished consumers' goods.

THE TEXTILE INDUSTRY

The textile industry is very complex. At this point, only an introduction can be given so as to provide a brief overview for some insight. It begins in agriculture with fiber production of cotton, flax, and other fibrous plants; in husbandry of sheep, other annuals, and silkworms; in mining of metals and minerals; in forestry for wood; in chemical research and production of synthetics. These fibers are processed into yarns and/or fabrics. The yarns are made into fabrics for industrial and consumer uses by various means such as weaving and knitting. The fabrics are converted into finished cloths, which provide particular appearances and performances. These fabrics are made into end-use products, including apparel, home furnishings, and various industrial applications. These products are then merchandised and sold. Every one of these aspects of the textile industry is a field in itself, and there is all interdependency with multiplying effects on other industries.

As one learns about the various aspects of the production of textiles and textile products, it becomes apparent that these activities play a major role in the economy The industry has so many facets that it is possible that the student's interests may develop in the pursuit of a career in one of them For example, consumers require the services of teachers of textiles, home economics, and interior decoration. The latter fields provide stimulating career opportunities in themselves. The retailer who serves them requires salespeople, buyers, merchandise managers, and related personnel who deal with textile products. The manufacturers of these products need fabric buyers, designers, production managers, salespersons, etc. The fabric manufacturers yarn producers, and fabric finishers need knowledgeable people. The chemical industry requires skilled personnel in a variety of areas. All of these fields utilize marketing and advertising specialists to promote textiles and textile-related products.

SEQUENCE OF FABRIC CONSTRUCTION

In beginning the study of textiles, you should have in your hand a sample of a woven fabric. Note that it is constructed by interlacing sets of yarns that run lengthwise and crosswise. It is from the interlacing, or weaving, of yarns that such textile materials are made. A close examination of any one of these yarns will reveal the fibrous substance from which the yarn is made. Such yarns comprise a multitude of fine, hair like fibers or filaments that have been separated, made parallel, overlapped, and twisted together by various processes.

There is a logical development of raw material into finished consumers' goods. Studying textile materials in the interesting sequence of "fiber to yarn to fabric" will help you understand the construction and ultimate qualities of the fabrics with which you will become familiar. Here are the steps in the manufacture of fabrics from raw material to finished goods:

1. Fiber, which is either spun or twisted into yarn or else directly compressed into fabric
2. Yarn, which is woven, knitted, or otherwise made into fabric
3. Fabric, which by various finishing processes becomes finished consumers' goods.

KINDS OF FIBERS

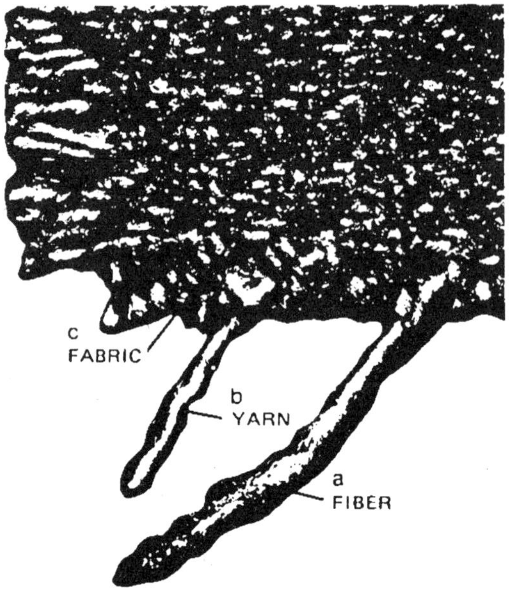

Fig.-1.1 : Many strands of (a) fiber are twisted, or spun, together to form a (b) yarn that is made into a (c) fabric

The textile industry uses many different kinds of fibers as its raw materials. Some of these fibers were known and used in the earlier years of civilization, as well as in modern times. Other fibers have acquired varied degrees of importance in recent years. The factors influencing the development and utilization of all these fibers include their ability to be spun, their availability in sufficient quantity, the cost or economy of production, and the desirability of their properties to consumers.

As a result of the development of new fibers, difficulties arose in the textile industry in terms of nomenclature, classification, and identification. The confusion was compounded by the trend of manufacturers to identify each of their fibers with a different trademark. Consumers became confused by these names and found it difficult and sometimes impossible to identify the fiber content of the products they saw in the stores. Often they did not know whether an identifying name represented a particular *kind* of fiber or a *trademark* for some kind of newly created fiber.

The label act has brought about some standardization, clarification, and easier identification of fibers. For the reader's further convenience, the natural and the manufactured, or manmade, fibers are identified in **Table 1-1** by classifying them according to type, name, and source or composition. A general description of each type is provided below.

Natural fibers that occur in nature can be classified as *vegetable, animal,* and *mineral.* Vegetable fibers, found in the cell walls of plants, are cellulosic in composition. Animal fibers, produced by animals or insects, are protein in composition. The mineral fiber, asbestos, is mined from certain types of rock.

Manmade fibers are derived from various sources. For instance, the natural material of cellulose has been taken from cotton linters and wood pulp, processed chemically, and changed in form and several other characteristics into fibers of various lengths. These are classified as *manmade cellulosic fibers.*

Noncellulosic polymer fibers are another group of manmade fibers. These synthetics have been and are still being created by research chemists as companies strive to imitate properties of other fibers, to develop other characteristics, or to combine certain properties. These fibers are synthesized by combining carbon, oxygen, hydrogen, and other simple chemical elements into large, complex molecular combinations or structures called *polymers.* Chemists, in fact, discover new chemical compositions and invent new substances that they form into fibers having certain desired characteristics.

The protein from such products as corn and milk has been processed chemically and converted into *manmade protein fibers.* However, they have not been commercially successful.

Manmade fibers created from other sources are *mineral fibers, metallic fibers,* and *rubber fibers.* Mineral fibers, such as glass fibers are produced by combining silica sand, limestone, and certain other minerals. Metallic fibers are produced by mining and refining such metals as aluminum, silver, and gold. Rubber fibers are made from the sap tapped from the rubber tree.

TABLE 1-1 : CLASSIFICATION OF FIBERS

TYPE	NAME OF FIBER	SOURCE OR COMPOSITION
	Natural Fibers:	
Vegetable	Cotton	Cotton boll (cellulose)
	Linen	Flax stalk (cellulose)
	Jute	Jute stalk (cellulose)
	Hemp	Hemp or abaca stalk (cellulose)
	Sisal	Agave leaf (cellulose)
	Kapok	Kapok tree (cellulose)
	Ramie	Rhea or China grass (cellulose)
	Coir	Coconut husk (cellulose)
	Pina	Pineapple leaf (cellulose)
Animal	Wool	Sheep (protein)
	Silk	Silkworms (protein)
	Hair	Hair-bearing animals (protein)
Mineral	Asbestos	Varieties of rock (silicate of magnesium and calcium)
	Manmade Fibers:	
Cellulosic	Rayon	Cotton linters or wood
	Acetate	Cotton linters or wood
	Triacetate	Cotton linters or wood
	Nylon	Aliphatic polyamide
	Aramid	Aromatic polyamide
	Polyester	Dihydric alcohol & terephthalic acid
	Acrylic	Acrylonitrile (at least 85%)
	Modacrylic	Acrylonitrile (35-84%)
	Spandex	Polyurethane (at least 85%)

Noncellulosic Polymers	Olefin	Ethylene or propylene (at least 85%)
	Vinyon	Vinyl chloride (at least 85%)
	Saran	Vinylidene chloride (at least 80%)
	Novoloid	Phenol based novalac
	Polycarbonate	Carbonic acid (polyester derivative)
	Polybenzimidazole	Tetraminobiphenyl and diphenyl isophthalate
	Alginate	Calcium alginate
	Fluorocarbon	Tetrafluoroethylene
	Graft	Molecular graft of polymers
	Matrix	Mixture of polymers
	Anidex	Monohydric alcohol and acrylic acid
	Lastrile	Acrylonitrile (10-50%) and a diene
	Nytril	Vinylidene dinitrile (at least 85%)
	Vinal	Vinyl alcohol (at least 50%)
Protein	Azlon	Corn, soybean, etc.
Rubber	Rubber	Natural or synthetic rubber
Metallic	Metal	Aluminum, silver, gold, stainless steel
Mineral	Glass	Silica sand, limestone, other minerals
	Ceramic	Aluminum, silica
	Graphite	Carbon

THE NATURAL FIBERS

Vegetable Fibers

Of the several vegetable fibers, each derived from a different plant, two are recognized as major textile fibers: cotton and linen. (The minor vegetable fibers are discussed in Table 1-1)

a) Cotton

The cotton fiber grows in the seedpod, or boll, of the cotton plant. Each fiber is a single elongated cell that is flat, twisted, and ribbon like with a wide inner hollow (lumen). It is composed of about 90 percent cellulose and about 6 percent moisture; the remainder consists of natural impurities. The outer surface of the fiber is covered with a protective wax like coating, which gives the fiber a somewhat adhesive quality.

This characteristic combined with its natural twist contribute to making cotton an excellent fiber for spinning into yarn. Cotton yarn is used to make fabrics that are universally used for all types of apparel, home furnishings, and industrial applications.

b) Linen

The linen fiber is obtained from the stalk of the flax plant. The hair like fibers, which are held together by a gummy substance called *pectin,* comprise the core of the flax stalk. It, too, has a lumen and is composed of about 70 percent cellulose and 30 percent pectin, ash, woody tissue, and moisture.

Linen fiber is relatively smooth, straight, and lustrous. Linen fiber is more brittle and less flexible than cotton. It is more difficult to prepare and spin into yarn. Linen yarn can be very strong and lustrous, and is used for apparel, home furnishings, and upholstery.

Animal Fibers

There are several animal fibers, each obtained from a different source, but only two are recognized as major textile fibers. They are wool and *silk.* (Minor *hair* fibers-camel, llama, alpaca, mohair, cashmere, vicuña, guanaco, rabbit, and qiviut)

a) Wool

Wool fiber grows from the skin of sheep. It is composed of a protein known as *keratin. Wool is* a relatively coarse fiber. It is crimpy (wavy) and has scales on its surface. Depending upon the breed of sheep, the appearance of the wool varies with some having a great deal of crimp and smaller, finer scales to those having little crimp and coarser scales. The finer, softer, warmer fibers have more numerous and smoother scales. The thicker, coarser, less-warm fibers have fewer and rougher scales. The better fibers with more crimp and finer scales are duller in appearance than the poorer quality wool fibers with fewer scales.

Underneath the scales is the main fiber body consisting of intermediate cells that hold the color pigment. These cells provide the fiber's strength and elasticity. In the center of the fiber is the *medulla,* which consists of spiral-shaped, air-filled cells. Some wool fibers that have no cortical (outer) layer are compensated with a larger proportion of medullary cells. This fact lessens the affinity for dyes, because the medulla has more fat than has the rest of the fiber. The finer wools, having no medulla, absorb dyes more readily.

Two striking characteristics of wool fiber are its susceptibility to heat and its felting property, which is caused by the scales on the surface. Because of this felting property, only pressure, heat, and moisture are required to make wool fibers into the type of fabric called *felt.*

b) Silk

Silk fiber is a fine continuous strand unwound from the cocoon of a moth caterpillar known as the silkworm. While silkworms are generally cultivated, another type, wild (or tussah) silk, is obtained from uncultivated silkworm cocoons. The latter produces a coarser fiber. Silk is essentially composed of protein.

Silk fiber is relatively lustrous, smooth, lightweight, strong, and elastic. Historically, it has always been a highly desired fiber, which has been used for apparel, home furnishings, and upholstery. Its desirability is one of the factors that prompted the production of manmade fibers to simulate silk.

MINERAL FIBERS

Asbestos

Asbestos is a natural fiber obtained from varieties of rock, It is a fibrous form of silicate of magnesium and calcium, containing iron, aluminum, and other minerals. Asbestos is acid proof, rustproof, and flameproof. Consequently, it has been used for materials requiring certain of these characteristics. However, asbestos fiber particles that lodge in the lungs have been found to be carcinogenous and its use has therefore been restricted.

THE MANMADE FIBERS

There are several categories of manmade fibers: cellulosic, non cellulosic polymers, protein, *rubber, metallic,* and mineral. Within each category, there may be found variations designed to provide certain characteristics.

I) Cellulosic Fibers

The three types of manmade cellulosic fibers – rayon, acetate, and triacetate – derived either from the cellulose of the cell walls of short cotton fibers (called linters) or, more frequently, from pine wood. Pure cellulose appears as a formless white substance that is converted by chemical treatment and produced into fiber form. Paper, for instance, is almost pure cellulose.

a) Rayon

There are two principal varieties of rayon now commercially produced: viscose and high wet-modulus. These, in turn, are produced in a number of types to provide certain specific properties. Thus, these rayons have been made to simulate natural fibers as well as to provide characteristics of their own. Accordingly, rayon is used for a wide variety of consumer and industrial products.

Rayon producers sell their fibers under their various trademarks. There are a large number of viscose rayon trademarks and two high wet modulus rayon trademarks: Avril, of which there are three types, and Zantrel.

b) Acetate

This fiber consists of a cellulose compound identified as acetylated cellulose – a cellulose salt. As a result, acetate possesses different qualities from the rayons. A variety of types are produced under different trademarks, according to the objectives of the manufacturers.

Acetate fiber is thermoplastic; that is, it can be formed into a desired shape by the application of pressure with heat. Fabrics made of acetate yarn are rather shape-retentive. They are used primarily for apparel.

c) Triacetate

This fiber consists of an acetylated cellulose that retains acetic groupings when it is being produced as triacetate cellulose. It is sold under the manufacturer's trademark of Arnel.

Triacetate has certain properties that arc different from acetate fiber. It is a thermoplastic fiber that is more resilient than other cellulosic fibers. Fabrics made of triacetate yarn have good shape-retentive properties. They are used primarily for apparel.

II) Noncellulosic Polymer Fibers

This group of fibers is distinguished by being synthesized or created from various elements into large molecules which are called *linear polymers* because they are connected in link like fashion. The molecules of each particular compound are arranged in parallel lines or rows in the fiber, similar to the way fibers are arranged in yarn. This arrangement of molecules is called *molecular orientation.* The properties of such fibers are dependent upon their chemical compositions and kinds of molecular orientation. There are several distinct varieties of synthetic long-chain polymers.

a) Nylon

Nylon is a manufactured fiber in which the fiber-forming substance is any long-chain synthetic polyamide in which less than 85 percent of the amide linkages are attached directly to two aromatic rings. The elements carbon, oxygen, nitrogen, and hydrogen are combined by chemical processes into compounds which react to form long-chain molecules, known chemically as polyamides, and are then formed into fibers. There are several forms of nylon; each depends upon the particular chemical synthesis. They are nylon 4; 6; 6, 6; 6, 10; 6, 12; 8; 10; and 11. There are different types under various trademarks within each of these forms of nylon.

Nylon is thermoplastic, resilient, elastic, and very strong. It is used for a wide variety of apparel, home furnishings, and industrial products.

Aramid

Aramid is a manufactured fiber in which the fiber-forming substance is a long-chain synthetic polyamide in which at least 85 percent of the amide linkages are attached directly to two aromatic rings. This definition indicates a relationship to nylon; the difference is in the percentage of linkage of the carbon, oxygen, nitrogen, and hydrogen amide groups directly attached to the two aromatic rings. Aramid fibers are produced in different forms, each dependent upon the particular percentage of linkage or chemical synthesis.

Aramid fibers are extremely strong and flame-resistant. They are used for certain consumer products and principally for industrial purposes. Aramid fibers are manufactured under two trademarks: Nomex and Kevlar.

Polyester

Polyester is a manufactured fiber in which the fiber-forming substance is any long-chain synthetic polymer composed of at least 85 percent by weight of an ester of a substituted aromatic carboxylic acid, including but not restricted to substituted terephthalate units and parasubstituted hydroxy-benzoate units. In producing such fibers, the basic elements of carbon, oxygen, and hydrogen are polymerized. Variations are possible in the methods of production, in the combination of ingredients, and in the ultimate molecular structures of the fiber-forming substance. Polyester fibers are produced by several manufacturers under their respective trademarks.

Polyester fibers are thermoplastic. They have good strength and are hydrophobic, that is, they do not absorb water well. Polyester is used for a wide variety of apparel, home furnishings, and industrial fabrics.

Acrylic

Acrylic is a manufactured fiber in which the fiber-forming substance is any long-chain synthetic polymer composed of at least 85 percent by weight of acrylonitrile units. By complicated processes, carbon, hydrogen, and nitrogen, the basic elements, are usually synthesized with small amounts of other Chemicals (to improve the fiber's ability to absorb dyes) into large polymer combinations. Variations are possible in the methods of production, in the combination of ingredients, and in the ultimate molecular structures of the fiber-forming substance. Varieties of acrylics are identified by such trademarks as Acrilan, Creslan, Orlon, and Zefran. Each of these has its own modifications, which have special properties and are designed to suit particular purposes.

In general, acrylic fibers have a soft, warm hand resembling wool or cashmere. They are resilient and shape-retentive and are used for apparel and home furnishings.

Modacrylic

Modacrylic is a manufactured fiber in which the fiber-forming substance is any long-chain synthetic polymer composed of less than 85 percent but at least 35 percent by weight of acrylonitrile units. As the definition indicates, variations are possible producing this type of fiber. Modacrylics are made from resins that are copolymers or combinations of acrylonitrile and other compounds, such as vinyl chloride, vinylidene chloride, or vinylidene dicyanide. These chemicals arc made of such elements as carbon, hydrogen, nitrogen, and chlorine, which are obtained from natural gas, coal, air, salt, and water. Trademarks of two modacrylics are Verel and SEF, which, in turn, have modifications.

These modacrylic fibers have similar properties to those of acrylics and are flame-resistant. They are used for apparel and home furnishings. A third modacrylic, Elura, is used for wigs.

Spandex

Spandex is a manufactured fiber in which the fiber-forming substance is a long-chain synthetic polymer comprised of at least 85 percent of a segmented polyurethane. As the definition indicates, variations are possible in producing this type of fiber. The basic elements of nitrogen, hydrogen, carbon, and oxygen are synthesized with other substances to ethyl ester compounds in polymer chains of soft segments or sections that provide stretch and hard segments that hold the chains together. Trademarks of three spandex fibers are Cleerspan, Glospan, and Lycra.

Spandex fibers are extremely elastic. They are used for such purposes as foundation garments, hosiery, swimwear, and sportswear.

Olefin

Olefin is a manufactured fiber in which the fiber-forming substance is any long-chain synthetic polymer composed of at least 85 percent by weight of ethylene, propylene, or other olefin units. As the definition indicates, variations are possible in producing this type of fiber. The carbon-hydrogen chains polymerized to produce this fiber are obtained from the cracking of petroleum. Polyethylene, the original olefin fiber, has been superseded by polypropylene. The fiber is produced by a number of manufacturers under their respective trademarks.

Polypropylene fiber is thermoplastic, resilient, lightweight, and resistant to mildew and many chemicals. It is used for apparel and carpets, particularly for outdoor use, as well as industrial applications.

Saran

Saran is a manufactured fiber in which the fiber-forming substance is any long-chain synthetic polymer composed of at least 80 percent by weight of vinylidene chloride units. As the definition indicates, variations are possible in producing this fiber. Originally, it was produced as a copolymer of vinylidene chloride and vinyl chloride synthesized from ethylene (from petroleum) and chlorine (from the salt of seawater).

Saran is in limited production. It is not suitable for general consumer use but it is used for outdoor furniture and industrial applications.

Vinyon

Vinyon is a manufactured fiber in which the fiber-forming substance is any long-chain synthetic polymer composed of at least 85 percent by weight of vinyl chloride units. This fiber is produced through the synthesis of the basic materials of chlorine, carbon, and hydrogen that are derived from salt water and petroleum. Variations are produced from copolymers.

This fiber is limited to industrial use and to certain bonded fabric applications for consumer use since it has a very low melting point.

Novoloid

This is a generic term for any manufactured fiber containing at least 85 percent by weight of a cross-linked novolac. The composition is that of a phenolic aldehyde. It is produced in crimped and staple form for spun yarn for specialized industrial and uniform purposes.

Polycarbonate

Although polycarbonate fibers are derived from carbolic acid and are chemically related to polyesters, they do not meet the technical description for polyester. Properties vary depending upon the particular chemical composition. Production is limited and dependent upon industrial end use.

Polybenzimidazole

Its principal characteristic is its resistance to heat or flame at high temperatures. It is therefore particularly useful for thermo-protective clothing and related industrial applications.

Alginate

Of minor importance is an alginate fiber made of a Jellylike calcium alginate derived from certain forms of seaweed. It is soluble in water and has been used as "scaffolding" in such fabrics as surgical dressings, which can be dissolved away.

Fluorocarbon

This fiber is polymerized from fluorspar and chloroform and is sold under Du Pont's trademark, Teflon. It is extremely difficult to dye and has excellent resistance to chemicals, mildew, bacteria, and insects. Another type of fluorocarbon is Halar, developed by Allied Chemical Corp. It has been found to have greater strength and better dyeability. Fluorocarbon is used primarily for industrial applications rather than for consumer fabric uses.

Matrix Fiber

A matrix fiber is defined as "a manufactured textile fiber that is essentially a physical combination or mixture of two or more chemically distinct constituents or components combined at or prior to the time of extrusion (i.e., produced in fiber form), which components if separately extruded would each fall within different definitions of textile fibers." Note that the matrix fiber is a physical mixture of its components. It therefore differs from bi component and bi constituent fibers, which are comprised of two or more chemically distinct compositions. Both components of these fibers are whole but adhere to each other to form one fiber.

Graft Fiber

The difference between the graft and matrix fibers is that the two or more components of the graft fiber are molecularly bonded to form a chemical hybrid from which the components cannot be subsequently isolated or regenerated by physical or chemical means. It is apparent that the appearances and characteristics of such graft fibers have almost limitless unique possibilities, although their present development and commercial production are in the early stages and are relatively minimal.

Protein Fibers

The protein from such products as corn and milk has been processed chemically and converted into fiber. However, such fibers have not been commercially successful.

Rubber Fibers

Rubber fiber is a manufactured fiber in which the fiber-forming substance is comprised of natural or synthetic rubber. The treated rubber is produced in strands, so that the cross section is either round or square and the longitudinal surface is relatively smooth. It is used to make certain elastic fabrics.

Metallic Fibers

Metallic fiber is a manufactured fiber metal-coated plastic, or a core completely covered by metal. This fiber is usually produced in flat, narrow, smooth strips with a gleaming luster. It is used as a decorative yarn for various apparel and home furnishings.

Mineral Fibers

Various minerals have been manufactured into *glass, ceramic,* and *graphite* fibers, having prescribed properties for specific uses.

Glass

Natural minerals such as silica sand, limestone, soda ash, borax, boric acid, feldspar, and fluorspar have been fused under very high temperatures into glass which can be processed into fiber. It is produced by a number of manufacturers under their respective trademarks.

Glass fiber is inert and highly flame resistant. It is used for such home furnishings as curtains and drapery. It has many industrial applications.

Ceramic

The fibers are multifilament, are highly heat-resistant, and are suitable for aerospace applications. Two trademarks are Avceram and Fiberfrax.

Graphite

Carbon fiber is derived from a precursor, usually rayon, polyacrylonitrile (PAN), or pitch subjected to high heat under carefully controlled conditions. Such carbon fiber is produced for such highly specialized purposes as reinforcement in airplane and rocket structures, as well as for golfstick shanks. Thornel and Magnamite are trademarks of graphite fibers.

2 CONVERSION OF FIBRE TO YARN

It was discovered that a succession of short fibers could be twisted into a continuous yarn. This was probably accomplished slowly and laboriously at first, but the greater strength thus produced and the many uses soon found for articles made from continuous yarns led to the invention of hand implements to aid and improve the process of twisting and spinning. Many such *implements* and methods are still used by *peoples in* various underdeveloped parts of the world as well as by persons interested in reviving artistic handicraft. At the same time, it was necessary to invent simple methods of disentangling, separating, and arranging the fibers according to their length, other than by just using the fingers. Thus, crude methods of carding *were invented* to separate the fibers according to their length of staple. Eventually, techniques were refined. In time, long filament strands unwound from silk cocoons, and still later, filaments formed by chemical synthesis were made into yarns. Now yarns are also made by integrating the staple and filament fibers.

STAPLE YARNS

Yarns can be made of staple (short) fibers by any one of several techniques. The method used is dependent upon such factors as the manufacturer's *preference of* equipment, the economic implications, and the fibers to be used and desired properties of the yarn to be produced. Ring spinning is the oldest and most widespread technique. Open-end spinning is another major method. Newer methods have been developed, and experiments to find more effective and suitable processes continue.

Flow charts of fibre to fabric:

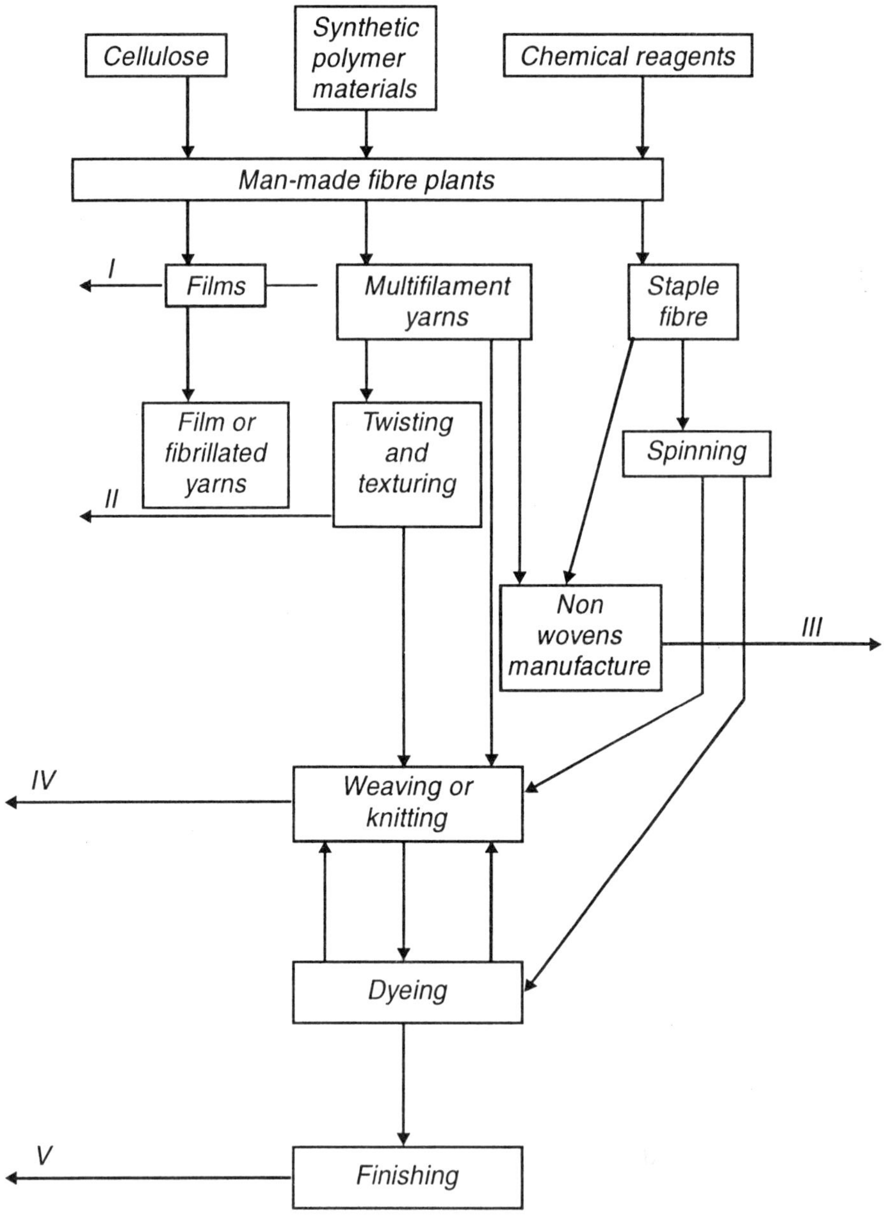

Manmade fibres/ filaments conversion into finished fabric

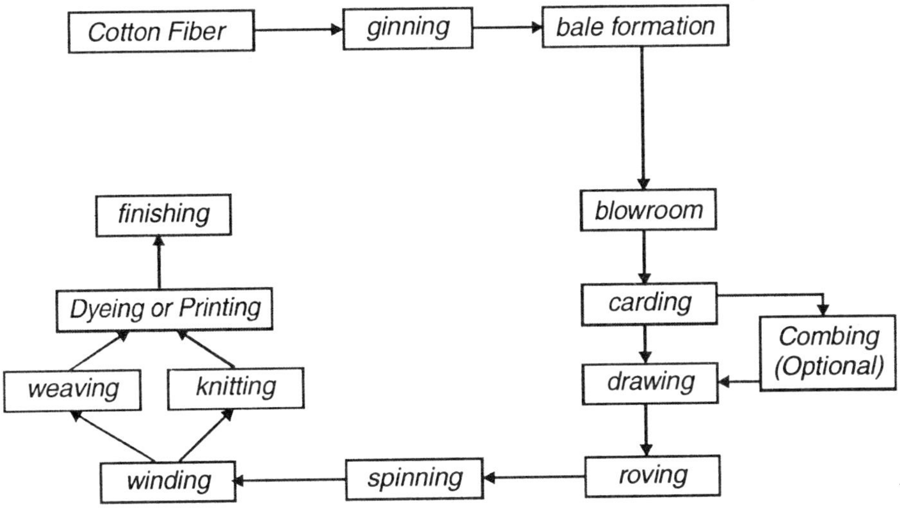

Flow chart of cotton fibre to fabric

Conventional Ring Spinning

The value and character of a yarn are determined by (1) kind and quality of fiber; (2) amount of processing necessary to produce fineness; and (3) amount of twist, which increases tensile strength in the finished yarn. The purpose of the yarn must be anticipated, as this determines the number and kind of manufacturing operations.

The formation of yarn from staple fibers by spinning becomes possible when they have surfaces capable of cohesiveness. This quality is exemplified by the natural twist of the cotton fibers which enables them to entwine around each other, the roughness of the linen fibers which cause them to cling together, and the scales on the surfaces of the wool fibers which cause them to grasp each other. Flexibility permits the fibers to be twisted around one another. Uniformity of staple gives yarns a required evenness and improves the quality.

Because the production of cotton yarn lends itself to a simple description of the manufacturing operations that make staple fiber into yarn, cotton fiber has been used in this chapter to illustrate the spinning process (see Figure 2-1). It must be remembered, however, that all other fibers pass through spinning operations, although, of course, there are differences that will be explained in the chapters dealing with the various fibers. One such difference occurs when long strands, or filaments, such as silk, are used rather than staple. In such instances, the required number of filaments is simply twisted together in a ropelike fashion.

The development of short fibers, or staple, into yarn, when stated in terms of basic manufacturing processes, is as follows: carding, combing, drafting, twisting, and winding. As the fibers pass through these processes, they are successively formed into *lap, sliver, roving,* and finally *yarn.* Here are the manufacturing operations in which these stages occur:

1. Lap to card sliver, by the carding process
2. Card sliver to comb sliver by the combing process (if the fiber is to be combed)
3. Sliver to roving by the drafting, or drawing-out, process
4. Roving to yarn by further drafting and twisting process
5. Yarn reeled on bobbins, spools, or cones by the winding process

Blending, Opening, and Cleaning. The cotton arrives at the mill in large bales weighing about 500 pounds [225 kilograms] each. The compressed mass of raw fiber must be removed from the bales, blended, opened, and cleaned. Blending is necessary so as to obtain uniformity of fiber quality opening is necessary in order to loosen hard lumps of fiber and disentangle them, cleaning is required to remove trash – such as dirt, leaves, burrs, and any remaining seeds – in order to prepare the fiber for spinning into yarn These functions are accomplished through a continuous series of stages

Mechanical bale pickers pluck thin,even layers of the matted fiber from each of a predetermined number of bales in turn and deposit them into a hopper .The fiber is mixed and passed to an opener. As the mass of fiber passes through the opener, cylinders with protruding fingers open tip the lumps and free the trash. The kind and number of cylinders or beaters, employed depend upon the type of cotton that is being processed; the commonly used porcupine beater revolves about 1000 revolutions per minute. As the cotton is opened, trash falls through a series of grid bars. When the cotton emerges from the opener it still contains small tufts with about two-thirds of the trash. It may be conveyed as a *lap,* which is a loosely entangled mass about 1 inch [2.5 centimeters (cm)] thick and about 40 inches [1meter] wide or it may be fed by chute directly to the card for further cleaning and fiber separation.

(a) BLENDING FEEDER

Fig.-2.1(a) Schematic of conventional ring spinning: (a) Cotton is passed from bales (1) onto apron (2). Apron moves cotton to blending apron (3). Blending apron has sharp spikes that raise cotton until part of it is knocked off by roll (4). Some of the cotton stays on apron. The cotton knocked back by roll (4) continues to churn and blend until picked up again by apron. Another roll (5) strips off cotton that was not knocked back by previous roll (4). Cotton falls on conveyor belt (6) and is carried to next process.

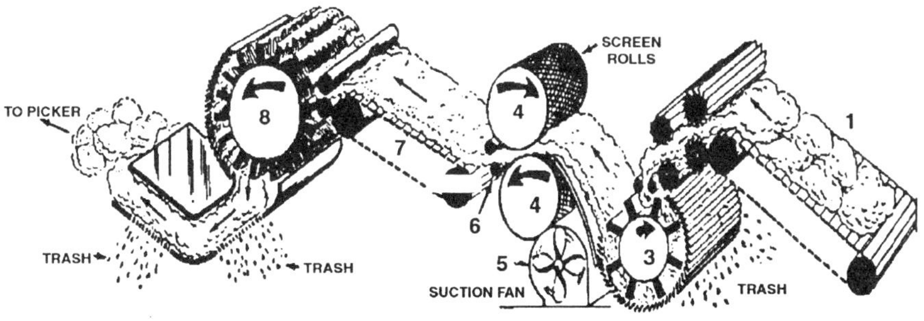

(b) OPENER

Fig.-2.1(b) Lint cotton falls on apron (1) and passes between feeder rolls (2) to beater cylinder (3). The rapidly whirling beater blades take off small tufts of cotton, knock out trash, and loosen up the mass. The two screen rolls (4) are made of screen material, and air is sucked out of them by fan (5). This draws the cotton from beater and condenses it on the surface of the screen rolls from which it is taken and passed on by the small rolls (6). Air suction through cotton takes out dirt and trash. Conveyor belt (7) passes cotton to another type of beater (8). (Beaters shown are typical of the many types used.) From beater, the cotton passes to a conveyor and is carried to picker.

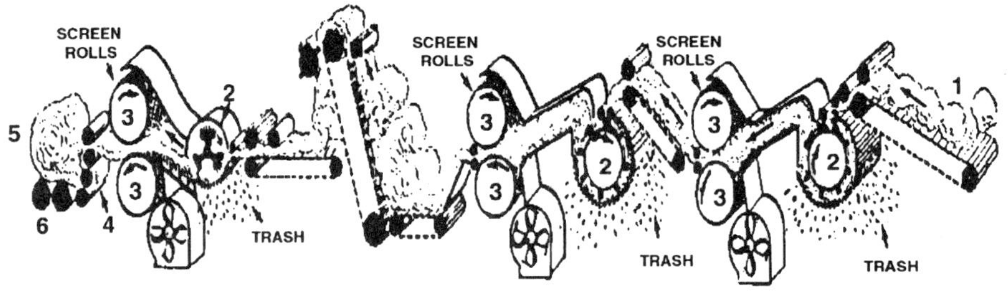

(c) PICKER

Fig.-2.1(c) Cotton in a loose mass enters picker, which is a series of beaters (2) and screen rolls (3) similar to those described under "opening" but progressively more refined. At the final output of beater and screen system (4) cotton has again been formed into a sheet, or lap. At this point, the "evener" operates to feed more or less cotton to make lap perfectly unifom as it is either wound up into a lap roll (5) on winding rolls (6) and then taken to the carding process, or conveyed as a lap by a chute feeder directly to the card.

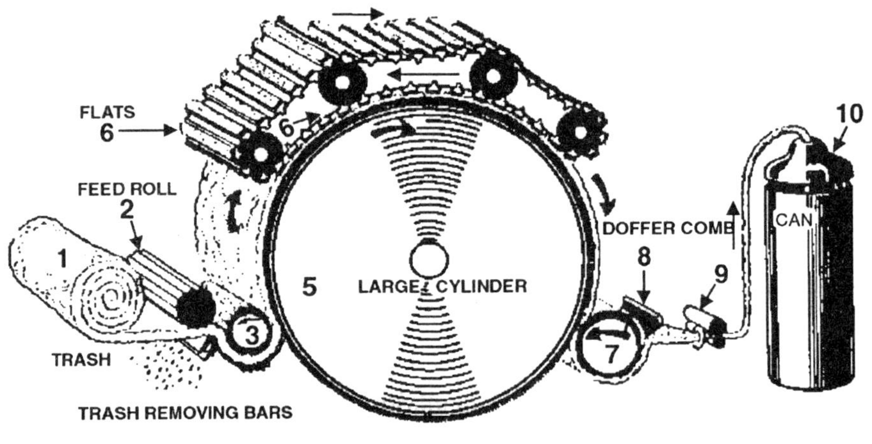

(d) CARDING

Fig.-2.1(d) The lap (1) from picker unrolls, and feed roll (2) passes cotton to the licker-in roll (3) (covered with sawtoothlike wire). The licker-in roll passes fiber against cleaner bars (4) and gives it up to large cylinder (5), which passes between the thousands of fine wires on surface of cylinder and on flats (6). The cotton follows large cylinder to doffer cylinder (7), which removes lint from large cylinder. The coffer comb (8) vibrates against doffer cylinder and takes lint off in a filmy web that passes through condenser rolls (9), coiler head (10), and then into can. The sliver may be passed from can to combing for further removal of foreign matter and parallelization of fiber or directly to drawing,

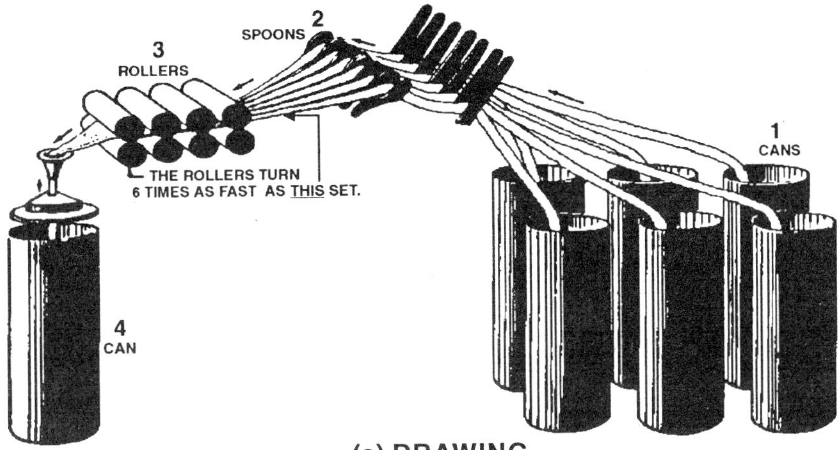

(e) DRAWING

Fig.-2.1(e) Here, six cans (1) that were filled at cards feed each drawing from delivery. The spoons (2) are connected so that if any one of the six slivers from can should break, the machine automatically stops. This prevents making uneven yarn later. Each of four sets of rolls (3) runs successively faster than preceding set. The last set runs approximately six times as fast as the first set; consequently, sliver coming out is the same size as each one of six going in, but is attenuated to six times the length per minute. The sliver is neatly coiled again in roving can (4) by coiler head. The sliver is now much more uniform and fibers are much more nearly parallel. The sliver is now ready for roving frames. In actual practice, drawing is usually repeated.

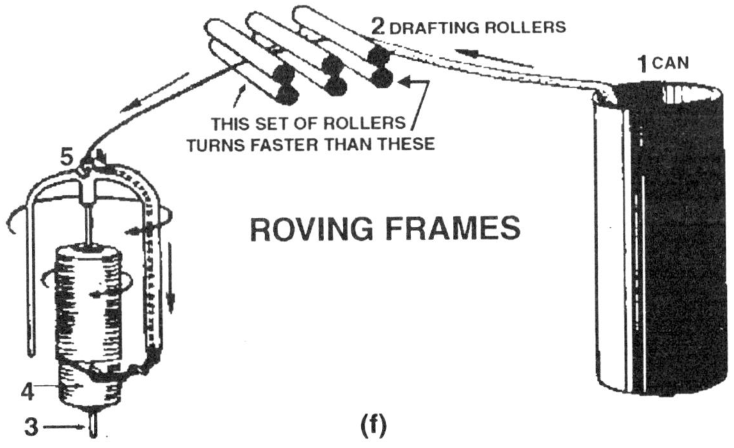

(f)

Fig.-2.1(f) The can of sliver (1) from drawing frames is fed between three sets of drafting rolls (2). Each following set of rolls runs faster than preceding set. This pulls sliver and thins it down, making fibers nearly parallel. The spindle (3) turns flyer (5) and is driven at a constant speed. The front rolls (nearest flyer) are set at a speed that gives strand coming out of the rolls a predetermined number of turns of twist per inch as it moves along between rolls and flyer. The bobbin (4) is driven by a source separate from gear that drives spindle and flyer. The bobbin is regulated to turn automatically at a speed sufficiently faster than flyer, which causes roving to wind on bobbin at same rate it is delivered by front roll.

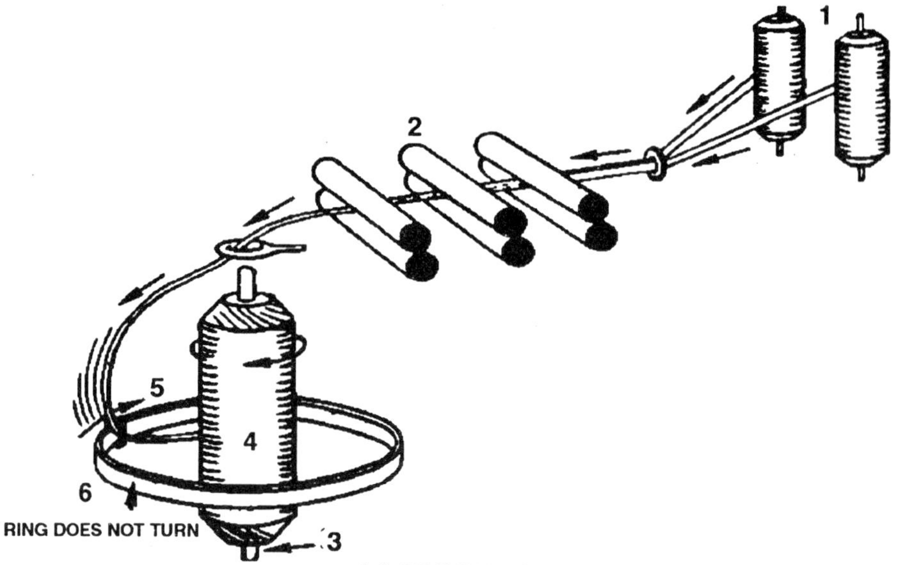

(g) SPINNING

Fig.-2.1(g) The principle for spinning is the same as that used for roving except that the operation is more refined and a ring and traveler are used instead of the flyer. From bobbin (1) roving is fed between sets of drafting rolls (2) to draw strand down to its final desired size. The spindle (3) turns bobbin (4) at a constant speed. The front set of rolls is adjusted to deliver yarn at a speed sufficient to insert desired amount of twist as strand moves along. The traveler (5) glides freely around ring (6). The tension caused by drag of traveler causes yarn to wind on bobbin at same rate of speed as it is delivered by rolls.

Carding. Before the raw stock can be made into yarn, the remaining Impurities must be removed, the fibers must be disentangled, and they must be straightened. The straightening process puts the fibers into a somewhat parallel lengthwise alignment. This is necessary for all staple fibers; otherwise, it would be impossible to produce fine yarns from what is originally a tangled mass. This initial process of arranging the fibers in a parallel fashion is known as *carding,* the work is done on a carding machine.

The lap is passed through a beater section and drawn on a rapidly revolving cylinder covered with very fine hooks or wire brushes. A moving belt of wire brushes slowly moves concentrically above this cylinder. As the cylinder rotates, the cotton is pulled by the cylinder through the small gap under the brushes; the teasing action removes the remaining trash, disentangles the fibers, and arranges them in a relatively parallel manner in the form of a thin web. This web is drawn through a funnel-shaped device that molds it into a round ropelike mass called *card sliver,* about the thickness of a broomstick. Card sliver produces *carded yarns* or *carded* cotton serviceable for inexpensive cotton fabrics.

Doubling. After carding, several slivers are combined. This results in a relatively narrow lap of compactly placed staple fibers. The compactness of these fibers permits this cotton stock to be attenuated, or drawn out, to a sliver of smaller diameter without falling apart.

Combing. When the fiber is intended for fine yarns, the sliver is put through an additional straightening called *combing.* In this operation, fine-toothed combs continue straightening the fibers until they are arranged with such a high degree of parallelism that the short fibers, called noils, are combed out and completely separated from the longer fibers. This procedure is not done when processing manmade staple fibers because they are cut into predetermined uniform lengths. Since these fibers do not need the combing separation, they are processed for spinning into yarns depending upon the desired end uses of the yarns. The combing process forms a comb *sliver* made of the longest fibers, which, in turn, produces a smoother and more even yarn. This operation eliminates as much as 25 percent of the original card sliver; thus almost one fourth of the raw cotton becomes waste. The combing process, therefore, is identified with consumers' goods of better quality. Since long-staple yarns produce stronger, smoother, and more serviceable fabrics, quality cotton goods carry labels indicating that they are made from *combed yarns* or *combed cottons.*

Drawing. The combining of several slivers for the drawing, or drafting, process eliminates irregularities that would cause too much variation if the slivers were put through singly. The draw frame has several pairs of rollers, each advanced set of which revolves at a progressively faster speed. This action pulls the staple lengthwise over each other, thereby producing longer and thinner slivers. After several stages of drawing out, the condensed sliver is taken to the slubber, where rollers similar to those in the drawing frame draw out the cotton further.

Here the slubbing is passed to the spindles, where it is given its first twist and is then wound on bobbins.

Roving. These bobbins are placed on the roving frame, where further drawing out and twisting take place until the cotton stock is about the diameter of a pencil lead. There are two stages of roving: intermediate and fine. The operations are identical, but each machine yields a finer product than the stock it received. Roving is the final product of the several drawing-out operations. It is a preparatory stage for the final insertion of twist. To this point, only enough twist has been given the stock to hold the fibers together. Roving has no tensile strength; it will break apart easily with any slight pull.

Spinning. The roving, on bobbins, is placed in the spinning frame, where it passes through several sets of rollers running at successively higher rates of speed and is filially drawn out to *yarn* of the size desired. Spinning machines are of two kinds: ring frame and mule frame. The ring frame is a faster process, but produces a relatively coarse yarn. For very fine yarns, such as worsted, the mule frame is required because of its slow, intermittent operation. The ring frame, which is in general use, is more suitable for the manufacture of cotton yarns for mass production. Its hundreds of spindles, whirling thousands of revolutions a minute and its constant spinning action provide a fast operation. The ring spinning frame completes the manufacture of yarn (1) by drawing out the roving, (2) by inserting twist, and (3) by winding the yarn on bobbins – all in one operation. The bobbins of yarn are removed for such processing as may be desired; for example, the yarn may be reeled into skeins for bleaching or may be wound on *cheeses,* or spools, for ultimate weaving.

Yarn Twist. The amount of twist is all important factor in finished consumers' goods. It determines the appearance as well as the durability and serviceability of a fabric. Fine yarns require more twist than coarse yarns. Warp yarns, which are used for the lengthwise threads in woven fabrics, are given more twist than are filling yarns, which are used for the crosswise threads. To retain the twist in the yarns and prevent any tendency to untwist or kink, the yarns are given a twist setting finish with heat or moisture, depending upon the kind of fiber used.

The amount of twist also depends upon the type of fabric to be woven

1. Yarn intended for soft surface fabrics are given only a slack twist. They are called *soft-twisted yarns.*

2. Yarns intended for smooth-surfaced fabrics are given many twists. Such *hard twisted yarns* contribute strength, smoothness, elasticity and some wrinkle resistance to fabrics.

3. Yarns intended for crepe fabrics (with rough, pebbly, or crinkled surfaces) are given a maximum amount of twist, which also adds wrinkle resistance.

The direction of twist may be observed by holding the Yarn in a vertical position.

If the spirals conform to the direction of the slope of the central part of the letter S, the yarn has an S twist, if they conform to the slope of the Z twist, the yarn has a Z-twist (see fig 2.2).

Permanent crepe effects, such as chiffon, georgette, crepe de Chine, canton, and flat and French crepes, are produced by the use of hard-twisted yarns some of which have left twist, others right twist. These yarns are placed alternately in the warp or in the filling, or in both. (Another satisfactory method of obtaining crepe effects during the construction of the fabric is by the use of slack warp yarns, which may or may not wound on a separate warp beam. These yarns are held less taut than the other warp Yarns and produce a permanent crinkled pattern. Seersucker and matelasse are produced in this way and prove very serviceable.) When the finished fabric is later washed or dyed such yarns kink in different directions, producing the crepe surface.

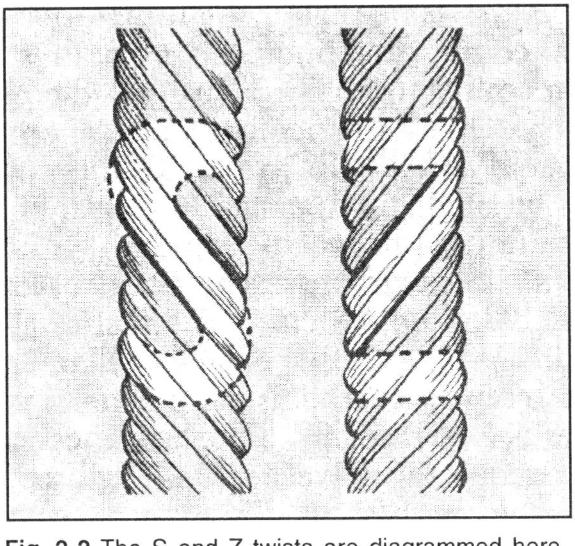

Fig.-2.2 The S and Z twists are diagrammed here.

Yarn Count. In the spinning process there is always a fixed relation between the weight of the original quantity of fiber and tile length of the yarn produced from that amount of raw material. This relation indicates the thickness of the yarn. It is determined by the extent of the drawing process and is designated by numbers, which are called the *yarn count.* This yarn count may be expressed according to the traditional method or by the newer *tex* system, which is based entirely upon the metric system of measurement.

The standard for the yarn count in cotton is 1 pound of fiber drawn out to make 840 yards of yarn, the resultant thickness or size is known as count number 1, or Ne

1. If the yarn is drawn out farther, so that 1 pound makes twice 840 yards, it is identified as Ne 2 or 2s. Thus Ne 2 yarn will be finer than Ne 1. A still finer yarn is Ne 10, as it indicates that 1 pound of cotton is drawn out to ten times 840 yards. The higher the number of the yarn count, the finer the yarn in size. Yarn counts up to Ne 20 are called coarse yarns; 20 to 60 are medium yarns; about 60 are fine yarns. Up to Ne 20, the count rises by single numbers. Only even numbers are used between 20 and 60. Above Ne 60, the count rises by intervals of 5 until 100, after which an interval of 10 is used. As an example of size or diameter, cotton sewing thread used for general purposes is Ne 50 or 60. The very finest cotton yarns spun have been as high as Ne 400, the product of 1 pound of cotton drawn out to a strand 336,000 yards long [almost 200 miles or about 300 kilometers]. Extremely fine yarns are difficult and costly to manufacture because of the greater care required in spinning and the greater amount of twist required.

The size of yarn to be used in a fabric is determined by the purpose of the fabric. Yarns may be twisted around each other, or *plied,* to obtain greater strength Yarns of varying sizes may be used to obtain the nubbed or novelty effects and rough textures such as characterized by ratine, boucle, or eponge .

There are different standards for yarn counts of different kinds of fibers. Although the standard base of 1 pound is used for all staple fibers, the length of drawing for each kind is different:

Fiber	Yards
Cotton and cotton blends	840
Linen	300
Wool and wool blends	1600
Worsted, worsted blends, and 100% staple acrylic	560
Spun staple silk	840
All 100% manmade staple fibers except acrylic	840

Furthermore, yarn counts of filament (continuous strand) fibers such as silk and nylon are designated according to denier, which is an entirely different system of measuring yarn diameter.

These differences of measurement have created difficulties, particularly In view of the number of fibers, the blending of these fibers into yarns, and the international textile trade. An increasing awareness developed for the need of a single common standard of measuring yarn diameter. Consequently, the tex system was introduced by The International Organization for Standardization (ISO) to overcome the confusing traditional yarn count measurements by providing a fixed relationship between the weight and length of all yarns: one tex equals 1 grain (g) per kilometer the greater the weight, the thicker the yarn, and consequently the higher the tex number.

The tex system can cover a wide range of yarn components and yarns, being useful to describe sliver or very fine filaments as well as the resultant yarn. As the tex is an accepted SI (metric) unit of measure, it may be multiplied or divided by factors of 10 or used with SI prefixes to form larger or smaller quantity units. The kilotex (1 ktex = 1000 tex) is normally used to describe tow or sliver, while the decitex (1 dtex = 0. 1 tex) is suitable to filaments or fine spun yarns, etc.

This system was initiated in 1960 with the support of the American Society for Testing and Materials (ASTM), which proposed a three-stage approach to the changeover. During the first stage, technologists and yarn manufacturers were urged to familiarize themselves with the new system and to include tex numbers in parentheses following the customary yarn count numbers. It was anticipated that after a period of time deemed sufficient

TABLE 2.1 : OFFICIAL ISO TEX CONVERSION STANDARD

DIRECT SYSTEM

Yarn Number System	Symbolic Abbreviation	Unit of Length	Unit of Mass	Unit of Yarn Count	Multiplying Factor, Yarn Number to Tex
Tex	Tt	1 Km	1 g	g/km	–
Denier	Td	9000 m	1 g	g/9000m	0.1111

INDIRECT SYSTEM

Yarn Number System	Symbolic Abbreviation	Unit of Length	Unit of Mass	Unit of Yarn Count	Constant for Conversion To Tex Values
Cotton Count*	NeC	840 yd (hank)	1 lb.	840 Yd/lb	590.5
Glass (U.K. and U.S.)	NG	100 yd	1 lb.	100 yd/lb	4961.0
Linen	NeL	300 yd (lea)	1 lb.	300 yd/lb	1654.0
Woolen (Amer. cut)	Nac	300 yd	1 lb	300 yd/lb	1654.0
Woolen (Amer. run0	Nar	100 yd	1 oz.	100 yd/oz	310.0
Worsted	NeW	560 yd (hank)	1 lb	560 yd/lb	885.8
Metric	Nm	1 km	1 kg	km/kg	1000.0

For familiarization, tex numbers would be used as the regular designation and the former yarn count numbers would be in parentheses. Eventually, only the tex number would be used. However, the system has still not been universally accepted.

Blending Fibers. It is important to observe that the production of staple yarn is, of course, not limited to composition from one kind of fiber. The staple of two or more different kinds of fibers may be combined, or blended, at any one of several stages discussed above. When different types of fibers are blended, the properties of these fibers are also combined, though modified, in the blended yarn. Fabrics made from such blended yarns are sometimes sold under registered trademarks; for example, Viyella is a trademark for a particular fabric made of blended cotton and wool yarn.

Blending may be done at any one of the fiber processing stages discussed. During the initial *opening* stage, appropriate amounts of each fiber can be weighed out and layers of them can be *sandwich blended* by spreading one on top of the other. Sections of the sandwich are then fed into a hopper or blending feeder for discharge into a mechanical mixer. When the fibers are *Feeder blended* each type of fiber is automatically weighed and fed directly from hoppers into a mechanical mixer.

When a lower percentage of one fiber is desired in a blend, it is *finisher picker blended.* Four of the breaker picker laps are blended together at the finisher picker stage and then fed to the carding machine.

Card blended fibers can be produced by feeding one lap of the different fibers into the carding machine to produce a blended sliver. However, this procedure does not produce a precise, well-distributed blend.

When the fibers are to be combed, the blending is not done until after the waste and the shorter fibers are removed Then, *drawframe blended* fibers are produced by combined slivers of previously carded, combed, and parallelized fiber.

Sometimes fibers are *rove* or spun *blended.* This produces a rather random arrangement that is usually limited to the blending of colored fibers for such fabrics as tweed.

Fibers may also be blended when spinning methods other than the conventional system aye used. The blending procedure varies with its compatibility with the particular spinning techniques described below.

Open-End Spinning

A relatively recent development in the production of spun yarn is the open-end, or break, spinning process. This technique was developed in Czechoslovakia during the 1960s. Other countries, notably England, Japan, and the United States, subsequently developed similar machines. The technique has reached wide acceptance as a satisfactory process for spinning coarser yarns of counts of upto about 40 (14.8 tex).

The open-end (O-E) spinning process begins with the carded sliver (combed sliver is not used), which is fed past a single-spiked roller or a succession of rollers, each advanced set of which revolves at a progressively faster speed, thereby completely opening tip the sliver so that the fibers call be fed virtually individually into the spinning operation (this, in effect, breaks apart the sliver; hence, the terms " open-end" and "break"). As the fibers are thus separated, they are transported forward by all air stream and are collected as a thin layer in a groove on the inner surface of a funnel-shaped rotor, which rotates at a very high speed. The centrifugal force of the rotor builds up a multilayer of fibers which is peeled away from the collecting groove as it is simultaneously twisted by the rotation of the rotor and withdrawn continuously, thus being formed into a yarn

The primary difference between the conventional ring spinning and the open-end spinning is that in the latter the spool does not need to be rotated in order to put twist into the yarn. Furthermore, much larger spools can be wound, thereby providing very long lengths of knot-free yarn and consequent reduction in handling the spools. The system also allows for greater automation in yarn production and therefore provides greater production economy. Open-end spinning can produce yarn spun at a rate of 3 to 5 times that of the conventional ring spinning. While the open-end spinning process provides better fiber elongation, the resultant yarn is only as even as a good ring spun yarn, but not better. The yarn produced has excellent dyeability, particularly with bright shades. The system homogenizes blends very well, even better than ring spinning utilizing the same preparatory blending techniques.

On the other hand, open-end spinning has its limitations. Problems arise in spinning yarns of 100 percent manmade staple (with the exception of rayon staple) on account of the fiber finish, which gets deposited in the rotor and causes clogging;and it is not possible to spin combed yarn. The yarn has a carded character and it has a rougher, sandier hand. The yarn counts are generally lower than 40 (14.8 tex), which hunts their use to heavier, coarser fabrics, such as denims, towels some poplins, and interlinings. Although open-end yarns are spun with 20 percent more twist, they are 15 to 20 percent weaker due to their coarseness. Also, the character of these yarns due to the twist formation is sufficiently different from that of ringspun yarns so that they, cannot be mixed in manufacture.

From the point of view of the manufacturer's further concern, it is essential that the slivers be free of foreign matter in order to operate the open-end system effectively. The power requirements increase geometrically with the increase in spun yarn count. Also, the longer the staple, the larger the rotor must be, which in turn reduces the maximum turbine speed and thus the productivity.

Friction Spinning

In the early 1970s, Dr. Ernst Fehrer received an Austrian patent for a friction spinning process which was subsequently commercialized under the trademark DREF. The system has since been modified and is identified as DREF II , a variation of the open-end spinning process. The principle of the technique is that of passing along the longitudinal drum axis a stream of carded fibers in the roll nip of the perforated drums both of which are moving in the same direction. This action forces the fibers to be wedged along the nip, thereby becoming compressed; the frictions of the rollers cause the fibers to twist around each other.

The process utilizes a current of air to transport the carded fibers to the longitudinal nip region of the two drums. To improve parallelization, parallel orienting disks with fingers are used to align the fibers in the take-off direction of the yarn. The air stream gives the sliver end the initial twist as it presses the disentangled fibers against the continuously forming yarn compound wedged into the roll nip. Air suction through the perforated drums produces a uniform twist effect as the yarn is drawn off the end of the drums. The amount of twist may be controlled by regulating the suction. The yarn count is determined by the thickness of the wedge in the yarn-forming nip and the width (diameter) of the nip itself (see Figure 2.3).

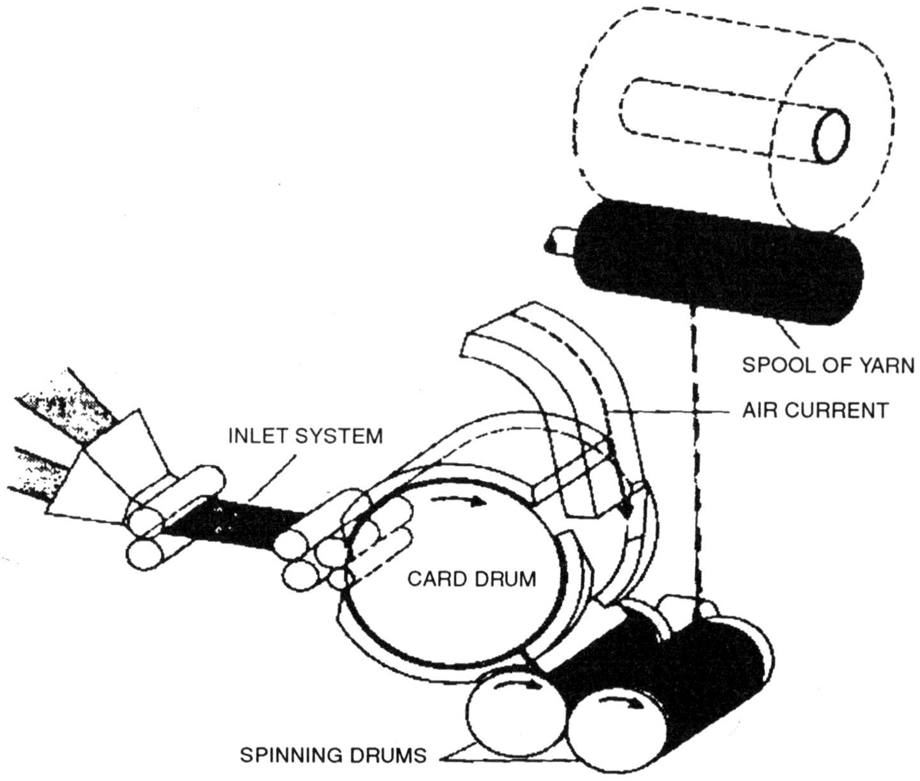

Figure 2-3 Schematic of DREF II friction spinning process: One or more card slivers are fed to the spindle, depending on the yarn count; maximum feeding weight 15-30 g/m. A rapidly rotating card drum opens the sliver to single fibers. A specially designed inlet system provides for the retention and the drafting of the fiber band. The centrifugal force strips the single fibers from the card drum and, supported by the air current the fibers are blown into the nip formed by the two perforated spinning drums.

There are certain advantages to the DREF II system. The fiber preparation costs are lower because direct feed of card slivers to the spinning zone is possible. The high-speed elements required for ring and rotor spinning are eliminated. Yarn breakage during spinning is avoided because there is no tension in the spinning area. The process allows the use of a wide variety and quality of fibers that can be used independently or blended into the slivers. However, the yarns produced may lack uniform distribution of twist through the cross section.

The resultant yarns are bulky and have surface and mechanical properties similar to those of woolen yarns. And since they do not have the wrapper fiber effect that is achieved by the rotor open end spinning, they have a low tensile strength. Improvements in the technique continue to be developed and there are a number of variations of this system.

Novelty specialty yarns, such as boucle' and nub, can be produced. Also, by feeding a filament core yarn axially into the center of the spinning zone, core spun yarns can be produced.

In 1979, Fehrer introduced the DREF III, an outgrowth of the DREF II. Yarns are spun from a wide range of fibers including cotton, rayon, nylon, aramid, polyester, acrylic, and polypropylene or blends of fibers into counts ranging from 6s to 18s. The process contains a dual yarn spinning system which can produce yarns by feeding either from two separate slivers or from one staple sliver feed and one filament feed. In the latter instance, the staple completely covers the filament which serves as the core of the yarn.

Yarn properties more closely resemble ring-spun rather than open-end rotor spun yarn, while lower production costs over both are emphasized. Weaving performance compares favorably with that of conventional yarns. A wide range of fabrics constructed of DREF III yarn are used for apparel, such as jeans home furnishings, such as upholstery; leisure goods; such as camping articles; and industrial products, such as cords.

Self-Twist Spinning

The self-twist spinning process for spinning wool or wool-like fibers was developed in Australia. Pairs of rovings are drawn out on a succession of drafting rollers the last set of which reciprocates axially, causing a rolling action of the strands as they emerge. This sideways movement of the drafting rollers causes the strands to wrap around each other. The twist is held by the texture of the yarn and the relatively rough texture of the fibers in the yarn; sometimes additives may be used for cohesion. After the rollers complete their sideways motion in one direction, the movement is then shifted in the opposite direction. The resultant yarn therefore has alternating lengths of right lefthand twist (see Figure 2.4).

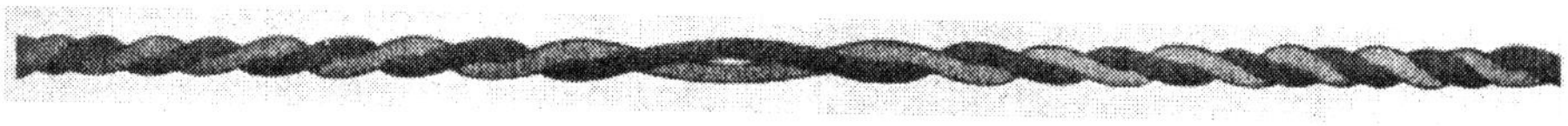

Figure 2-4 Alternating S and Z twist created in the self-twist spinning process.

Under certain circumstances, depending upon the nature of the fibers used and the ultimately desired yarns, these self-twist spun yarns may subsequently be put through a further conventional spinning process to increase strength and produce yarns in which all the twist is in the same direction.

The self-twist process can spin worsted yarn of good quality up to 10 times faster than conventional spinning. Labor and power costs are considerably lower, and the self-twist spinning machine occupies much less floor space, thereby saving on capital costs.

Electrostatic Spinning

Mindful of the facts that each bale of cotton may have as much as 8 to 12 percent very short fibers and that a reduction in short-fiber content will result in an increase in yarn strength and a substantial improvement in spinning efficiency, researchers tried to develop a system that would improve the uniformity, strength, and appearance of cotton yarn. They also sought a more efficient and less expensive means of processing cotton fiber which is more difficult to spin than other fibers.

The researchers began by exploring the possibility of removing the short cotton fibers from the longer ones by an electrostatic process. The principle is based upon the knowledge that widely differing materials can be separated from each other electro-statistically. The idea of separating different sizes of the same material, and more particularly cotton, was a novel approach.

Ultimately, research showed that under carefully controlled conditions of humidity, it is possible to separate short fibers from long ones in an electrostatic field. The technique utilizes a non uniform electrostatic field in which the gradient between the electrodes varies at a curved rate from minimum to maximum intensity. A mechanism was also developed to remove the short fibers from the long fibers as they passed through the electrostatic field and transport the desired long fibers by an air current.

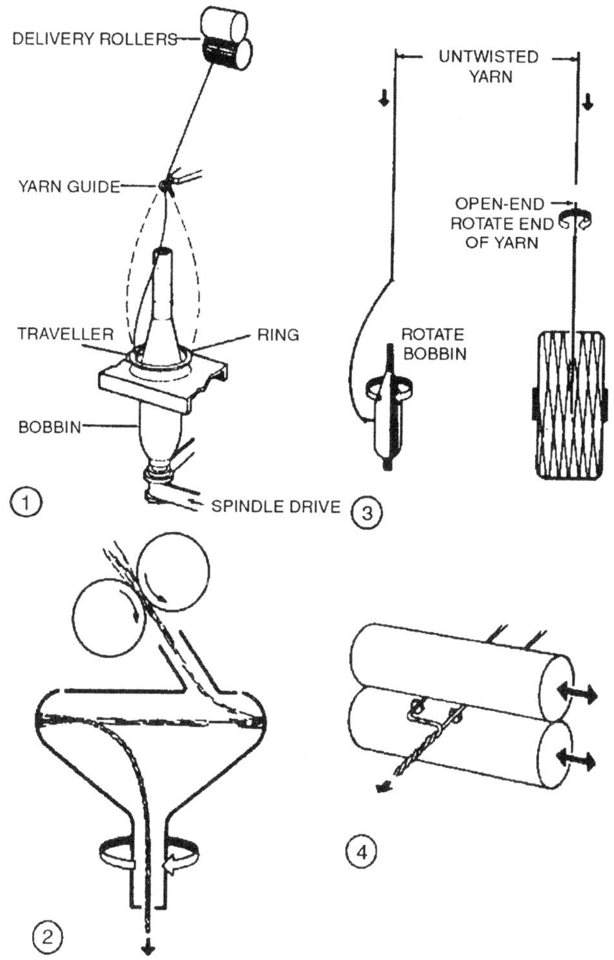

Figure 2-5 Primary yarn-spinning techniques : (1) Ring-spinning sliver is fed from deliver rollers through the traveler (a wire loop) onto the bobbin. As the rotation of the spindle drags the traveler around the ring, one turn of twist is inserted into the yarn. The drag of the traveler against the ring causes the traveler to lag behind the spindle and the twisted yarn is wound onto it. (2) Open-end spinning-an open sliver produces loose fibers which are fed by an airstream onto the inner surface of a funnel-shaped rotor driven at high speed. A thin layer of the fibers is depösted by the centrifugal force onto a collecting groove on the inner circumference of the revolving rotor. As this layer of fibers is peeled from the groove, twist is immediately inserted into it by the rotor's rotation, thus foming a yarn. (3) Comparisn of ring spinning and open-end spinning showing that the latter method does not require the collecting package, or spool, to be rotated in order to insert twist into the yarn. (4) Self-twist spinning-pairs of rovings are drawn out into finer strands on a rolle drafting system in which the front rollers move axially (side-ways) causing the strands to rool over each other forming a twist -first in one direction and then in the other-as they are moved forward. Pairs of these twisted strands are brought together shortly therafter in a manner that causes them to wrap around each other to form "piled"yarn that has alternating S and Z twist at regular intervals along its length.

Thus, from the carded stage, the fibers are drawn out, or drafted, by rollers and are fed over rotating cylindrical electrodes of high field intensity which direct the long fibers to either an air current or an electrostatic field for transport to the combed sliver stage. The short fibers, which move more slowly, are carried by rotating electrodes of low field intensity to where they are removed to a receptacle.

Of far greater significance than the removal of short fibers is the fact that preliminary research with a modification of this electrostatic device has shown that it can replace all textile processing equipment from opening through spinning. Fed cotton from the bale, a small machine can produce a clean, relatively nep-free strand with excellent fiber orientation. The apparatus has required refinement, production rate has been low, and there are still problems to overcome.

This electrostatic technique has been examined by some mill equipment manufacturers. One of the leading manufacturers has developed a commercial prototype designed to meet the initial Objectives of lower cost of production, greater efficiency improve uniformity, strength and appearance of yarns.

Vortex Spinning

A variation of the open-end spinning technique is the vortex principle developed in the mid-1970s in Poland. The rotor is eliminated and replaced by a tangential air inlet that draws fibers down a tube. As a seed yarn is rotated in the air stream, a twist is inserted causing the fibers to grasp onto each other forming a continuous yarn.

The technique is of interest because moving parts in the machine are eliminated, providing a considerable cost savings. However, the yarns produced are weak and irregular.

Air-Jet Spinning

A further variation of spinning yarn with the aid of an air stream was developed in Japan and commercially introduced in 1981. It is a patented pneumatic process that produces yarn directly from high quality drawing sliver of wool, manmade staple, or manmade and cotton staple blends. This air-jet spinning technique drafts the sliver to a predetermined size and passes it through rollers over a friction plate (to prevent backtwist) into a cylindrical pneumatic twisting chamber. As compressed air is released from jets set in the walls of the chamber at predetermined angles to the central axis of the tube, the fibers are whirled around each other. Special rings and specific grooves within the tube are used to loosen the fibers from the sides and to control the twist and strength parameters of the forming yarn. As the fibers are whirled through the first chamber, they are given either all S or Z twist. With the aid of air suction, the strand is passed into a second chamber where it is first stabilized and then given an equal amount of twist in the opposite direction. The strand is again stabilized to prevent back twist as delivery rolls draw off the yarn which is wound onto a take up package.

The air-jet spinning produces a yarn of uniform diameter without thick or thin areas. However, it has a somewhat harsh hand. Yarn can be produced in counts equal to or somewhat finer than those made by open-end spinning. Although the tensile strength of air-jet spun yarn has been reported to be less than that of ring-spun yarn it may be greater than that of open-end yarn. It weaves and knits well, but performance and durability in the fabric remains to be fully determined.

Twist Less Spinning

Other techniques for making yarns of staple fibers without the need for twisting them around each other to achieve cohesiveness and strength are being developed. The methods are basically designed to place the fibers parallel to each other and have them adhere together with the aid of a bonding agent that is removable after the yarns are constructed into fabrics.

Twilo. After a number of years of experimenting the Fibre Research Institute TNO in Holland produced a twistless spinning process called Tek-Ja. Further research resulted in improvements and led to the development of the Twilo twistless yarn.

The Twilo twistless spinning process forms yarn by temporarily binding the fibers together with an adhesive and subsequently removing the adhesive after the yarn has been made into a fabric. A carded silver of cotton, rayon, polyester, or acrylic staple is blended on a drawing frame with a sliver of water-soluble polyvinyl alcohol (PVA) binder fibers, which accounts for 5 to 10 percent of the ultimate sliver depending upon the particular need. The blended sliver is then drafted 5 to 10-fold in a dry condition, wetted to activate the binder, wet-drafted, given a tangential water injection which causes a vortex that imparts a false twist, drafted 6 to 40-fold in its wet condition, and again passed through the false twister while steam or hot water is applied. The wet, untwisted yarn is dried on a rotating heated drum and wound on a cheese at the rate of about 1300 feet (400 m) per minute.

The resultant yarn is ribbon -shaped and consists of parallel fibers held together by the water-soluble binding agent. After the Twilo yarn is woven or knitted into a fabric, the binder is removed by washing. The fabric is, in effect, constructed of fibers; it is held together by the frictional resistance wherever the yarn crosses. Since the fibers can move slightly in the fabric, the fabric's appearance may be affected in the finishing process and have a different appearance from that of comparable fabrics made of other yarns.

Fabrics made of this twistless yarn have an attractive luster because the fibers in the yarn are relatively parallel to each other, thereby providing a flat, smooth surface. Dyes are more accessible to the fibers and deeper shades can be achieved. Also, since the fibers in the yarn are not found together, they can be spread out to provide much better cover than can be achieved with twisted yarn. Such fabrics may appear heavier and denser but are actually lighter and thinner. Fabrics of twistless yarns have been found to shrink less than those made of conventional yarn. The strength of fabrics made of Twilo yarn depend upon the inherent strength of the particular fiber used in that yarn and the strength of twisted yarn that may be combined in the structure, such as in the warp (lengthwise yarn) of a woven cloth.

FILAMENT YARNS

With the advent of manmade fibers, it became possible to produce endless, fine strands of fiber. These filaments are produced by different methods, and they can be formed directly into yarn without the use of techniques to connect fibers together to form the required lengths.

Wet Spinning

The first commercially successful method for the manufacture of manmade fiber was the wet spinning of the cellulosic fiber, rayon. This method is still used today. Essentially, the process involves the use of an appropriate liquid solution which is pumped through a small nozzle, which is called a spinneret; into a chemical bath that coagulates the extruded solution of endless strands of filaments. These coagulated continuous fibers are drawn out of the bath, purified by washing, dried, and then wound onto spools.

The construction of the spinneret may be varied according to the desired results. If the spinneret has one extrusion hole, then a multifilament yarn will be produced.. The size and number of the holes of spinneret may be varied. Thus the thickness, or denier, of the yarn is determined by the number and size of the filaments of which it is constructed. Also, the amount of twist given the processed yarn will affect its texture and strength.

Dry Spinning

Another method for the manufacture of manmade fibers is referred to as dry *spinn*ing. An example of this is the process of making; acetate. The process involves the use of an appropriate liquid solution which is pumped through a spinneret into air chamber. The air reacts with the extruded streams causing them to solidify. These coagulated continous fibers are then drawn out of the chamber, twisted and/or processed further, and then wound onto spools.

As in the case of wet spinning, monofilament or multifilament can be produced, and the diameter of the yarn will depend upon the number and size of the spinneret holes. Again, the amount of twist given to the yarn will determine its texture and strength.

Melt Spinning

A third method of manufacturing manmade fibers is referred to as *melt spinn*ing. An example of this is the process of making polyester .Polymer chips obtained from previously reacted chemical combinations are melted and then pumped through a spinneret into an air chamber. The extruded streams cool and solidify into continuous filaments and are then drawn out of the chamber, twisted and/or processed further, and subsequently wound onto spools.

Monofilament and multifilament yarns of various diameters can be produced as is done with the other extruded filaments. Texture and strength are also determined by the amount of twist put into the yarn.

Bicomponent Spinning

During the research of such manmade polymers as nylon, various forms of the same polymer were created. While each variety had certain common characteristics, each also had certain different qualities. In the quest for yarns that would have combined certain desired properties of a particular manmade fiber, a variation of melt spinning was devised. The technique involves the extrusion through a spinneret of two different types of the same polymer to produce a bicomponent fiber.

There are three techniques of bicomponent fiber production. One method is the side by side extrusion through one spinneret hole of two varieties of the same polymer. As the two variants cool and solidify, they adhere together as one filament, one side of which is composed of one type of the polymer and the other side of which is composed of another type of the same polymer.

Another means of manufacture of bicomponent fiber is basically that of using one spinneret inside another. One variant of the polymer is pumped through the center, or core, spinneret while another is pumped through the outer, or surrounding, spinneret. Both varieties of the polymer emerge as one through the common hole of the surrounding spinneret so that the fiber is formed of a core of one polymer variant surrounded by a ring of the other variant.

The third method of composition of bicomponent fiber is the distribution of drops of one molten polymer variant into another molten form of the same polymer. This composite mixture is then extruded through the single spinneret hole. The result is a matrix, or conglomerate, of minute, short strands of one fiber suspended inside another variety of the same fiber.

Biconstituent Spinning

Another variation of filament yarn production is *biconstituent spinning.* Essentially, the techniques used are the same as those for bicomponent spinning. The difference is that biconstituent spinning utilizes two *different* polymers that are combined and extruded in the same manner.

Film Splitting

Filament fibers are also produced by melt extrusion of a polymer through a very wide die but with a very narrow slit to form a sheet of film. There are several methods of producing fiber from these sheets. The film may be stretched and oriented along its direction of extrusion and then either broken or cracked (technically called *fibrillating)* by mechanical means into a mat of fibers. Another technique is to emboss with a roller a fiber pattern of indentations of specific dimensions on the film and then mechanically to fibrillate the film to produce the fibers.

The same technique may also be used with bicomponent or biconstituent film.

INTEGRATED MULTICOMPONENT YARNS

Since there are distinct advantages unique to yarn spun of staple fiber and others to Yarn made of filament fiber, techniques have been developed to produce yarn by combining staple and filament fibers in order to obtain certain of the characteristics of each. The kinds of staple and filament fibers used and the methods of production vary but such combinations are designated as *integrated multicomponent yarns.*

Integrated Composite Spinning (ICS)

In the late 1960s, the father and son team of Emilian and Andrew Bobkowicz of Montreal, Canada, introduced an integrated multicomponent spinning technique, which they identified as the Bobtex ICS process. Since then, advances have been made in technique and yarn varieties which have led to applications in industrial, environmental, and a wide range of consumer products.

Production of ICS Yarn. The process entails passing a monofilament or multifilament strand through a molten proprietary polypropylene alloy and then immediately embedding part of the length of staple fibers into the polymeric resin. The filament may be round, flat, fibrillated tape, or tubular monofilament, each of which may be highly oriented or of nearly crystalline structure (the latter aids acceptance and retention of the subsequent twist). The resin is fed into the system in pellet form and melted (as for melt spinning) to serve as a bonding agent. After the filament (the carrier or core) is passed through and coated with the polymeric resin, a predetermined variety and length of staple fiber is superimposed upon and

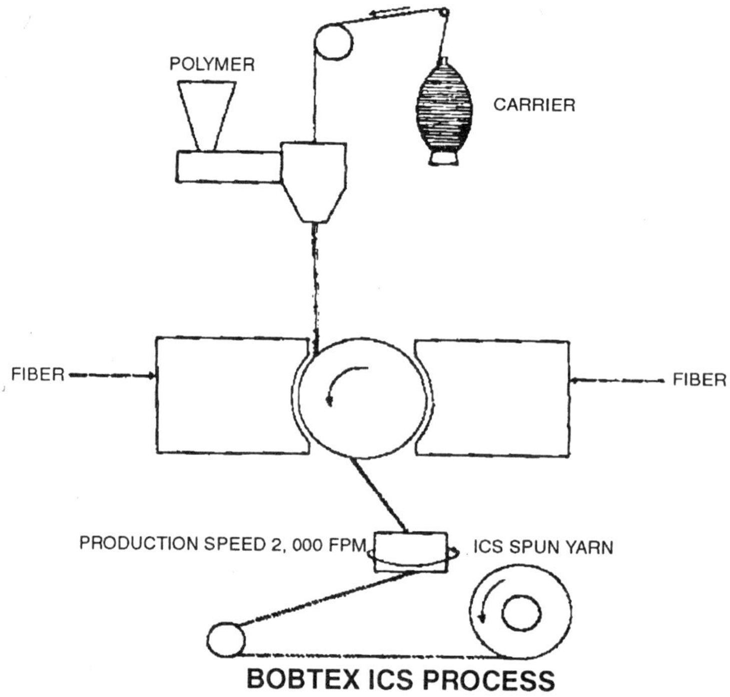

Fig.-2.6(a) Schematic Diagram

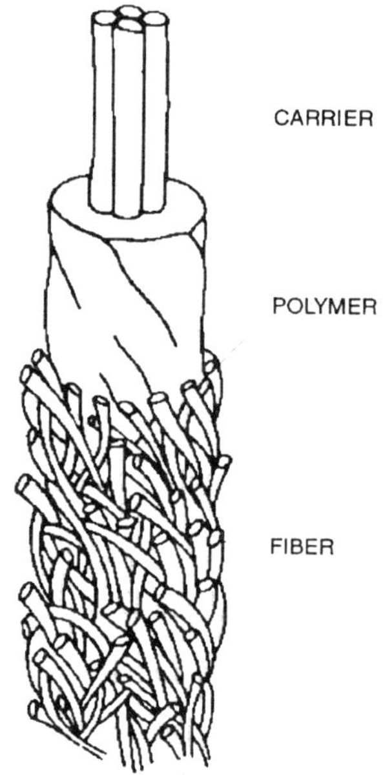

Fig.-2.6(b) Schematic of ICS Yarn Structure.

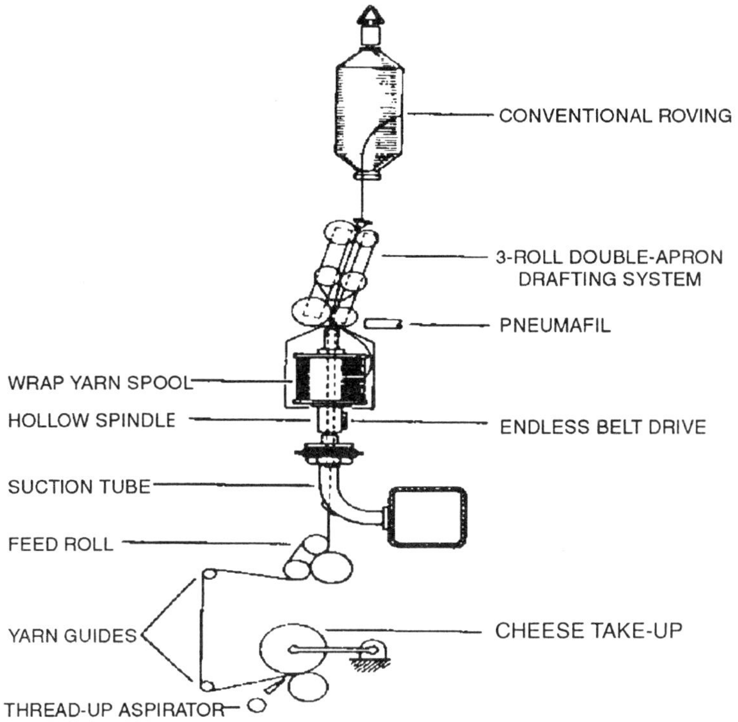

Fig.-2.6(c) Schematic of the Converspun process

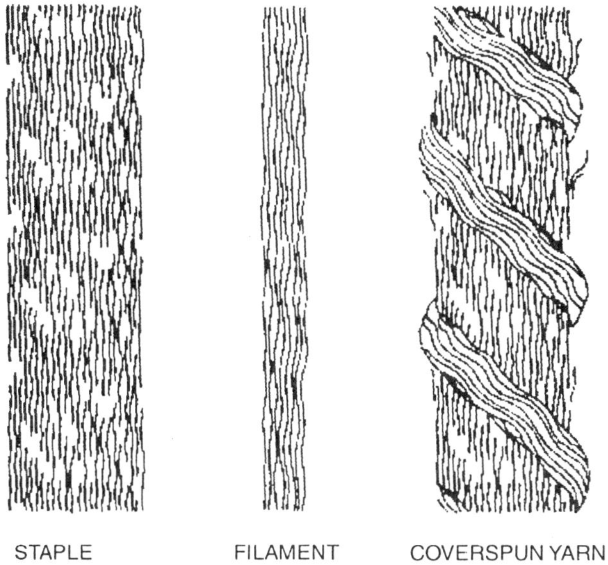

Fig.-2.6(d) Sketch of the structure of Coverspun yarn.

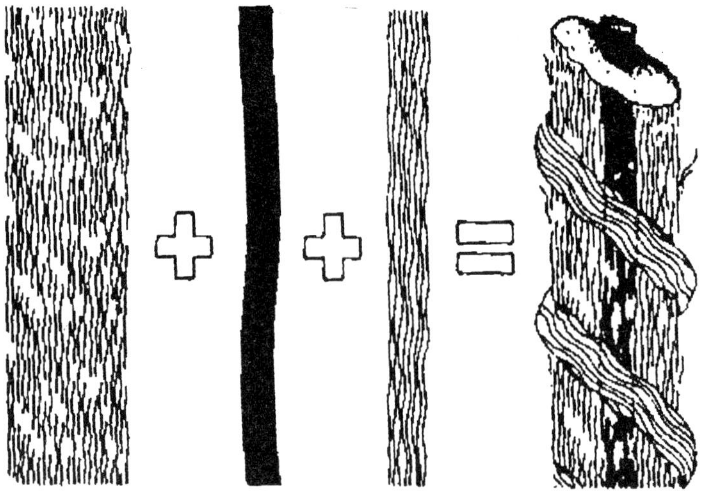

Fig.-2.6(e) Sketch of the structure of a Coverspun stretch yarn.

bonded by compression to the polymeric coated continuous filament core. The ICS yarn is then given a twist at high speed, cooled, and wound on spools (see Figure). This is all done in a continuous sequence of operations on one machine at rates of up to 2500 feet (750 m) per minute.

Significant economics can be achieved in ICS yarn production. Cost of manufacture is substantially lower than that of ring or open-end spinning, while production speed is greater. The carrier filament is less likely to break during production, which reduces downtime (loss of production due to interruption of operation). Any short or medium randomly arranged staple fibers can be used without involving carding, drawing, or roving operations. Further raw-material economies are realized since the finished yarn will contain 20 to 50 percent of the polymer resin, which is lower in cost than the staple fibers used in conventional ring or open-end spinning.

Characteristics of ICS Yarn. ICS yarn can have high tensile strength, depending upon the filament core, the polymer resin substrate, the staple, and the twist. The synergistic effect of the components contribute to the strength. The yarn tends to be uniform in diameter. Abrasion resistance of fabrics made of ICS yarn is good because after the staple is rubbed away, the polymer substrate must be worn through, and then the filament core must be abraded.

Different types of staple fibers of different staple lengths and different colors can be used to incorporate desirable properties, effects, and appearances. However, there is difficulty in obtaining uniform color in dyeing due to the difficulty of dye penetration into the polymer substrate; the result is a heather effect. Work on improved dyeing techniques is being pursued.

The yarn can be permanently crimped and otherwise engineered to produce a wide variety of yarns of various compositions for a great variety of purposes. ICS yarns are described by a numbering system that indicates the percentage by weight of each of the components: staple fiber/carrier filament/binder, resin; in that order. Thus, 35/40/25 signifies 35 percent surface staple fiber, 40 percent filament core, and 25 percent polymer resin. The nominal yarn count range is 300 to 30 tex.

To obtain the desired characteristics for ICS yarns, certain amounts of each component are required. The outer staple fiber content must be 30 to 60 percent to produce a satisfactory fiber cover and acceptable yarn. The filament core may constitute 10 to 60 percent of the yarn to provide strength and flexibility. The polymer resin content should be 20 to 50 percent for proper blending and consolidation. Within these constraints, a wide variety of general-purpose yarns can be produced (see Figure).For example, yarn for such uses as carpet or upholstery backing can be composed of 30 percent oriented polypropylene monofilament, 30 percent resin, and 40 percent short-staple cotton, linters, Rite, sisal, flax, etc. A low-stretch warp yarn for home furnishings or industrial fabrics can be made of 20 to 30 percent glass multifilament, 30 percent resin, and 30 to 40 percent any staple fiber, depending upon desired texture and appearance. Woolen and worsted yarns with permanent press properties can be made of 10 to 30 percent nylon or polyester multifilament, 30 to 40 percent resin, and 40 to 50 percent fine wool fibers. A low-cost, easy-care yarn for such applications as clothing, curtains, and upholstery can be composed of 30 percent nylon or polyester multifilament, 30 to 40 percent resin, and as little as 30 percent silk staple.

Coverspun

Another type of integrated multicomponent yarn spinning is Coverspun developed in England in the early 1970s. Two models of machinery have been designed: one for cotton system fibers of 1 to 2 inches (2- 5 cm) staple length and one for midfiber and worsted staple lengths of 21/2 to 8 inches (6- 20 cm). The technique wraps fine continuous filament manmade fiber around a core of untwisted natural or manmade staple fiber to produce yarns in a wide range of counts.

Production of Coverspun. Coverspun yarn is made by drafting conventional roving to the desired fineness and passing it directly into the top of a hollow vertical spindle that has a spool of filament mounted on it. The filament is fed into the top of the hollow spindle and as the spindle turns the filament wraps around the untwisted core. As the fully constructed yarn leaves the bottom of the hollow spindle, it is pulled through a nip roll and wound on a cheese package. Virtually all kinds of staple fiber may be used for the core; either nylon or polyester monofilament or multifilament of 26 to 55 denier (22.2-61.1 dtex) is used for the binder. The proportions are 85 to 90 percent staple core and 10 to 15 percent filament binder. The number of wraps are dependent upon the yarn count desired.

The count ranges on an equivalent cotton system of Ne 2 to 100. Yet, only about one-half the normal number of fibers per cross section are used to produce yarn counts equivalent to those produced by ring spinning. It is also possible to use coarser staple in moderately fine count yarns.

The technique of production has been found to be more efficient than ring spinning. Fewer filament wraps are required than staple twists for similar count ring-spun yarn, and there are fewer spinning interruptions from core and filament breaks, Labor and energy demands are lower.

Characteristics of Coverspun Yarn. The multicomponent construction of Coverspun results in yarns that are generally more even, uniform, fuller, and stronger than comparable yarns produced by conventional ring spinning. The greater strength rests primarily upon the wrapping filament, which carries the tension load, and secondarily on the interfiber friction caused by the compression of the parallel staple fibers.

Such specific properties as appearance, texture, durability, absorbency, warmth, and care will vary according to composition and structure of the yarn. The nature of the staple used in the core, the kind of filament wrap employed, the fineness and number of the filament used, the number of twists or wraps of the filament around the core, and the fineness of the yarn itself will all influence the properties of the yarn.

Coverspun yarn is used in woven and knitted fabrics. Finishing techniques are influenced by the combination of staple and filament yarns used. The fabrics may be used for apparel ranging from half hose and sweaters to stilts and dresses to drapery.

Selfil

The Selfil spinning technique, developed in Australia in the early 1970s and produced by Repco Limited, combines the self-twist principle for staple fibers.

Production of Selfil Yarn. The self twisted core is initially wrapped with a filament yarn in alternating S and Z phases; a second filament yarn is then wrapped around these in alternating opposite Z and S twists (see Figure 2.8) The filaments account for about 10 percent of the yarn content. A balanced three-strand yarn of counts equivalent to the cotton system of 20s to 60s can be produced at the rate of about 985 feet (300 m) per minute. The machine is said to require considerably less energy than ring spinning equipment, generally functions more economically, and has a low noise level.

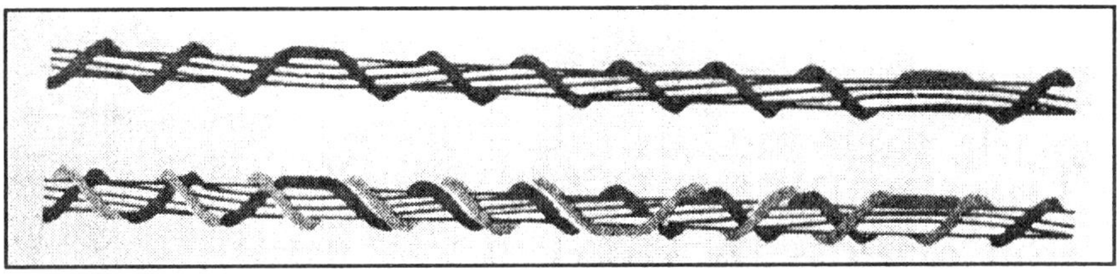

Fig.-2.7 Schematic of Selfil yarn construction. Upper diagram shows first continuous filament wrapped alternately in S and Z twist around self twisted staple core. Lower diagram depicts second continuous filament wrapped around the first in alternating Z and S twist and out of step by half of one twist zone.

Characteristics of Selfil Yarn. Good surface uniformity with a low rate of defects and freedom from snags are major features of Selfil. It has good resistance to pilling, high abrasion resistance, and relatively good strength depending upon its composition. Selfil yarns are considered well-suited for single and double jersey, hosiery , full-fashioned, mid warp-knit garments.

Aerodynamic Spinning

The aerodynamic spinning system passes continuous multifilament yarn together with staple fiber through a pneumatic device which causes the filaments to twist and curl, entrapping the staple fibers in the snarls. The yarn that is produced has an untwisted continuous multifilament core covered with twisted and entangled staple fibers. Such yarn, which is claimed to be similar in appearance to but stronger than ordinary spun yarn, can be produced about 4 times faster than yarns spun on the conventional ring-spinning system.

TYPES AND CHARACTERISTICS OF YARN

There are various types of yarn, each having its own characteristics. These characteristics vary according to the treatment given in the manufacture of the yarn.

Ply Yarns

The previous discussion of yarn production has concentrated on single strands. When two or more strands or yarns are twisted together, they are designated as ply yarns. They are termed two-ply, three-ply, and so on, according to the number used in their construction. A single yarn may be of relatively good quality; but where durability is all-important, ply yarns are preferable, assuming that the yarns have the same length of staple. Good-quality broadcloth for men's shirtings, for example, is made with ply yarns.

Yarn construction and yarn count are expressed differently according to the kind of staple or the filament fiber used. When yarn is sold, it is sold by weight but identified as to size and type by number.

Cotton and cotton blend yarns are designated by two numbers: the first identifies the yarn size and the second indicates the number of yarns used. For example, whereas 30/1 denotes a single yarn having a count of 30, a 30/2 yarn is two size 30 yarns plied together (this would be equivalent in size or diameter to a single yarn count of 15). Such a yarn would be referred to as 30 two ply or 30s two. In the same way, 30/3s denotes the use of a three-ply yarn-that is, three strands twisted together, each having a separate yarn count of 30. A three-ply, yarn, indicated by 30/3s would be equivalent to a single yarn having a yarn count of 10.

Worsted yarns, based upon the system used for spinning long staple wool into fine yarn, are designated in the reverse order. For example, 1/60 denotes a single yarn having a count of 60, and a 2/60 yarn) is two size 60 yarns plied together (this would be equivalent in size or diameter to a single yarn of 30). Such a yarn would be referred to as a *two sixty yarn.*

Linen yarns are designated by the term *lea,* such as 40 *lea* yarn, etc. They are almost never plied and, unless specifically indicated, are considered to be singles.

Filament yarns are also not generally plied. When they are, the designation is usually by the number of plies and the denier (diameter), such as three-ply 60 denier.

Cabled Yarns

Two or more plied yarns may be twisted together to form a cabled yarn. In general, it is constructed by twisting the plied yarns around each other successively in the opposite direction of the preceding twist, i.e., **S/Z/S or Z/S/Z.** As a result, the opposite twist directions cause the plies to grip each other and maintain adherence. These yarns are hard, rough, and strong.

Doubled Yarns

Another type of yarn construction is the *doubled yarn,* This consists of two or more Single strands treated as one in the weaving process, but the strands are not twisted together. The doubled yarn must not be confused with ply yarns, which are stronger because they are twisted. Doubled yarns are used for ornamental effect, they do, of course, contribute a certain amount of additional strength. Because doubled yarns have little twist, they produce luster and softness.

Novelty Yarns

The spinning process can produce decorative effects by varying the amount of twist or by twisting together yarns of different diameters, each of which may have different amounts of twist in them (Figure 2.9). Such yarns can give fabrics almost limitless textural effects of various color combinations. Fabrics made of novelty yarns cannot generally be as durable as fabrics made of uniform yarn, that have been evenly spun. A safe rule for the consumer is to remember that, longer service may be expected from flat, smooth fabrics made from evenly spun yarns rather than from novelty yarns of complex character.

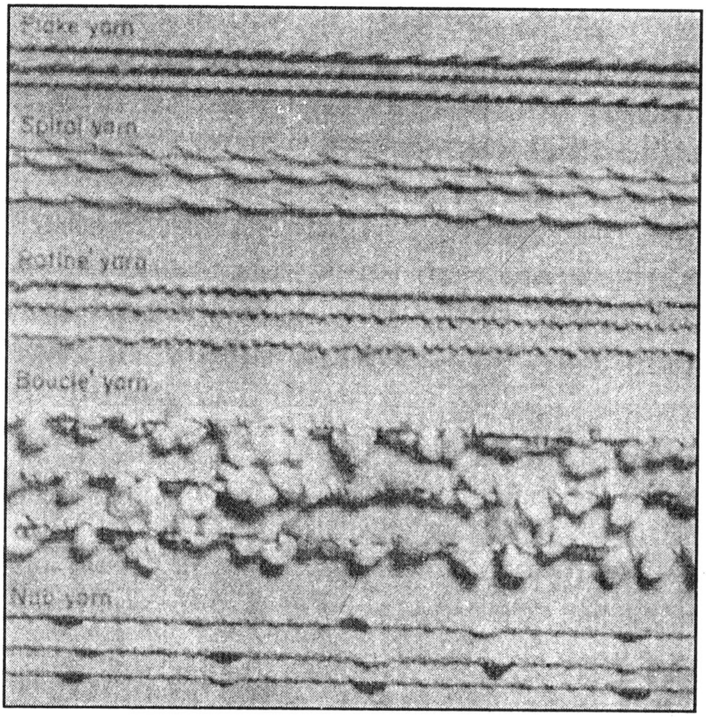

Fig.-2.8 Novelty Yarns

Slub Yarns. The consumer's desire for ornamental effects has popularized the production of yarns that are given only a small amount of drawing out. Such yarns, called *slub yarns,* have soft, untwisted areas at frequent intervals throughout their length. They are coarse, with slight twist, having varying diameters that show irregularities typical of all incomplete spinning operation.

If simulation of linen is desired, the use of slub yarns is easily understood. Where durability is a main consideration, their practicability is justly questioned, because a heavy yarn protruding above the level of surrounding yarns is subjected to friction and the fabric soon shows signs of wear at those points after continued use. In the past, slub yarns were generally used in fabrics that possessed an especially compact construction and consequently were characterized by marked durability. Today, slub yarns do not always imply compact construction in the fabric of which they are a part. They furnish ornamental effects and are often used for that purpose in shantung and tweed.

Flake Yarns. Flake yarns are variations of the slub yarns. The flake or slub effect is made by inserting soft, thick tufts of roving between binder yarns at intervals. The result is a flake yarn of varying thickness and softness, caused by the soft-effect ply held in place by the uniform binder. This type of yarn is limited to fancy-effect uses .

Spiral Yarns. The general appearance of a spiral yarn is that of a coarse yarn wound around a fine yarn, giving the effect of a spiral. The thicker yarn is given a slack twist and wound spirally around the fine yarn (sometimes referred to as the *core yarn),* which is given a hard twist. Other names for the spiral yarns are corkscrew and eccentric. Spiral yarns may be made for different purposes. They may be constructed in such a way as to give the decorative spiral effect of a candy-cane pattern. Sometimes the core yarn is completely hidden by the spiraling outer yarn, as in the case of Lastex where the core yarn is rubber while the outer yarn may be of cotton, nylon, or other textile.

Ratine Yarns. Ratine yarns are a variation of the spiral yarn type, although the method of manufacture differs. The outer (effect) yarn and the core yarn are twisted in a spiral manner, but at intervals a longer loop is thrown out by the effect yarn, which kinks back on itself and is held in place by a third (binder) yarn. The binder is added in a second twisting operation going in the opposite direction of the effect yarn. The ratine yarn's small loops on its surface give the yarn a taut, rough-surfaced effect. The technique may be applied to all major fibers and is popular for combinations of yarns made of such fibers as cotton and rayon.

Boucle, Loop, or Curl Yarns. Boucle loop, or curl yarns are comparable to the ratine yarn type, but in boucle yarns the surface is softer and has a more pronounced novelty effect. This effect is accomplished by allowing one of the plies to remain slack during the twisting operation, causing it to twist on itself and form a loop. The size of the loop will vary depending on the speed of the rollers. These yarns are popular for knitted fabrics. They are also used to create fabrics with a looped pile to resemble fur, such as karakul, for trimmings and coating fabrics.

Nub, Knop, Knot, or Spot Yarns. Nub yarns are made by twisting the effect ply around the core ply many times within a very short space, causing bumps or nubs that may be spaced at intervals along the yarn. Variations are possible where, for example, two effect plies, each of different color, may be used, and the nubs arranged so that the colors are alternated along the length of the yarn. In some instances, nub yarns are wound by a binder or third thread; in other cases, the effects can be created without the binder.

Chenille Yarns. The term *chenille is* derived from the French for "caterpillar," and the yarn does somewhat resemble one. It has a soft, fuzzy, lofty (springy) surface. The effect is achieved by a core of two yarns plied together and firmly holding short tufts of soft-twisted yarn between the twists along the core's length. The result is a yarn with a velvet like or pile surface.

A common method of manufacturing chenille yarn is to construct a fabric on a leno weave using soft twisted yarn in the filling . The warp yarns usually are 1/8 to 1/4 inches (3-7 mm) apart. The fabric is then split into strips between the warps and the soft filling yarns held within the twists of the warps form the characteristic fuzzy pile surface of chenille yarn.

Chenille is generally made from cotton, wool, rayon, nylon, or polyester and is made into fabrics that are soft and have good draping effects. These fabrics are used for such varied purposes as dresses, drapery, and bedspreads. However, the soft chenille yarns are vulnerable to rubbing and the fabrics do not wear well because of the low abrasion resistance.

Sewing Thread

Sewing threads are specifically designed for efficient, smooth stitching that will not break or become distorted for the useful life of the sewn product. The adequacy of the thread depends upon its composition, construction, and finish as well as its proper selection for the fabric and type of seam to be used.

Construction of Thread. Sewing threads are made of cotton, linen, silk, rayon, nylon, or polyester. The properties of the fiber determine its use and application. For example, cotton is the most widely used because of its high versatility and low cost; rayon, which is much -weaker, is used primarily for fancy stitchwork; polyester is used where strength and water repellency are important.

All Sewing threads are made of ply yarns. The single yarns, which may be spun, filament, or multicomponent are highly twisted (plied) to form a firmer and more uniform thread than ordinary yarn. Sewing thread may be given special finishes, such as mercerizing, glace, or water repellency to serve particular uses .

Thread Sizes. Identification of thread size, called *ticket number, is* undergoing a transition. Different kinds of yarns had different numbering designations. On January 1, 1980, The Thread Institute adopted a standardized ticket numbering system based on the tex system of numbering yarn . The system is to be used on a voluntary basis by its member manufacturers, converters, and jobbers. Adoption by the American Society for Testing and Materials (ASTM), the American National Standards Institute (ANSI), and the International Organization for Standardization (ISO) is expected. Pending full acquaintance and acceptance by industry and consumers, both the past systems and the tex system will be used. It is therefore necessary to describe the several ticket number systems for appropriate application.

The size of spun thread had always been expressed in terms of its diameter: the higher the number, the finer the thread .At one time, thread had been made only from three-ply spun yarns. Therefore, a spun yarn thread of 50 *three ply* (50/3) had a ticket number of 50, a thread of 60 *three ply* (60/3) had a ticket number of 60, and so forth. Subsequently, the number of plies in sewing thread was extended to two, three, four, and six ply. A ticket number of 50 could therefore indicate a 50 two ply (50/2), a 50 three ply (50/3), a 50 four ply (50/4), or a 50 six ply (50/6); but the thickness of the thread in each case was the same, while each ply was thinner. The greater number of ply yarns implied greater thread strength.

The sizes of mercerized cotton sewing thread were identified by letter as well as number. The range was from F (coarsest) to A (medium), and then from 0 to 00000 (finest).

Sewing thread is also made of filament fiber. The denier designation had been used, and the lower the number, the finer the thread. The size of filament sewing thread had been identified by denier, except that the last digit was omitted. For example, a 180 denier thread had a ticket number 18.

The tex system is intended to give an orderliness by providing one ticket numbering system based upon the metric *System* which is expected to become universally adopted. Since tex is the weight in grams of a 1000-meter length and is a direct numbering system, the greater the weight the thicker the thread and therefore the higher the number. Ticket numbers are based on actual tex size of the thread in the griege state, i.e. twisted, braided, or extruded before any dyeing, special processing, or finishing. The purpose of the stipulation is intended to obviate the alteration of the thread's apparent size by any finishes.The following is the system adopted:

STANDARD SEWING THREAD
TEX TICKET NUMBERS

1	10	35	105	300
2	12	40	120	350
3	14	45	135	380
4	16	50	150	400
5	18	60	180	450
6	21	70	210	500
7	24	80	240	Above 500, in
8	27	90	270	increments of 100
9	30			

One important caution should be noted when using the tex ticket numbers. When selecting proper thread size, threads of the *same* fiber and type must be compared. Since the tex ticket numbering system is based on weight and since different kinds of fibers and/or types have different weights, the same tex number of threads of different fibers or types will not necessarily be of the same thickness and may therefore not be interchangeable.

Thread Selection. Selection of the appropriate kind and size of sewing thread is important. The thread should be as fine as possible, consistent with the nature of the fabric and the strength requirements of the stitching. Finer threads could be less obvious, they become hidden below the surface of the cloth, and they are less subject to abrasion than heavier threads. Also, finer threads require finer needles which cause less fabric distortion than heavier needles. Threads composed of the same kind of fiber as that of the fabric is also important because of such factors, as general appearance, color fastness, finish retention, elasticity and strength.

3 COMFORT YARNS

The yarns discussed are made of fibers in their normal forms.

While they are produced in many varieties to provide various effects, each yarn's characteristics are limited by the normal condition of the fiber's shape, its thickness, its length and surface texture, as well as such inherent qualities as elasticity, resilience, and warmth.

Consumers often desire certain characteristics combined into one yarn for a particular kind of fabric. They welcome new, interesting, and useful properties in fabrics made from yarns that normally cannot provide these characteristics. Consequently, techniques have been developed that change the surface or shape and texture of the fibers and, in turn, affect the characteristics of the yarns. These *textured* yarns provide consumers with variations in fabric properties that they seek. For convenient identification, they may be grouped into three types: stretch, high bulk, and loop bulk.

TEXTURED YARNS

Textured yarns made of filament fibers may be produced either by the fiber producer, the throwster, or trade-texturizer who serves as an intermediary between the fiber producer and the fabric Manufacturer, or the user-texturizer. The yarn may be textured from undrawn, partially drawn, or fully drawn filaments.

A major source of textured yarns is from fully drawn filaments. Fibers such as nylon or polyester (the two major fibers that are textured) are produced by extrusion through small orifices in spinnerets as tacky streams of filaments. The number of filaments and the denier, or diameter, of the yarns depend upon the desired effect and intended use. They are attentuated to a desired denier (diameter) by being drawn through a series of rollers. This process causes the molecules in the fibers to be longitudinally reoriented into a chainlike connected series and makes the filaments into uniform, stronger, and stable. The filaments are thus fully drawn, and the yarns are referred to as parent yarn (PY) or fully oriented yarn (FOY). Traditionally, the texturizer purchases the fully oriented yarn from the producer and processes it into the desired texture. This division of labor has additional built-in costs and results to some degree in lack of uniformity in the ultimate texturing process.

One alternative to this approach is to produce filaments without attenuating them after they emerge from the spinneret, thereby producing undrawn (UD) yarn. Since the fiber is not subjected to any significant linear orientation, it must be specially handled by meticulous packaging and by controlling the humidity, temperature, and oxygen to retain its viscous state. The fiber producer or texturizer subsequently draws and textures the yarn, but it must be done within a relatively short period of time of about two weeks in order to obtain the desired results. The fragility of this technique provides much risk.

Another approach is that of texturing from partially oriented yarn (POY). Fiber manufacturers produce filaments which are partially or incompletely drawn to yarns of a predetermined size. This drawing only partially aligns the molecules in the lengthwise direction of the fiber. These partially oriented yarns, sometimes called partially drawn yarns (PDY) depending upon the technique used, may be draw-textured by either the fiber producer itself, the trade-texturizer, or the user-texturizer. the conversion of POY yarn by *draw texturing is* done either by the sequential or the simultaneous method.

The sequential method the fibers are drawn through rollers and the resultant drawn yarn enters a heater unit attached to the texturing machine and then feeds into the appropriate texturing treatment. This procedure is the one more widely used. It is particularly more suited to draw texturing of nylon.

In the simultaneous system POY yarn is simultaneously drawn and textured in the first heater unit of the texturing inachine itself and then subjected to final annealing, or curing, in a second heater zone. This method seems to be better for draw texturing of polyester.

Draw texturing from partially oriented yarns has been shown to be an adaptable technique. Although it has some aging and handling problems, it is less troublesome than draw texturing from undrawn yarn. As the denier of the POY yarn decreases, the yarn becomes more oriented and has greater stability. Consequently, its aging period call be longer. In general, that period ranges between three and eight weeks. Longer delays could result in higher costs, create production problems, and reduce manufacturing efficiencies. Other advantages of the use of partially oriented yarn for texturing are lower production costs, more even yarn, and consequently greater ease and uniformity in dyeing.

The kinds and characteristics of the yarns produced are dependent upon the texturing processes. There are two major types of textured yarns: stretch and bulk.

STRETCH YARNS

There are five kinds of stretch yarns: (1) those made bv giving a special mechanical heat-setting treatment to thermoplastic filament fibers such as nylon or polyester; (2) those made of elastomeric fibers, such as spandex or rubber; (3) those made of bicomponent fibers, such as two different types of nylon produced as a single filament, (4) those made of biconstituent fibers, such as two different polymers produced as a single filament; and (5) those made of specially chemically treated natural fibers, such as cotton.

There are also several different techniques that are used in producing each kind of stretch yarn. These stretch yarns are then selected for use in producing stretch fabrics of two general types: *power stretch* and *comfort stretch*

Heatset Thermoplastic Yarns

The long, smooth, endless strands of man made filament fibers, such as nylon, have various, amounts of natural ability to stretch when pulled and to spring back to their original sizes when allowed to relax. However, when subjected to certain methods that use heat to set crimp in these thermoplastic filament yarns, the crimp greatly increases their stretchability.

A *thermoplastic yarn is* one that can be put into any shape or position desired and, after being subjected to a predeterinined level of heat for a specific period of time, will retain that shape despite washing, dry cleaning, stretching, or compressing. This heat-setting technique is employed in many ways, and depending on the method of manufacture and the fibers used, the properties of the yarn will also vary.

Thermoplastic stretch yarns have many advantages over untreated filament yarns. They have a soft touch and a dull appearance like that of wool rather than the sometimes undesirable sheen of some flament yarns, the resultant textural appearance of stretch yarns provides opportunity for desirable novelty effects. Fabrics or garments made of these yarns have a higher degree of absorbency and adsorbency than ordinary filament yarns, since stretch yarns provide loops and kinks to hold the moisture. This results in providing better perspiration conductivity and consequently increases comfort to the wearer. The pockets of air caused by the coils in the yarns also act as an insulative barrier, making the garment warmer.

Garments made of such stretch yarns wash easily and dry clean readily. They are as strong and durable as garments made of yarns of similar fibers that have not been processed into stretch yarns. In fact, the stretch characteristic is more likely to result in less strain on the yarns, fabrics, and seams of garments during the ordinary stress of putting on, wearing, and taking off. The stretchability also provides greater comfort, shape retention, and wrinkle resistance and allows the garment to conform to the figure and to fit better. Solving the fitting problem is an advantage not only to the consumer but also to the mnufacturer, who finds it more economical to produce fewer specific sizes, and to the retailer, who needs less space to store fewer sizes and finds it easier to fit the consumer.

There are four general types of heatset thermoplastic yarns: coil, curl, crimp, and wavy. All are treated to provide a spring like or accordionlike characteristic to the yarn. The methods of accomplishing this vary, thereby giving different shapes to the yarns but producing somewhat similar effects.

Coil Types: Conventional Method. This method utilizes conventional twisting equipinent with heat-setting techinques. It consists basically of untwisting nylon or polyester yarns inserting a measured twist [from 47 to 114 turns per inch (18-45 turns/cm)] depending upon denier, heat-setting the yarn in that condition in a high-pressure steam autoclave at approximately 260 degrees Fahrenheit [130 degrees Celsius for an hour or less, and then untwisting the yarns to a predetermined level. As a result, the torque or tendency to twist back to its heat-set condition causes the filaments to bulk tip into a spring like condition. To give balance to the yarn, a set of filaments previously given an S twist is generally plied a few turns with a previously Z-twisted set of ends.

Helanca nylon, a well-known stretch yarn introduced by the Heberlein Patent Corp. in 1947, is produced by this conventional method. It is now produced under license by many compaines. This yarn can be stretched 3 times its relaxed length in heavier weights and from 4 to 5 times in lighter yarns. Helanca has excellent recovery to its original size on release of the tension and will provide a snug fit and shape retention to garments made from it. It has a firm, crisp hand and a bulking power up to 3 times its uncoiled condition. Different types of Helanca stretch yarn are produced to meet specific requirements and end uses. They vary from high stretch to low stretch with high bulk.

Coil Types: **False-Twist Method.** Most of the world's stretch yarn is made by this method because it is more economical and much faster to produce. It is basically a technique of temporarily putting a very high twist in a multifilament yarn, heat-setting the yarn in this twisted condition, cooling it quickly,and then untwisting the yarn (see Figure 3.1). The operation is based on the principle that a stationary multifilament yarn that is held at both ends and twisted at the center by art eccentrically placed hook will develop equal amounts of twist in opposite directions on each side of the guide hook. The opposite direction of the twist in the yarn as it passes out of the false-twist spindle cancels out the twist in the yarn. However, since the yarn is made of a thermoplastic fiber that has been heat-set in a coiled condition, the yarn develops a Coil like, bulky, springy character (Figure3.2).

On emerging from the false-twist spindle, the yarn has a built-in torque (or twist) in either the S or the Z direction, which depends upon the direction of the rotating spindle. Since fabrics made of yarns in this condition would be distorted, yarns of opposite torques are usually plied or sometimes doubled to provide balance.

The amount of stretchability and the texture of the yarn is dependent upon such factors as its diameter, the amount of false twist used, the amount and method of heat applied, and the ply of the yarn. The principal varieties are as follows:

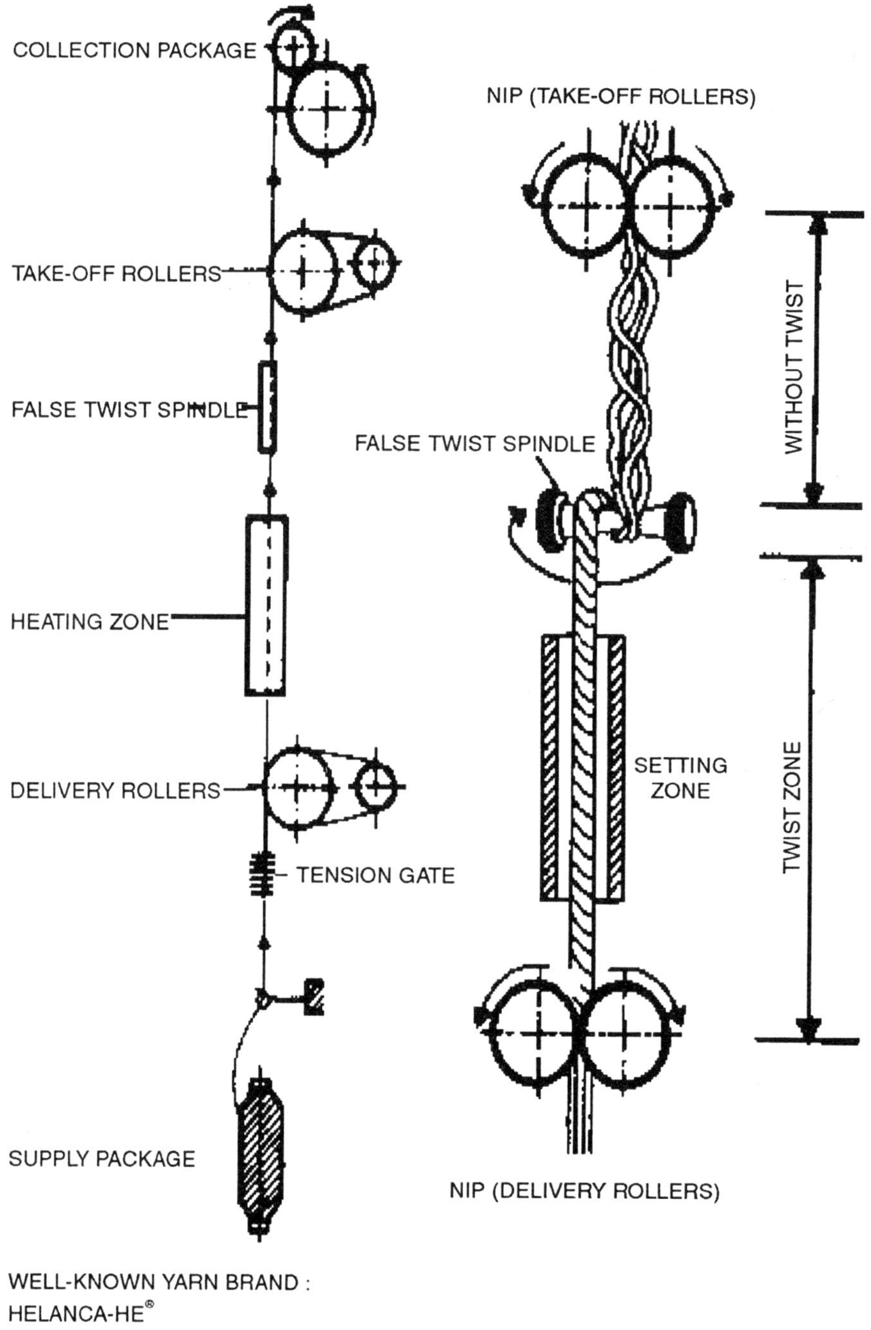

Fig.-3.1 Schematic representation of false-twist coiling.

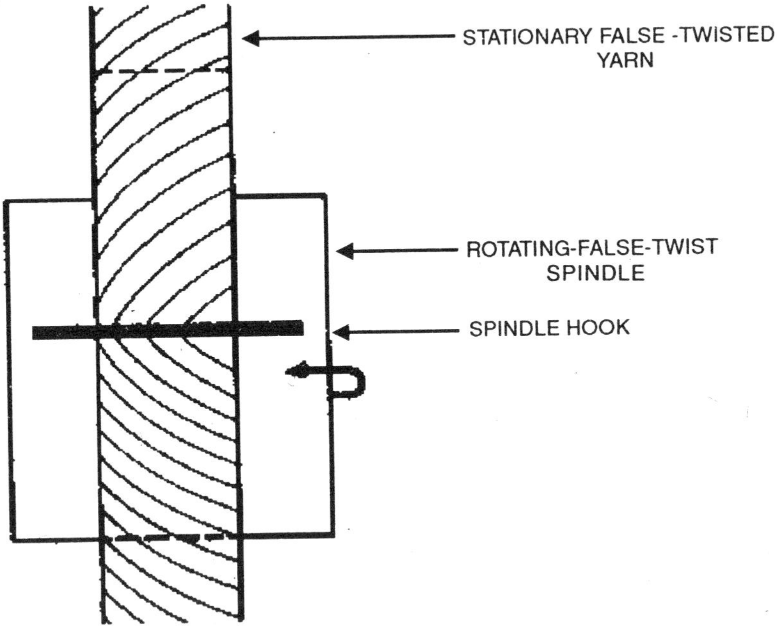

(a)

Fig.-3.2 (a) Schematic representation shows insertion of false-twist in a stationary yarn.

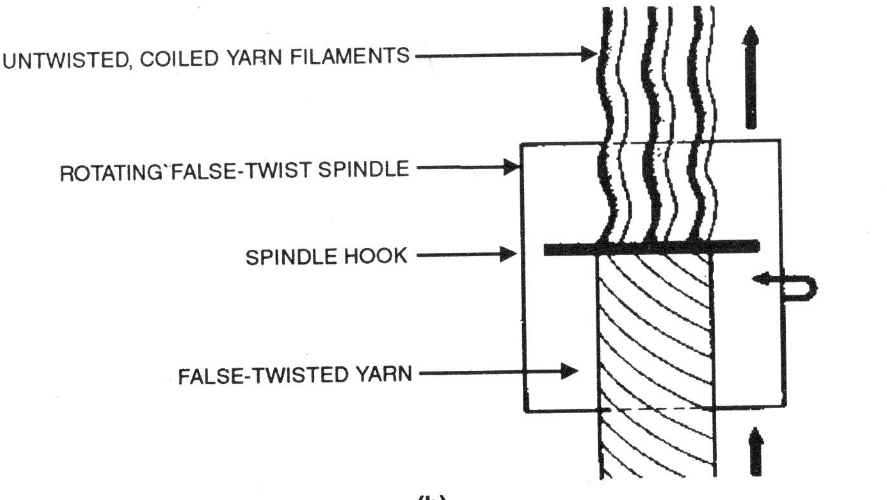

(b)

Fig.-3.2 (b) insertion of false-twist in a moving yarn. As the yarn is drawn through the spindle, the twist is resticted to that part of the yarn reaching the spindle hook; it leaves the false-twist spindle with the filaments untwisted but coiled.

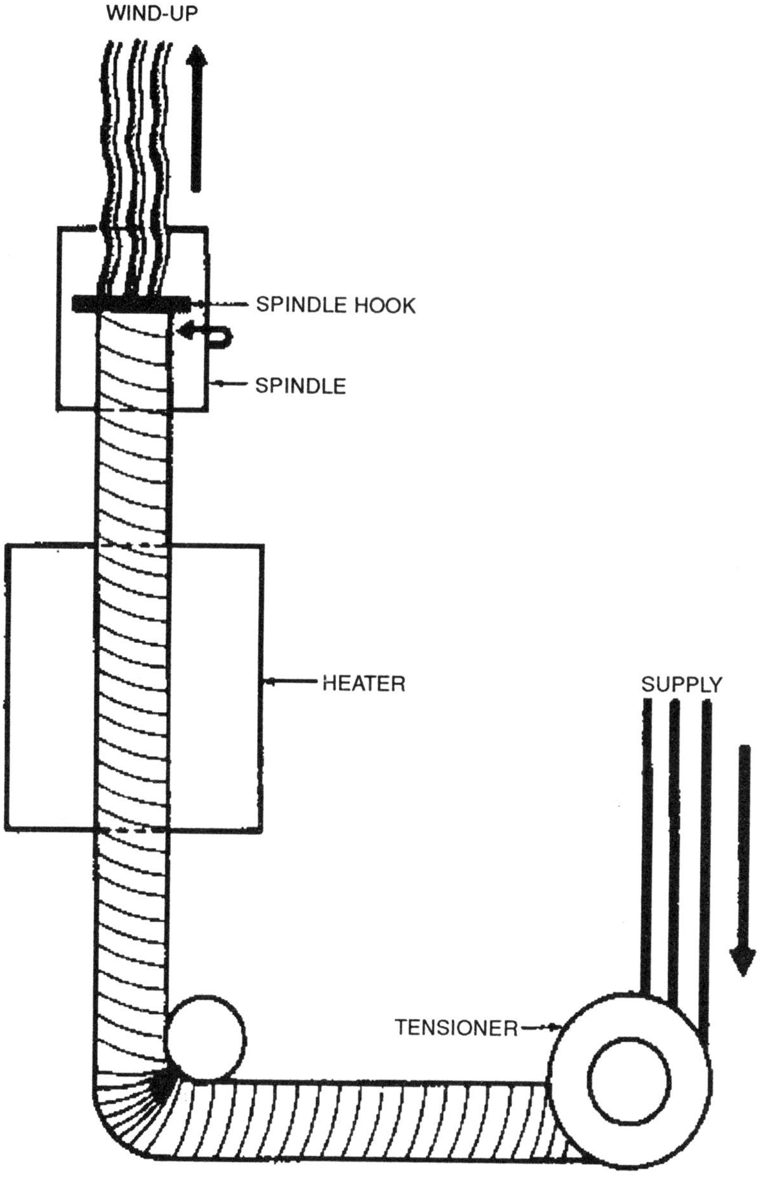

(c)

Fig.-3.2 (c) Schematic shows the false-twist texturing process. The untwisted yarn is given a false twist and is then heatset just below the false-twist spindle. The spindle hook holds the twist below itself and permits the yarn to be untwisted above it as it leaves the false-twist spindle, but the heat-set coil in the filaments is retained.

Helanca generally has less stretch than the other stretch yarns made by the false-twist method. It is used for sweaters and crepe-textured fabrics that need a more relaxed fit.

Fluflon yarn, which is produced on machines manufactured by the Leesona Corp., is usually made of nylon but could be made of other thermoplastic fibers. The yarn may be made into singles or plied. It has a high degree of elasticity, stretches up to 4 times its original length, and relaxes to its normal size. It has a very soft hand and a variety of uses.

Superloft, which is also produced on Leesona machines, is another trademark for stretch yarns made of any thermoplastic fiber. It has good bulk but less stretch than Fluflon.

Whitin ARCT, manufactured by the Whitin Machine Works, is a nylon stretch yarn. It can be stretched up to 5 times its relaxed length and, when relaxed, it can bulk up to 3 times its stretched diameter.

Cumuloft is a MonsantoTextiles Co. nylon stretch yarn. Its characteristics are the same as Whitin ARCT.

Saaba is a false-twist yarn that has been modified by a second heat-setting treatment at a lower temperature. The technique reduces the stretch but increases the bulk. The trademark is owned by Leesona Corp. (see Figure3-3)

Coil Types: Autotwist Principle. This process is similar to the false-twist principle. Two thermoplastic yarns are twisted around each other and then are passed over the surface of a heated tube to set them. The yarns are subsequently separated and the tension in them is equalized, but their coil, which provides the strech characteristic, is retained (see Fig 3.4).

Duo-Twist is a trademark for a stretch yarn which is made by this process and developed by the Turbo Machine Co. (see Figure 3.5).

Curl Types: Stress-curled Method. This is essentially an adaptation of the method of obtaining a random curl in a paper ribbon by pulling it between one's thumb and the edge of a dull blade (see figure3.6).

Agilon is the trademark of the stretch yarn first developed by this process and patented by the Deering Milliken Research Trust. This thermoplastic yarn is softened by heating and passed with a slight pressure

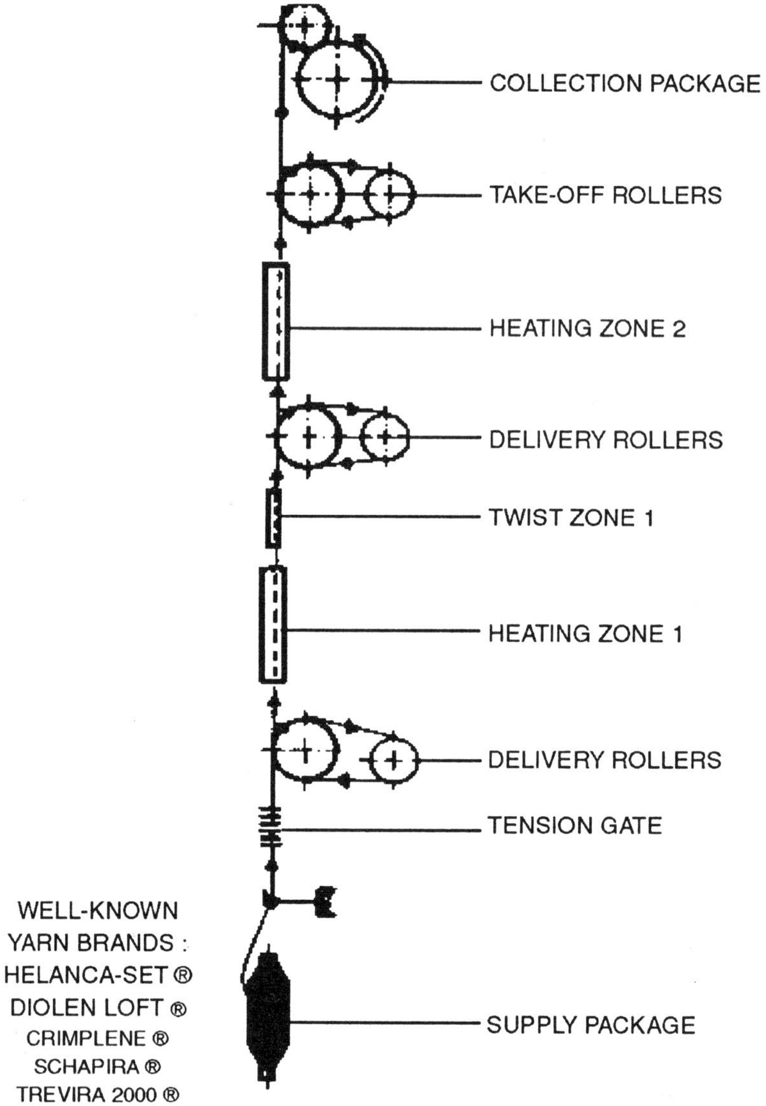

Fig.-3.3. Schematic representation of yarns with reduced stretch; false-twist coiling with postseting.

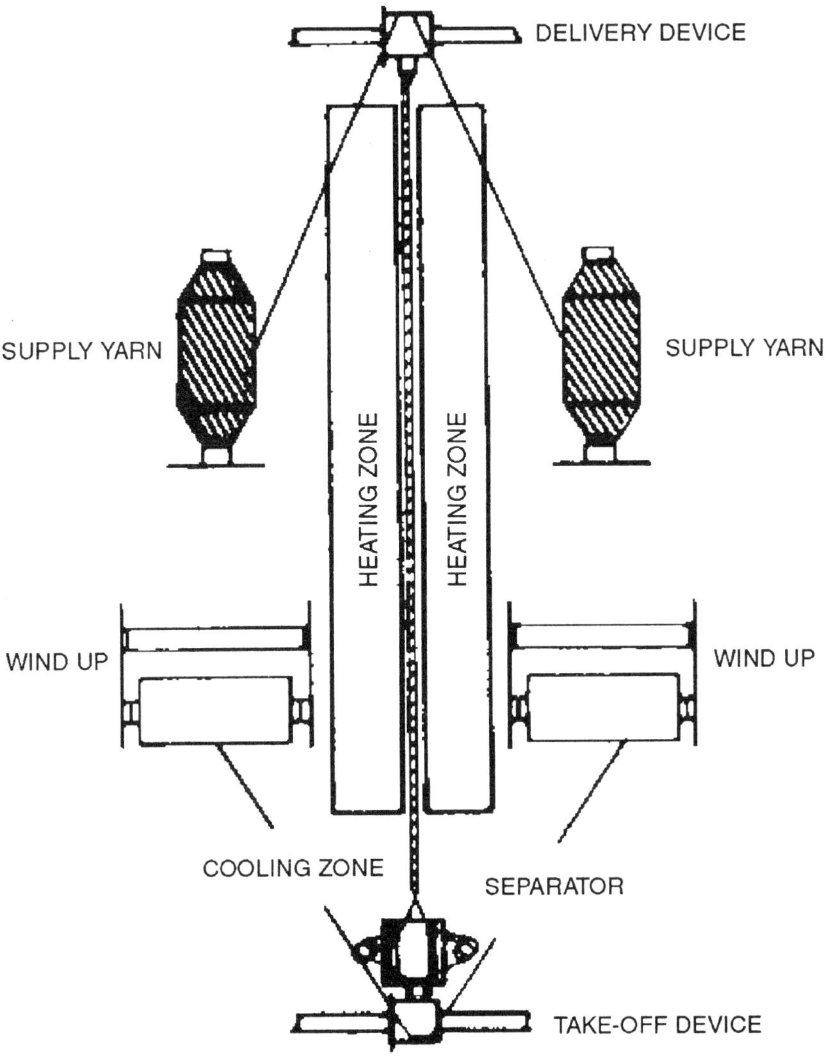

Fig.-3.4. Schematic representation of autotwist principle.

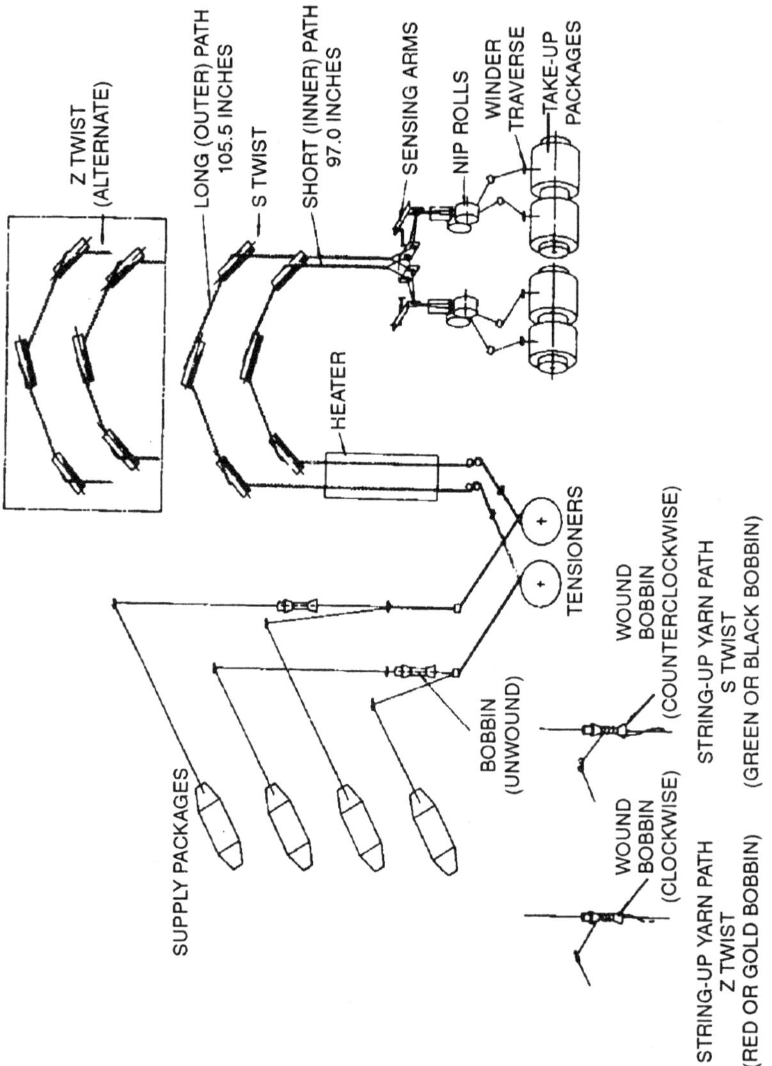

Fig.-3.5. Schematic Do-Twist yarn patern.

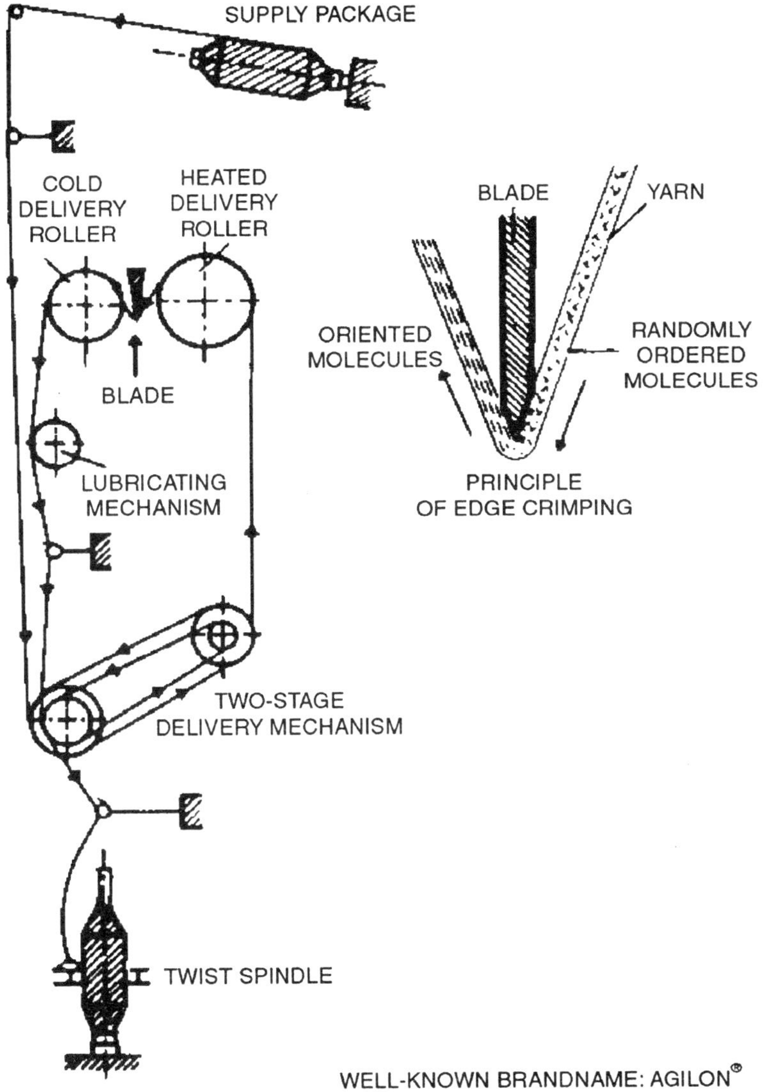

Fig.-3.6. Schematic representation of edge curling.

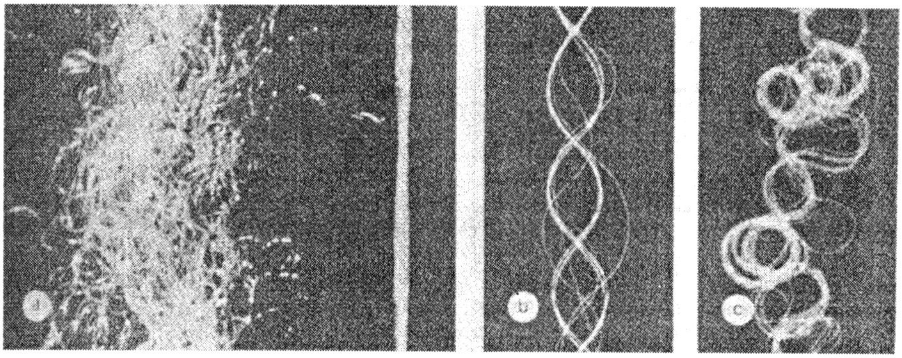

over a dull knife edge, which deforms the filaments by flattening one part of their curved surfaces. The actual contracting and stretching characteristic of the yarn is added to the fabric made from this yarn in the washing or scouring process, which is part of the finishing operation. The yarn develops very short sections of marked curl and torque, but since they change position at random, the net result is a balanced no-torque effect in the fabric.

Agilon yarn is producсd in monofilament and multifilament forms. It has an additional distinguishing feature in that a filament fiber, such as nylon, can have a staple fiber, stich as cotton or wool, spun around it. Therefore, the textural characteristics can vary; Agilon yarn can simulate any kind of yarn made of any kind of fiber, whether smooth or rough, soft or harsh.

Depending on the denier and processing of the yarn, Agilon can stretch up to 3 times its length and return to its original length on release of the tension. Unlike some other stretch yarns, Agilon yarn does not immediately snap back with an almost rubber-band action after it has been released. It recovers its original shape more slowly. This gentle elasticity results in less strain on the fabric and no binding to the wearer, which insures increased comfort. Garments made of Agilon yarn include men's, women's, and children's hosiery, creped fabrics for women's blouses and lingerie, and pile fabrics, such as velvets, artificial furs, and fleeces.

Crimp types: **Stuffer Box Method.** This process is essentially one of tightly cramming thermoplastic yarn into a container and heat-setting it in this cramped condition, thereby forming a random zigzag crimp (see FIgure 3.8)

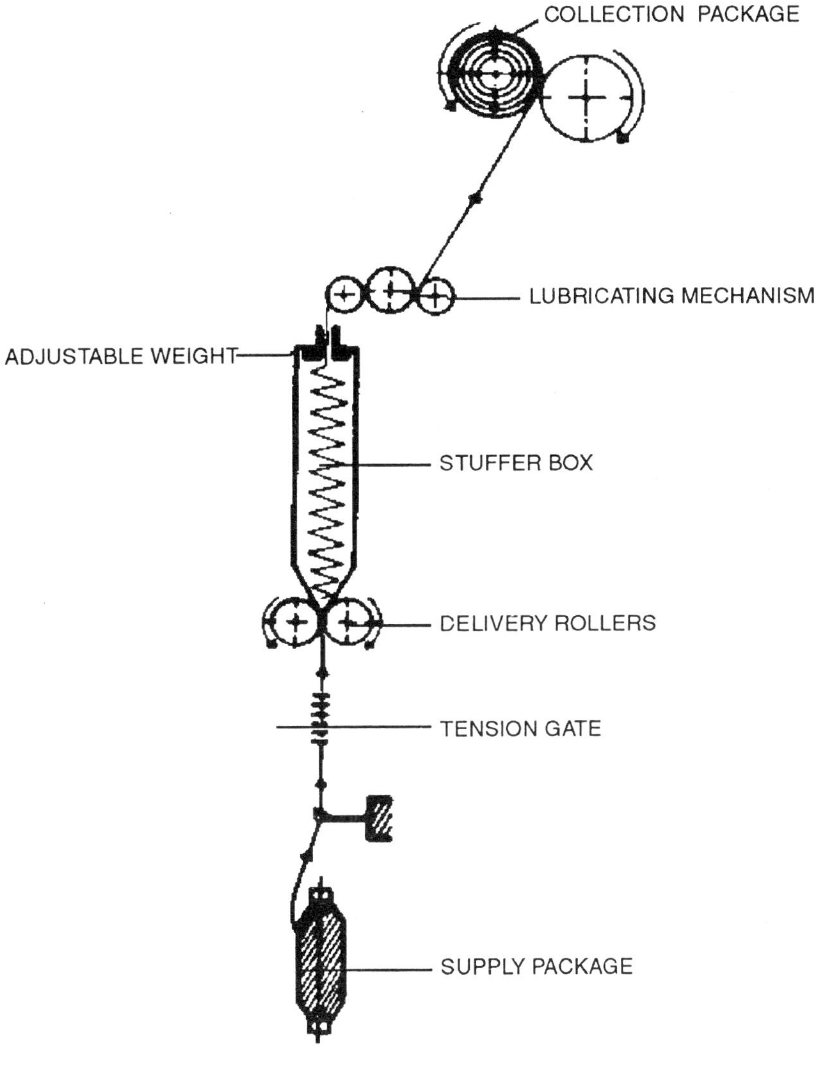

Fig.-3.8. Schematic representation of stuffer crimping.

Spunized yarn is an example of this method. It is produced by the Hartford Spinners process from thermoplastic yarn in a laced-chain arrangement, passed through a stuffer box, and heat-set. The yarn is soft and quite bulky, but it has limited stretch.

Crimp Types: Gear Method, Another method of putting crimp into thermoplastic yarn employs the teeth on heated gears wheels, car wheels. As the is passed between the wheels, it is crimped into a Jagged fashion in conformation to the gears and is heatset. The permanently crimped yarn is then wound on spools (see Figure3.9).

Crimp Types: IWS Crimp Method. IWS Crimp is related to the stuffer-box method, yet, it is different. It was developed by the International wool Secretariat specialy to increase the crimp of some types of wool that do not have much crimp. The process is based upon the natural thermoplasticity of wool. The procedure is incorporated into the carding process for spinning wool sliver into yarn.

A device causes the fiber to be fed into the crimping zone 4 times faster than it emerges, causing the wool fiber to be compressed in its length and thereby becoming crimped. Steam is jetted onto the fiber to set the crimp permanently.

The crimped fiber is then immediately moved into another chamber where high velocity Jets of hot air dry the fiber. The yarn of this crimped fiber, called Programmed Pile, is used for rugs (see Figure 3-10).

Wavy Types: Knit-Deknit Method. This technique requires that a thermoplastic yarn to be knitted into a fabric and then heat-set. The yarn is subsequently unraveled from the fabric. The loops, formed in knitting and then heat-set, remain permanently in the yarn and give it a wavy or crimpy character (see Figures 3.11 &3.12)

Elastomeric Yarns

All these yarns are elastic because of the inherent nature of the basic fiber: rubber or spandex.

Rubber. Everyone is familiar with the elasticity of rubber. In fact, it is this characteristic that brought about the production of rubber yarn as the first stretch yarn. It has been produced for many years under the trademark Lastex. This type of yarn has a rubber core with a ply of cotton

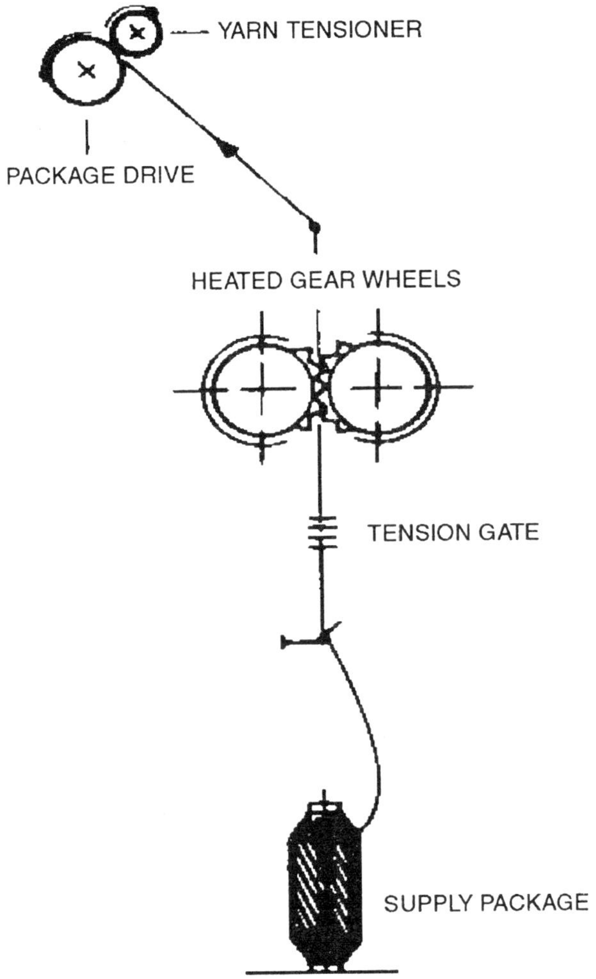

Fig.-3.9. Schematic representation of gear crimping.

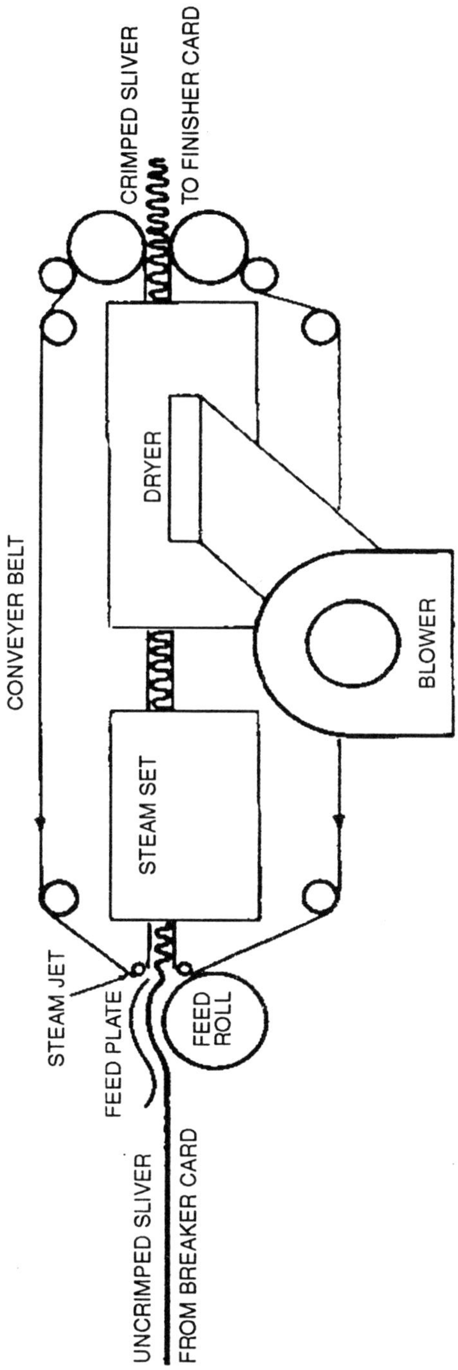
CRIMPED SLIVER
TO FINISHER CARD
CONVEYER BELT
DRYER
BLOWER
STEAM SET
STEAM JET
FEED PLATE
FEED
ROLL
UNCRIMPED SLIVER
FROM BREAKER CARD

Fig.-3.10.

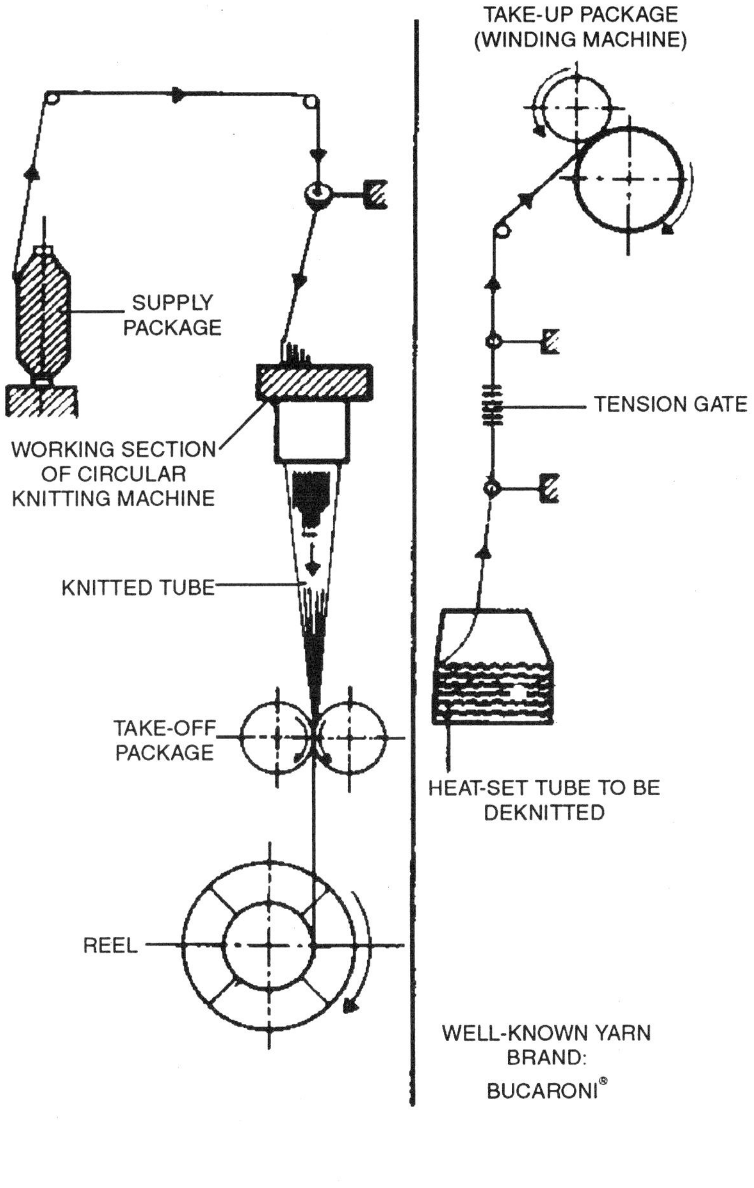

Fig.-3.11. Schematic representation of knitdeknit routine.

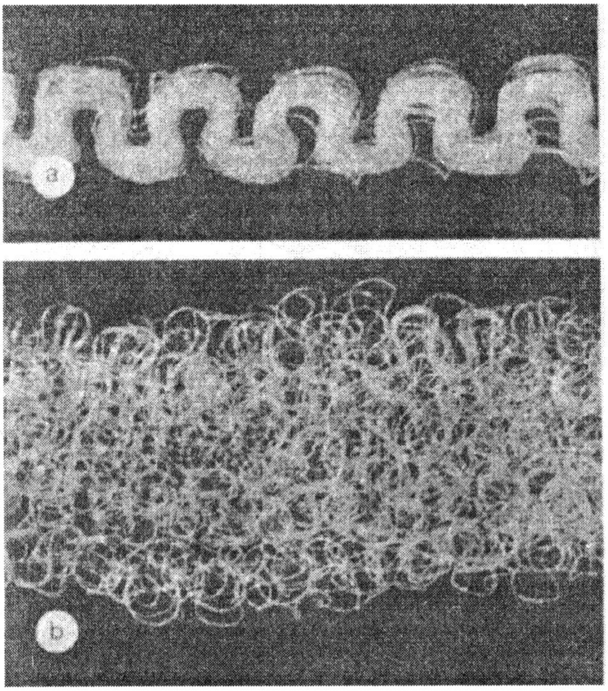

Fig.-3.12. (a) A heat-set nylon yarn as it first appears from the knit-deknit process. (b) A stretch high-bulk nylon yarn produced by the knit-deknit process.

or some other yarn wound around it, thus combining the elasticity of rubber with the texture and hand of the other fiber, which hides the rubber.

Rubber yarn can be produced in weights fine enough for sheer fabrics and laces and heavy enough for foundation garments. Stretched rubber has a strong tendency to return to its relaxed condition, which makes it an excellent yarn for power stretch fabrics for supportive or holding purposes. It is not affected by laundering or dry cleaning, but the use of chlorine bleach or excessive amounts of dry-cleaning fluid should be avoided. Over a period of time, rubber loses its elasticity as the rubber tends to dry out and deteriorate. Fabrics of rubber yarn are heavier than fabrics made of other types of stretch yarns.

Spandex. Spandex is a manmade fiber and has the distinctive property of stretching about 4 to 7 times its relaxed state without breaking. This high degree of elasticity, along with its relatively light weight and its resistance to most solvents (including the common dry-cleaning and laundering agents), make it superior to rubber. Spandex fibers have a comfortable hand, wear very well, and retain their natural whiteness. They do not dye easily and may fade.

Spandex fibers, such as Lycra, are also produced as core-spun yarns. These yarns have a spandex core (which could be as little as 5 to 15 percent of the entire yarn) with a layer of any staple fiber spun around the core as it is held under a predetermined amount of tension. When it is relaxed after spinning, the spandex core returns to its normal length, which pulls the outer layer of spun fibers into a more compact formation. This technique can control the degree of stretchability of the core-spun yarn from a very low degree to twice its relaxed state. Since the core yarn is encased in a layer of staple fibers, the yarn takes on the hand and appearance of these fibers.

Depending upon the kind of spandex fiber used and the type of yarn construction, spandex yarns can have various degrees of either power or comfort stretch Spandex yarns differ from the heat-set thermoplastic stretch yarns in that they have a stronger pull or tendency to recover to original size. This provides more positive support to the body. They are therefore very useful for foundation garments, support hose, and swimsuits. They are also used in various modified stretch capacities for garments ranging from lingerie to ski stilts.

A variation of the use of spandex fiber in yarn that has been under development is called *intimate blend spinning.* The objective is a stretch yarn spun of a blend of spandex staple with any other staple fiber that is desired in the yarn by the fabric producer. As with other blends, the characteristics of the yarns and fabrics produced depend on the kind and the amount of fiber blended, the kind of spun yarn, and fabric construction.

Bicomponent Yarns

This yarn is made of a filament of two types of a manmade fiber extruded simultaneously through the spinneret opening. The fibers adhere in simese fashion. As the yarn is processed , one type, which shrinks more than the other, pulls on the other type attached to it and causes the whole filament to become distorted and crimped. Such yarns are free of torque. Cantrece, which is used for hosiery, is a nylon bicomponent yarn produced by Du Pont.

Biconstituent Yarns

This yarn is made of two different kinds of manmade polymers extruded simultaneously from the spinneret opening The polymers adhere together to form a single filament, in the production of stretch yarns, one polymer may be spandex, for elasticity, and other nylon, for such purposes as added strength.

Chemically Treated Natural Fiber Yarns

Manufacturers of cotton fabrics have been interested for a long time in the development of yarns and fabrics that have stretch. The natural properties of cotton -cool hand, texture, absorbency, washability, and durability- could be enhanced by the addition of stretch capability. The competitive production of ingenious manmade stretch yarns has given great impetus to the experimentation and development of cotton stretch yarns. There presently are three techniques.

Heatset Thermoplastic Cotton Crimping Process. Cotton yarn can be treated with one of several polymeric chemicals, which gives it thermoplastic properties. The yarn is then processed by the same heat-setting and crimping methods that are applied to manmade thermoplastic yarns. Cotton yarns produced by this method have as high as 200 percent stretch, and fabrics woven of these yarns may have up to 100 percent stretch. The higher the thread count, the lower the stretch. Return to original size is not immediate and is generally about 75 percent, though it is completely restored by washing or dry cleaning.

Cotton Yarn Cross-linking Process. Cotton yarn can be treated with a resin similar to the ones used for cotton wash and wear finishes. This resin is known as a cellulose cross-linking chemical. It gives cotton yarns and fabrics a "memory" and causes them to return to their original state (the same principle as wrinkle resistance). After the yarn has been treated, it is twisted and set with heat. It is subsequently *back-twisted* in the reverse direction. As the treated yarn tries to return to its original twist, it pulls itself up into tiny coils. This provides the springlike action of stretch.

A variation of this process is that of *false-twisting* the resin-treated cotton plied yarns, heat-setting them, and then untwisting the plies. The cotton singles retain their coiled characteristics and thus have the springlike stretch action. Performance of the yarns and fabrics is similar to that of the heat-set thermoplastic crimping process.

Slack Mercerization Process. Another method used to provide stretch in cotton is to give the woven cotton fabric a speciat finish by the *slack mercerisation* process.

Essentially, it is a technique of passing the cotton fabric through caustic soda as the warp is held at constant tension while the width is allowed to relax. The resultant slack in the filling causes the yarns to contract. Under tension, the filling in the finished fabric may stretch 15 to 20 percent. The fabric returns to about 80 percent of its original size, and it is completely restored by washing. The advantages of this method over the others are increased strength and low cost of production.

BULK YARNS

High-Bulk Yarns

The high-bulk yarns are relatively thick and soft, and they may also have the additional characteristic of stretch. They are always made of crimped staple synthetic fibers that are usually an acrylic, such as Orlon, Acrilan, or Creslan. Blends of these fibers can also be made with other manmade as well as natural fibers. Some high-bulk yarns are spun with a slack twist, sometimes with crimped staple, to produce a soft, thick, spongy yarn; such yarns generally do not have much natural stretch. Frequently, high-bulk yarns are made by blending stretched fibers with fibers that have been stretched and relaxed. During the dyeing operation, the stretched fibers relax; and their contraction causes the other already relaxed fibers to crimp and curl. This produces a soft, thick, but lightweight stretch yarn. Agilon and Fluflon yarns may be produced as stretch high-bulk yarns.

High-bulk yarns have the soft hand of wool or cashmere. Although they are lightweight, they are warm because the crimped fibers form air spaces within the thick yarn providing insulation. Highhulk yarns have good water adsorbency,water droplets will accumulate on the surface of the fibers in the air spaces. The fabrics do not feel clammy when moist, and they tend to dry more quickly than wool fabrics. Garments made of highbulk yarns wash and dry-clean readily. But they may pill-that is, form little balls of fiber on the surface of the fabric. To avoid this garments should be turned side out and washed gently. Light brushing with a very soft brush will help reduce the pilling. When knitted garments made of these yarns are washed, it is best to block them, since knitted garments of slack-twisted yarns tend to sag.

The durability of garments made of high-bulk yarns depends primarily on the durability of the synthetic fiber used and the amount of twist in the yarn. The more twist in the yarn, the greater the durability, however, the more twist, the less bulk in the yarn. Among the products made of high-bulk yarns are blouses and sweaters .

Loop-Bulk (Air-Jet) Yarns

These yarns are made of the continuous-filament fibers, such as rayon, acetate, nylon, or polyester. The textured appearance and hand of

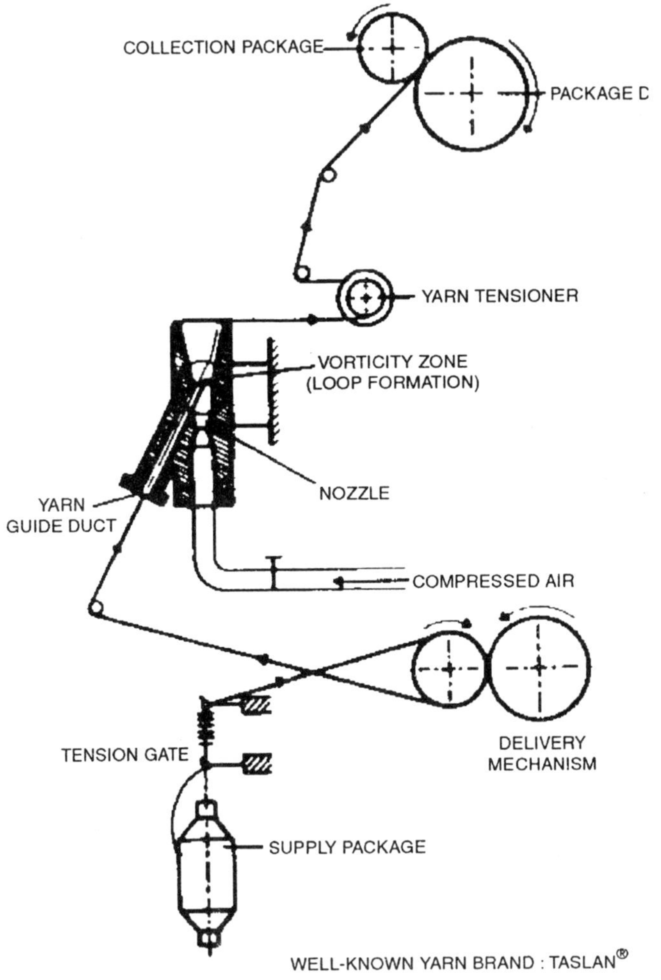

Fig.-3.13. Schematic representation of air-jet texturing.

the yarns resemble that of cotton or fine wool. Yet the yarns have many of the desirable characteristics of the filament fibers used. There are variations in the technique of making textured yarns. They all involve the process of passing smooth filament yarn across high-pressure air Jets that cause the individual filaments to loop up and become tangled so that a permanently textured surface of randomly situated tiny loops develops along the yarn. Different textures and effects are possible, depending on the size of the loops, the closeness of the loops, the yarn size, the amount of twist in the yarn, the number of plies, and the nature of the plies. Boucle yarns can be produced; core and effect yarns can be made by twisting bulkyarns around spun yarns (Figure 3.16).

Loop-bulk yarns are dull and have the fuzzy or rough appearance and texture of staple yarns. They have bulk without weight, which provides high cover power of 50 to 150 percent of the untreated filament yarn as well as opacity. These yarns have little stretch, depending upon the fiber used. Garments made of loop-bulk yarns launder and dryclean readily, dry quickly, and need little or no ironing. The air spaces caused by the loops provide for moisture adsorption and some insulation, which makes the fabrics comfortable to wear. These fabrics will not pill, as will those made of some staple fibers, such as nylon or acrylic staple. Loop-bulk yarns are used for a wide variety of textile products, such as shirts, blouses, upholstery and rugs.

4 PROPERTIES OF NATURAL FIBRES

IMPORTANT CHARACTERISTICS

To make a satisfactory textile choice for a particular use, one must understand not only the separate and combined properties of the various textile fibers but also comparative merits of the fibers.

The commercial value of any fiber depends largely on the extent to which it possesses certain characteristics, such as tensile strength, elasticity, fineness, and cohesiveness, all of which facilitate the process of spinning fibers to yarn to produce satisfactory fabrics for the consumer. The effectiveness of finishes and the care of fabrics depend upon such properties as the effect of heat, reaction to alkalies and acids, and affinity for dyes. The consumer is also concerned with serviceability, performance, and ease of care. Therefore, consideration must be given to such factors as absorbency, cleanliness and washability, effect of bleaches, shrinkage, resilience, drapability, and resistance to mildew and perspiration.

STRENGTH

Fibers differ in their resistance to tearing apart when subjected to tension. The serviceability and durability of a fabric are also affected by the length of the fiber. Tensile strength is a prime necessity in fibers if the resultant fabric is to withstand the strain of wear. The ability of a fiber to resist wearing away by friction or rubbing, referred to as abrasion resistance, is another aspect of durability. Yet, it does not follow that tensile strength and abrasion resistance go together.

ELASTICITY

Elasticity means that when the fiber is elongated or stretched, on release of tension, it will tend to return to its original length. Consequently, the less stress that is necessary to stretch the fiber and the more nearly it returns to its original length, the more elastic it is. The greater the elastic quality, the more the fiber will resist tearing. This elasticity contributes not only to the strength of a fiber but to the strength of a fabric as well. Elasticity permits materials to drape well on the body. Because elastic fibers do not break as easily as inelastic ones, this quality also facilitates the spinning process.

RESILIENCE

Resilience means that the fiber can be compressed or crushed and, on release of pressure, will tend to return to its original shape. When a fiber is resilient, it can be spun or twisted into springy yarns and the resultant fabric is also resilient. This quality causes the fabric to be wrinkle-resistant, with the resistance varying according to the degree of elasticity inherent in the fiber. Resilience also contributes to the abrasion resistance of a fabric. Some fibers have both elasticity and wrinkle resistance, but it is possible for a fiber to have none or little of either. It is also possible for a fiber not to have one quality, such as stretchability, but to have the other quality of wrinkle resistance.

Fibers that are not inherently resilient can be given a degree of resilience by reducing them to short staple. Short-staple yarns contribute softness to a fabric and help to make it somewhat wrinkle-resistant, but some strength is sacrificed. A chemical finish can be used to obtain wrinkle resistance, but this method may also affect the strength of the fiber.

DRAPABILITY

The drapability of a fabric, or its ability to hang and fall into graceful shape and folds, is dependent upon the finish, construction, the kind of yarn used, and the libers in the yam. The other factors being equal, the pliability and springiness of the various fibers will contribute different amounts of capability.

HEAT CONDUCTIVITY

The ability of a fiber to conduct heat has great significance in textiles. The degree of heat conductivity helps determine whether fabrics are suitable for winter or for summer use.

In addition to the heat conductivity inherent in the fiber, the kind of yarn, fabric formation, and finish will also affect this quality. When a fabric is loosely constructed, for example, it has air spaces, which have an insulative property. The captive air pockets contained in a napped surface add warmth to a fabric. These are the more important considerations concerning the warmth or coolness of a fabric along with the following generalities about the heat conductivity of the fibers themselves.

ABSORBENCY

The quickness with which a fabric absorbs moisture and gives it up again in evaporation has an important bearing on health and comfort. Textile fibers vary in their natural absorptive capacity, but absorbency may be increased by fabric construction or by a finishing process. A loosely constructed fabric or one with a napped surface, for example, is more absorptive than a smooth-surfaced fabric.

CLEANLINESS AND WASHABILITY

The consumer is interested in knowing what textiles are hygienic, how long a garment may be expected to remain clean, and whether it will require special care when laundering or dry cleaning is necessary. The fibers with smooth surfaces produce fabrics that are easy to launder: thus garments made of linen, silk, and rayon wash easily. A napped surface on any one of these materials makes it necessary to give the garment more care in washing. The fact that a fiber does not absorb much water does not imply that the fiber is unhygienic. Actually, such fibers usually do not absorb dirt particles and have relatively smooth surfaces. The water then washes the dirt off the surface, and the fiber dries quickly.

REACTION TO BLEACHES

Sometimes fabrics are bleached to get them whiter or to remove stains. When a bleach is used, it should be put into the water and thoroughly mixed before garment is added. This will prevent the possiblity of damaging the fabric with bleach that is too concentrated.

Most white manmade fibers do not usually turn gray or yellow. Sometimes however, the finish on the fabric may cause the discoloration. It is therefore a good idea to wash garments first without a bleach to determine if one is necessary.

EFFECT OF LIGHT

Textiles are constantly exposed to the out-doors and light. Some need to be very resistant to degradation by sunlight.

RESISTANCE TO INSECTS

Certain kinds of insects may attack textile fibers that provide a source of food for them. They may also be attracted by substances that may be deposited on fabrics. In the latter instance, appropriate cleaning and storage should prove helpful in preventing damage by insects.

REACTION TO ALKALIES AND ACIDS

A knowledge of the reaction of textile fibers to alkalies and acids is important, as alkalies destroy protein fibers and acids, even in a weak solution, destroy cellulose fibers. For example, chemical tests tor determining the fiber content of fabrics are made by noting the disintegration of wool and silk when exposed to a strong alkali, and there is a similar reaction when cotton and linen are exposed to acids. Good results in the bleaching, finishing, and dyeing processes depend on the reaction of the fibers to alkali or acid chemical agents. Not only is this reaction important in testing and manufacturing, it also closely touches the consumer when the care of fabrics is considered.

This reaction to alkalies and acids is most important to the consumer when fabrics are washed. Proper soaps and detergents should be selected for laundering the various kinds of textiles.

AFFINITY FOR DYES

The readiness with which a fiber absorbs and retains dye affects the appearance and serviceability of a fabric. Affinity for dyes is usually determined by the porosity of a fiber.

RESISTANCE TO PERSPIRATION

Aside from the fact that perspiration may affect the color of fabrics and may stain some, it will cause deterioration of some textile fibers. To minimize this, frequent cleaning is advisable.

A) COTTON

Cotton is a fiber that grows from the surface of seeds in the pods, or bolls, of a bushy mallow plant. It is composed basically of a substance called *cellulose*.

KINDS AND TYPES OF COTTON

Different kinds and types of cotton are grown in various parts of the world. Some of their basic characteristics differ. Variations among cotton fibers also occur because of growth conditions including such factors as soil, climate, fertilizers, and pests. The quality of cotton fiber is based on its color (degree of whiteness), length (or staple), fineness, and strength. Usually, the longer fibers are finer and stronger.

The particular kind of cotton is often identified by the name of the country, or geographical area where it is produced, and although a major portion of the world's cotton is Upland type, it is still known by the place of production whether Brazil, Zaire, Greece, Pakistan, Russia, Syria, Turkey, Uganda, or San Joaquin Valley. The quality is associated with the name. The better known kinds and types of cotton used in the United States are Upland, American pima, Egyptian, and Asiatic cotton.

Upland Cotton

American Upland cotton constitutes over 99 percent of the United States cotton crop and is used for many fabrics either wholly or as a component of blends with manmade fibers. The particular kind of Upland cotton from which these fabrics are made is important because the quality and characteristics vary among the kinds.

Generally speaking, Upland cotton fibers are fairly white, strong, and dull, and range in staple length from 78 to 1 1/4 inches (22- 32 mm). The Upland cottons are usually categorized as short-, medium-, and long-staple. The short-staple cottons are less than 1 inch (25- mm) and

American Pima

The staple length is 35- 38 mm and the fiber is fine, strong, lustrous, silky, and creamy-brown-white in color. American Pima fiber is used primarily for sewing thread.

Egyptian

The fibers are light brown, fine, strong, and 32- 38 mm in length. They are used in the same applications as American Pima.

The fiber is light brown, fine, strong, and 35-41 mm in length. It is used in applications where fine yarns or strong yarns are required.

Asiatic

Asiatic cottons are produced in India, China, and the Near East. For the most part these are coarse fibers less than I inch (25 mm) in length.

Ginning and Baling

When the raw cotton is harvested, it contains seeds, leaf fragments, dirt, and other material that must be removed before the fiber can be baled. Cottonseeds alone constitute approx. two-thirds of the weight of the raw cotton when first picked. The seeds are removed by the cotton gin.

Essentially, the cotton gin has rows of revolving saw-toothed bands that pull the fiber away from the seeds as well as remove other extraneous material.

BYPRODUCTS OF COTTON

The raw cotton passes through several cleaning processes before it is baled as well as after it is unbaled at the cotton mill. As a result, the grower obtains valuable by products that amount approximately to one-sixth of the entire Income from the cotton plant. Cotton is therefore important because of its contributions to other industries as well as to the textile industry.

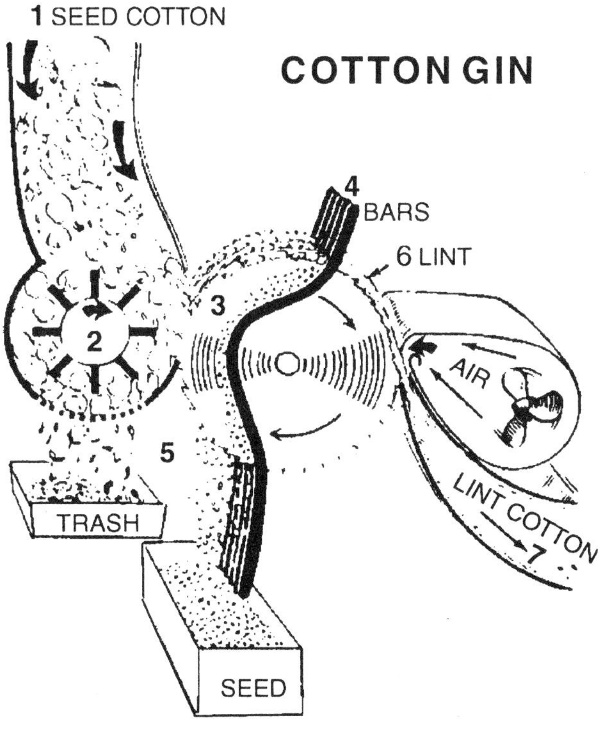

Fig.-4.1. (a) Shown in the drawing are the following basic principles of the cotton gin : (1) Seed cotton enters gin. (2) Roll throws seed cotton against bars. (3) Saw teeth take cotton up and against bars. (4) Bars near saws on both sides let lint pass through but hold back seed. (5) Seed falls into conveyor. (6) Lint on sawtooth is struck by blast of air, and (7) blown into lint cotton conveyor pipe.

Cotton linters

Linters are the short, fuzzy hairlike fibers that remain on the seeds after they have been separated from the fiber in the cotton gin. The cotton linters are removed by a second ginning process. They are used in the manufacture of rayons and acetates, plastics, shatterproof glass, guncotton, photographic film, and fast-drying lacquers, and for other purposes.

Hulls

The hulls, which are the outside portion of the cottonseeds, are obtained after the linters have been removcd. The hulls are rich in nitrogen .

Inner Seeds

The meat of the seed inside the hull yields *cottonseed oil, which* is used in cooking oils and compounds and in the manufacture of soap. The residue of the inner seed becomes cattle feed.

PROCESSING, BLENDING, AND MIXING COTTON

Cotton fiber may be spun alone or blended with other fibers in making yarns. Cotton yarns are also combined or mixed with other yarns in making fabrics. These techniques contribute to fabrics such desirable cotton properties as softness, strength, absorbency, and affinity for color.

FINISHING COTTON FABRICS

The finishing processes given to cotton may be summarized as follows:

Name of Finish	Purpose
Ammoniating	for strength, abrasion resistance, luster, and affinity for dyes
Antibacterial finish	for hygienic protection
Beetling	for flattened effects
Bleaching (full)	for clear whiteness
Calendering	for luster
Compressive shrinkagc	for maximum preshrinking
Crepe effects	for wrinkle resistance and textured surface
Drip-dry	for no ironing
Embossing	for decoration

Flame retarding	for fire inhibition
Glazing	for luster
Insulating	for warmth
Mercerizing	for strength, luster, and affinity for dyes
Moireing	for variable luster and variable pattern
Napping	for softness, warmth, and increased absorbency
Permanent pressing	for easy care Preshrinking- for serviceability
Schreinerizing	for luster
Singeing	for smoothness
Slack mercerizing	for stretch
Stain repelling	for easy care
Stiffening	for smoothness and body
Water repellency	for resistance to water and rain
Weighting	for bulk
Wrinkle resistance	for retention of appearance

Simulating Linen

Cotton yarn can be spun to simulate the irregularities characteristic of linen fiber. The fabric is woven in the damask and other patterns usually associated with linen fabrics and is then sized, beetled, and calendered similarly to linen.

Simulating Wool

Cotton fibers can be treated with chemicals to give them the roughness characteristic of wool fibers. The fibers are spun into thick yarns to increase the similarity. The finished fabric is napped or roughened to produce a wool-like surface. Because cotton fiber has crimp, an inherent similarity to wool fiber, it is sometimes mixed with American Upland cotton to simulate wool.

Simulating Silk

The highest quality of cotton fiber, when spun to a high yarn count and then mercerized, simulates silk. The use of the satin construction in weaving produces a silk like luster. The cotton fabric may be singed and calendered to smooth its surface and to increase the luster. Cotton fabrics are frequently Schreinerized to obtain an added lustrous effect.

EVALUATING COTTON FABRICS

Manufacturers put labels on finished consumer's goods to give such vital information as the thread count, fiber content, expected shrinkage, permanency of crispness (if any), fastness of dye to strong light, washing, dry cleaning, and general instructions on the maintenance and care of the fabric. Such labels are designed to protect and help the consumer. If one understands them, one can estimate how long the fabric or garment that one is purchasing may be expected to give good wear. These labels also protect the manufacturer from the consumer's possible misunderstanding of the quality and durability of a fabric and from complaint if it is improperly handled when washed or drycleaned.

The information gained in previous chapters of this book concerning the essential qualities of the fibers and their spinning into yarn and construction into fabric can now be applied to the purchase of consumers' goods.

Strength. Strength of a fiber is indicated by the ability to resist being pulled or torn apart when subjected to stress or tension. Cotton fiber is relatively strong due to the intrinsic structure of layers of crisscrossed, minute, spiraled fibrils that, compose the fiber cell (see Figure 4.2). Strength is also determined by the character of the cotton yarns, which should be of long staple tightly twisted. Compact construction, represented by high thread count, helps a fabric keep its shape and give longer wear. A sample of the fabric may be tested for strength by holding it in both hands and pressing down firmly with the thumbs while pulling. If the cloth gives easily, It will not stand the strain of wear. Strength can be improved by mercerizing or ammoniating.

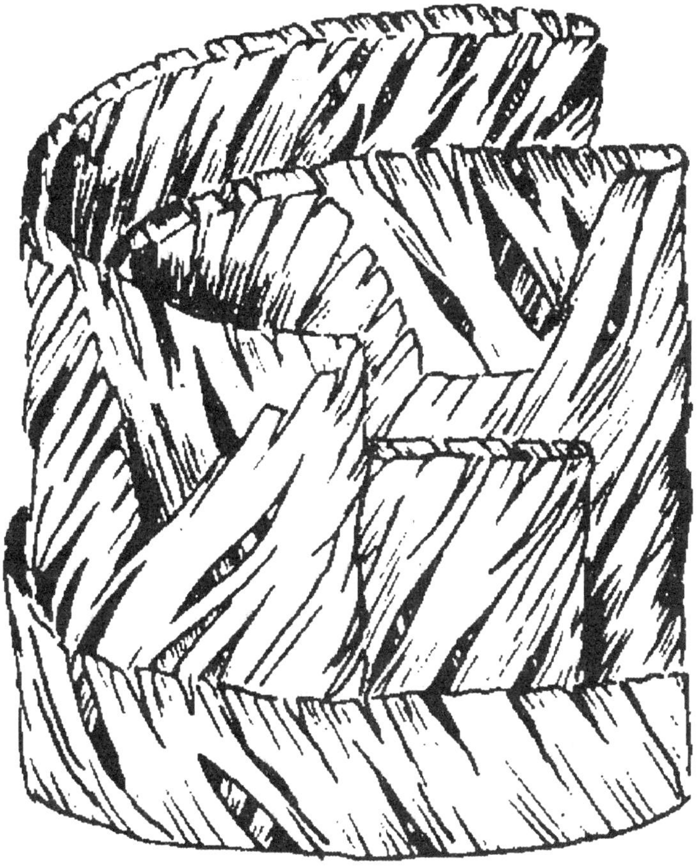

Fig.-4.2. Diagram of inner layer of an enlarged cotton fiber shows how fibrils crisscross and double back. This structure contributes greatly to the strength of cotton.

Elasticity. Elasticity refers to the extent to which a fiber can be elongated by stretching and then returning to its former condition of size or length. Cotton fiber has very little natural elasticity. This characteristic can be altered to varying extents by hard-twisting fibers into creped yarns and by using fabric construction techniques such as knitting. The slack mercerization technique may be used to give cotton fabrics some stretch in the warp and/or filling, thereby reducing the binding characteristics of the cotton fabrics.

Resilience. Resilience refers to the extent to which a fabric can be deformed by compression or crushing and return to its original condition. The tendency of cotton fabrics to wrinkle easily may be offset by finishing processes that give a wrinkle resistant quality.

Drapability. The ability of a fabric to hang easily and fall into graceful shape and folds indicates its drapability. It is dependent upon the kindof fiber, yarn, and construction of the fabric as well as finish given to it. Cotton does not have the body and suppleness required for good drapability.

However, the nature and compactness of the fabric construction can improve it,This can be enhanced further by sizing and other finishes.

Heat Conductivity. The extent to which heat can be conveyed through a fiber or a fabric indicates its heat conductivity. Cotton has a relatively high degree of heat conductivity. Therefore it is a cool fiber.

Absorbency. The ease and extent to which moisture can penetrate into a fiber determines its absorbency, Once the outer protective cuticle of the cotton fiber is broken down by finishing processes, such as kiering and mercerizing, the fiber becomes very absorbent, Cotton fiber is composed primarily of cellulose.,which is very absorbent. Such factors as the amount of twist in the yarn will also affect the absorbency, since a low-twisted yarn will be more absorbent than a high-twisted one. Fabric structure, such as 2 pile weave, will affect absorbency. Also, the compactness of the weave influences the absorbency because the looser the structure the more absorbent the fabric will be.

Reaction to Bleaches. bleaches are chemical solutions designed to remove discoloration (and sometimes color). While hydrogen peroxide may be used, the more common household bleaches for cotton are solutions of sodium hypochlorite, or sodium perborate, which is a milder type. These bleaches, used as directed, will effectively bleach cotton fabrics. Bleach should be put into the rinse water after washing so that it is thoroughly mixed and diluted to avoid the oxidizing or yellowing that may be caused by over concentration. Labels on wash-and-wear fabrics should be observed since some of these finishes are chlorine retentive-they turn yellow when subjected to sodium hypochlorite bleaches.

Shrinkage. When cotton fiber is wet, it tends to contract or shrink as it dries. As a result, cotton yarns and fabrics can shrink considerably, particularly those that are loosely constructed. However, preshrinking finishing processes minimize shrinkage in cotton fabrics. Labels should be read for the amount of residual shrinkage that a fabric or garment has and care instructions should be followed to retain the required size and shape.

Effect of Heat. Cotton will withstand moderate heat. If pressed with an iron that is too hot or if a hot iron is allowed to remain too long in one place on the fabric, it will scorch and ultimately burn. It is therefore best to either iron cotton material that has been dampened or use a steam iron.

Effect of Light. Cotton fiber oxidizes, turning yellow and losing strength from exposure to sunlight over a protracted period of time. Cotton fabrics should therefore be shaded from direct sunlight.

Resistance to Mildew. Cotton fabrics, especially sized fabrics, mildew readily, when permitted to remain in a damp condition. Small greenish-black or rust colored spots caused by mildew fungus develop and a musty odor may be detected. Therefore, cotton material should be kept in a dry atmosphere. Where this is not possible, a mildew resistant finish or a mildew inhibitor is advisable when stored.

Resistance to Insects. Cotton is not digestible by moth larvae, so the fabric will not be attacked by moths. But in fabrics containing cotton and wool, the larvae may damage the cotton to get at the wool. Certain other insects that may be attracted to its cellulose content may damage cotton, but this is not common.

Reaction to Alkalies. Cotton is not harmed by alkalies. In fact, a solution of sodium hydroxide is used to mercerize cotton, making it stronger, smoother, and more lustrous.

Reaction to Acids. Cotton is not damaged by such volatile organic acids as acetic acid (vinegar). However, it is tendered if such nonvolatile organic acids as oxalic and citric (found in orange, lemon, and grapefruit juices) are allowed to remain on it, particularly if heat is also applied. They should therefore be rinsed with cool water as soon as possible. Concentrated cold or diluted hot mineral acids, such as sulfuric acid, will destroy cotton.

Affinity for Dyes. Cotton has a good affinity for dyes. It is dyed best with vat dyes, but oxidation bases, azoic, and reactive dyes may also be effectively used. Colorfastness is generally good, but specific conditions should be considered. Fastness of dye to washing can be tested by washing a sample in hot water. Fastness to light can be tested by exposing a sample to light for a week or more. Penetration or thoroughness of dye can be tested by raveling a yarn and examining its unexposed surfaces.

Resistance to Perspiration. Perspiration may be alkaline or acidic, depending upon the individual's metabolism. Since cotton is resistant to alkali, alkali perspiration does not deteriorate cotton. However, acid perspiration has a slightly deteriorating effect. In either case, discoloration may occur.

COTTON BLENDS

Cotton is blended with many other fibers so that certain of the desirable properties of cotton, that other fibers may lack, will contribute to the general characteristics of the blended yarns and fabrics. As discussion of the properties of the other fibers proceeds, consideration will be given to the effect of cotton fiber when blended with each of these fibers, respectively.

B) LINEN

Linen yarn is made from fibers removed from the stem of the slender flax plant. These fibers, held together under the stem's bark principally by a gummy substance (pectin), form the body of the flax plant. The flax fiber is composed basically of the substance, *cellulose.*

Preparation of the Fiber

The seeds and the leaves are removed from the stems of the flax plant by passing the stalks through coarse combs. This process is called rippling. The bundles of plants are then steeped in water so that the tissue or woody bark surrounding the hairlike flax fiber will decompose, thus loosening the gum that binds the fiber to the stem. This decomposition is called retting

Retting only loosens the woody bark. If flax is not retted enough, the removal of the stalk without injury to the delicate fiber is difficult. If flax is overretted, the fiber is weakened. The retting operation, as well as all other processes for producing linen fabric, therefore requires great care.

Dew Retting. The flax straw is spread on the grass and is exposed to the atmosphere for three to four weeks. This method produces strong flax, dark gray in color.

Pool, or Dam, Retting. It requires less time than dew retting, from ten to fifteen days. As stagnant pools of water are used, this method sometime causes overretting, which is responsible for brittle and weak flax fibers. Pool retting darkens the flax, giving it a bluish gray color.

Vat, or Mechanical, Retting. This method shortens the retting process.

Chemical Retting. Chemical retting, can shorten the retting process, but chemicals will affect the strength and color of the flax fiber. Soda ash, oxalic soda, and caustic soda in warm water or boiling in dilute sulphuric acid solution are the chemical methods used.

MANUFACTURING PROCESSES

Breaking

The stalk becomes partially separated from the fiber when the wet plants are placed in the fields to dry . When the decomposed woody tissue is dry, it is crushed by being passed through fluted iron rollers. This *breaking* operation reduces the stalk to small pieces of bark called *shives.*

Scutching

The scutching machine removes the broken shives by means of rotating wooden paddles, thus finally releasing the flax fiber from the stalk. This operation can be done by hand as well as by machinery.

Hackling (Combing)

The simple combing process known as hackling straightens the flax fibers, separates the short from the long staple and leaves the longer fibers in parallel formation, For very fine linen, hackling is done by hand. For faster and more efficient combing, hackling is done by machine. A finer comb is used progressively at each stage

Spinning

The short-staple flax fibers, called tow, are used for the spinning of irregular linen yarns. Tow is put through a carding operation, similar to the carding of cotton staple, which straightens the fibers and forms them into a sliver ready for spinning into yarn. The long-staple fibers are used for fine linens. These are called line, sometimes *dressed flax.* Line fibers are from 12 to 20 inches (30- 50 cm) in length. They are put through machines, called *spreaders,* which combine fibers of the same length, laying them parallel so that the ends overlap. The sliver thus formed passes through sets of rollers, making a rove for the final spinning process, which inserts the necessary twist

The standard measure of flax yarn is the cut. If 1 pound of flax fiber is drawn out to make 300 yards, the yarn is known as Ne 1. When drawn out to make twice 300 yards, it is labeled Ne 2. The higher the yarn count, the finer the yarn. Exceptionally fine linen yarns for fine laces have been spun as high as 600s (2.7 tex).

Although flax is one of the strongest fibers, it is inelastic and requires a carefully controlled, warm, moist atmosphere for both methods of spinning.

Dry Spinning. Dry spinning does not use moisture. It produces rough, uneven yarns, which are not especially strong. These yarns are used for making coarse, heavy, and inexpensive linen fabrics.

Wet Spinning. This method requires a temperature of 120 degree F (50 degree C), which is conducive to the production of soft, fine, even yarns. By passing the roving through hot water, the gummy substance on the fiber is dissolved, permitting drawing out the roving into a fine yarn of high yarn count .

LINEN FABRICS

The inelasticity of the flax fiber presents a problem in the weaving process because the fiber breaks easily under strain. A dressing, applied to the warp yarns by passing them over rotating brushes, helps linen yarns to withstand the strain of being lifted by the heddles during weaving. A very moist atmosphere is also required.

Linen yarns are generally not knitted because of their inherent stiffness and resistance to being formed into loops. Special surface treatment of the yarns, which must be uniform and of high count, and specialized knitting machines would be required. However, research has demonstrated that linen fiber properly blended with manmade fibers can produce yarns that can be knitted into fabrics having certain advantageous features contributed by the respective fibers.

General Applications

Linen fabrics usually have a balanced or squared construction, with the exception of double damask and certain sheer linens. The thread count, therefore, is always expressed as one number.

Linen has long been used for a wide variety of apparel and home furnishings. In fact, the oft-used term of "linens," which refers to such home furnishings as sheets, pillowcases, towels, tablecloths, and napkins, now usually made of cotton and cotton blends, stems from their original composition of linen. Linen is now used to a very limited extent. Fabrics for apparel are usually made of plain or basket weaves. Twill weaves are used for drill fabrics, drapery, and wall coverings. Damasks for tablecloths and drapery are made in jacquard patterns using satin weaves

FINISHING PROCESSES

Linen is generally scoured before it is given a finish, and the finish used depends upon the intended purpose and use of the fabric. The most common treatment given to linen is bleaching.

Bleaching

Linen is usually bleached in the piece except when it is to be used for such purposes as yarn-dyed fabrics and dress linen. The two methods used are *grass bleaching* and *chemical bleaching.*

Grass bleaching produces the finest results. It is accomplished by spreading the linen out in the fields so that it is gradually -bleached in the sun. This process is time-consuming but less injurious to the linen; it is therefore considered more desirable.

Although chemical bleaching is the method chiefly used, it may adversely affect the durability of the finished fabric owing to the weakening effects of the chemicals. The process requires boiling the linen in a lime solution for eight to ten hours to remove such impurities as wax, then rinsing it in water, bleaching it with hydrochloric acid, washing the fabric again, and then, finally, treating it with caustic soda to neutralize any acid that still remains.

Bleaching produces four grades in the finished product: fully bleached, three quarters bleached, half or silver bleached, and quarter bleached. Unbleached linen makes a fifth grade. A fully bleached linen fabric is less enduring than any other grade. Unbleached linen is the strongest because the natural strength of the fiber has not been weakened by the bleach. It is sometimes called gray linen or brown linen.

Other Processes

The natural characteristics of linen are enhanced by the following finishing processes.

Name of Finish	Purpose
Beetling	for flexibility and uniform thickness
Calendering	for luster and smoothness
Mercerizing	for luster
Sizing	for added body
Wrinkle resisting	for resilience and easier care

Linen is never napped. The fiber does not lend itself to this process, nor would napping be desirable for long-staple yarns of hard surface. Where some crease resistance is obtained by reducing the yarn to short staple, the strength of the linen, which is its chief attribute, is sacrificed. Thus, any fuzziness in a linen fabric indicates the use of short staple or the presence of another fiber.

DYEING LINEN

Linen is seldom yarn-dyed. The surface of the natural flax fiber is hard and nonporous and is, therefore, impenetrable to dyes. The cells of the fiber are held together with tissue that can be broken down only in a severe bleaching process. Highly colored linens, therefore, will not give lasting service because they must have been fully bleached to absorb the dye. The colors are therefore usually pastel or dark but dull shades.

EVALUATING LINEN FABRICS

Reference has already been made to the general use of the term "linen" for a variety of household goods. Therefore, when a consumer does want articles made of linen, the fiber identification should be noted ; a fabric may be labeled "linen," "pure linen," or "pure flax" only if it is made of 100 percent linen. A fabric that contains linen and other fibers must be so labeled, indicating the percentage of each fiber used in the order of weight predominance. However, fabrics made of fibers other than linen, such as rayon, but made to resemble linen may be labeled by such terms as "rayon linen."

Even when a fabric is labeled "pure linen," it is best to know whether the yarns are line or tow. Fine linen fabrics, such as high-grade table damask and dress linens, are usually made of line, the long uniform staple. Line may be distinguished from tow by untwisting and examining the length of the fibers.

Pure linen is free from lint; therefore, the presence of lint indicates adulteration with cotton, or possibly oversizing. Cotton yarns are frequently mixed with linen to produce inexpensive fabrics. The name Union Linen is given to a fabric of which half or more is cotton. Linene is a name for an all-cotton fabric that simulates linen.

Strength. Linen is especially durable being two to three times as strong as cotton. Among the natural fibers, it is second in strength to silk. In linen, weight may be considered a criterion of durability. Damask weighs from 4 to 7 ounces to the square yard (135-235 g/m^2)

Elasticity. Linen has no significant elasticity. It is, in fact, the least elastic of natural fibers. In order to fit comfortably, linen garments should neither bind nor pull at the seams.

Resilience. Linen fiber is relatively stiff and has little resilience. Therefore, it wrinkles easily, which somewhat offsets its otherwise excellent qualities as a fabric for summer apparel.

Due to its stiffness, linen fabrics should not have creases pressed firmly into them. Deep repeated folds, as in tablecloths, should be avoided because these creases eventually cause the otherwise strong yarns to crack and break long before they ordinarily would.

Drapability. Linen has more body than cotton and drapes somewhat better.

Heat Conductivity. Linen is most suitable for summer apparel, as it allows the heat of the body to escape.

Absorbency. When absorbency is the main consideration, linen is preferable to cotton. It absorbs moisture and dries more quickly. It is therefore excellent for handkerchiefs and towels.

Cleanliness and Washability. Linen launders well and gives up stains readily; its softness is enhanced by repeated washings. Because of its stiffness, linen must be thoroughly damp when it is ironed, or a steam iron may be used. Some linen apparel requires dry cleaning because of construction and fabric finish (or lack thereof). Care label instructions should be observed.

Reaction to Bleaches. Linen does not stain as readily as cotton, but it is also more difficult to bleach. Like cotton, it is weakened by sodium hypochlorite bleaches. Sodium perborate bleaches are effective and safer.

Shrinkage. Linen does not shrink a great deal; in fact, it shrinks less than cotton. But preshrinkage finishing is desirable.

Effect of Heat. Linen scorches and flames in a manner similar to cotton.

Effect of Light. Linen is more resistant to light than cotton, but it will gradually deteriorate from protracted exposure.

Resistance to Mildew. Like cotton, linen is vulnerable to mildew.

Resistance to Insects. Like cotton, linen is not damaged by moths. Damage by other insects is uncommon.

Reaction to Alkalies. Linen, like cotton, is highly resistant to alkalies. Linen may also be mercerized.

Reaction to Acids. Linen is damaged by hot dilute acids and cold concentrated acids-but not by cold dilute acids.

Affinity for Dyes. Linen does not have good affinity for dyes. However, it is possible to obtain dyed linen that has good colorfastness. When buying colored linens, look for the words "Guaranteed Fast Color" on the label or get a guarantee of colorfastness from the store. If a label states that the fabric is vat-dyed, it has been given the fastest color possible to withstand washing.

Resistance to Perspiration. Acid perspiration will deteriorate linen. Alkali perspiration will not cause deterioration. But in either case discoloration may occur.

LINEN BLENDS

Linen fiber is blended with other fibers so that certain of its desirable properties, that other fibers may lack, will contribute to the general characteristics of the blended yarns and fabrics. One may sometimes find on a linen blend fabric the trademark, Linron, which identifies linen fiber that has been put through a series of mechanical and chemical processes that produce crimped, prebleached, preshrunk linen fiber intended for spinning on cotton or woolen systems.

Linen and Cotton

As with any blend, the amount of each fiber used is significant in its contributing effects. In any event, linen offers prestige. It also provides body and improved drapability. Linen adds greater strength and absorbency, Cotton is very compatible with linen. It spins well with it to provide good quality yarn and fabrics while keeping the cost lower than it would be as an all-linen material.

3) WOOL AND HAIRS

Wool fiber and hair fiber are the natural protein fibres & hair growth of certain animals and are composed of protein.

CLASSIFICATIONS FOR WOOL

Classification by Sheep

'There are about forty breeds of sheep. Counting the crossbreeds, there are over 200 distinct grades of sheep. Those that produce wool may be classified into four groupings according to the quality of the wool produced.

Merino Wool. Merino sheep produce the best wool . The variety originated in Spain and was so prized for its outstanding quality that during the middle Ages it was a capital offense to export merino sheep from Spain. The staple is relatively short, ranging from 1 to 5 inches (25 -125mm), but the fiber is strong, fine, and elastic and has good working properties. Merino fiber has the greatest amount of crimp of all wool fibers& has a maximum number of scales, totaling as many as 3000 to the inch(118/ mm)-two factors which contribute to its superior warmth and spinning qualities. Merino is used in the best types of wool clothing. The Ohio Merino, Austrianl Silesian, and French Rainbouillet are all varieties of Merino sheep. Other types are now found in Australia, New Zealand, South America, South Africa, and Spain.

Class-Two Wools. This class of sheep originated in England, Scotland, Ireland, land Wales. They helped make the British Isles famous for their fine wool fabrics. They are, however, no longer limited to that area and are now raised in many parts of the world. While not quite as good as the Merino wool, this variety is nevertheless a very good quality wool. It is 2 – 8 inches (50- 200 mm) in length, has a large number of scales per inch, and has good crimp. The fibers are comparatively strong, fine, and elastic and have good working properties. Some of the betterknown sheep of this variety include Bainpton, Berkshire, Blackface, Cornwall, Devonshire, Dorset, Hampshire, Hereford, Exmoor, Kent, Norfolk, Shropshire, Southdown, Sussex, Oxford, Welsh Mountain, Wiltshire, Westmoreland, Irish, and Ryeland.

Class-Three Wools. 'This class of sheep originated in the United Kingdom. The fibers are about 4 to 18 inches long (100 -455 mm), are coarser, and have fewer scales and less crimp than Merino and the class-two wools. As a result, they are smoother, and therefore have more luster. These wools are less elastic and resilient. They are nevertheless of good enough quality to be used for clothing. In fact, some of these sheep, such as Leicester, Cotswold, Cheviot, Harris, Lewis, and Shetland, have given their names to wool fabrics.

Class-Four Wools. This class is actually a group of mongrel sheep sometimes referred to as half-breeds. The fibers are from 1 to 16 inches (25- 400 mm) long, are coarse and hairlike, have relatively few scales and little crimp, and are therefore smoother and more lustrous. This wool is less desirable, with the least elasticity and strength. It is used mainly for carpets, rugs, and inexpensive low-grade clothing.

Classification by Fleece

Sheep are generally shorn of their fleeces in the spring, but the time of shearing varies in different parts of the world. In the United States, shearing takes place in April or May; in Australia, in September; in Great Britain, in June or July. Texas and California sheep are shorn twice a year because of the warm climate.

Sheep are not washed before shearing. Sometimes, they are dipped into an antiseptic bath, but this is done only when prescribed by law. Formerly, sheep were shorn with hand clippers; today the fleeces are removed in one piece by machine clippers, which shear closer as well as faster.

A skilled worker can shear up to 200 sheep a day. Wool shorn from young lambs differs in quality from that of older sheep. Also, fleeces differ according to whether they come from live or dead sheep, which necessitates standards for the classification of fleeces.

Lamb's Wool. The first fleece sheared from a lamb about six to eight months old is known as *lamb's wool* and sometimes referred to as *fleece* wool, or *first clip.* This wool is of very fine quality; the fibers are tapered because the ends have never been clipped. Such fibers produce a softness of texture in fabrics that is characteristic only of lamb's wool. Because of its immaturity, however, lamb's wool is not as strong as fully developed wool of the same sheep.

Hogget Wool. Hogget (hogg or teg) wool comes from sheep twelve to fourteen months old that have not been previously shorn. The fiber is fine, soft, resilient, and mature, and has tapered ends. Hogget wool is a very desirable grade of wool and, because of its strength, is used primarily for the warp yarns of fabrics.

Wether Wool. Any fleece clipped after the first shearing is called wether wool. This wool is usually taken from sheep older than fourteen months, and these fleeces contain much soil and dirt.

Pulled Wool. When sheep are slaughtered for meat, their wool is pulled from the pelt by the use of lime, by sweating, or by a chemical depilatory. Such wool fiber, called *pulled wool, is* of inferior quality for two reasons: (1) because sheep that are raised for meat generally do not have a good quality of wool, (2) because the roots of the fibers are generally damaged by the chemicals and the tension exerted in pulling.

Dead Wool. The wool fiber known as *dead wool is* sometimes mistaken for pulled wool. The term is correctly used for wool that has been recovered from sheep that have died on the range or have been accidentally killed. Dead wool fiber is decidedly inferior in grade; it is used in low-grade cloth.

Cotty Wool. Sheep that are exposed to severe weather conditions or lack of nourishment yield a wool that is matted or felted together and is hard and brittle. This very poor grade is known as *cotty* wool.

Taglocks. The torn, ragged, or discolored parts of a fleece are known as *tag*locks. These are usually sold separately as an inferior grade of wool.

WOOL PRODUCTS LABELING ACT

There has never been a sufficient supply of new wool stocks to take care of a steadily increasing demand for wool. To meet this situation, wool fibers have had to be recovered from old clothing, rags of all kinds, and waste from wool manufacturing; all are important sources. This wool is variously called salvaged, reclaimed, reworked, or remanufactured, but it is best known in the textile industry as *shoddy.* This term is misunderstood by the average consumer, who is inclined to believe that wool fabric containing remanufactured fibers is necessarily of inferior quality. This is not so.

The hardier, though less resilient, remanufactured fibers, when obtained from good original stock and combined with new wool from lamb, hogget, or wether fleeces, add durability to the soft new wool. Thus, remanufactured fibers contribute ability to withstand hard wear, although there is some sacrifice in warmth, softness of texture, and resiliency. They also make wool clothing available to consumers who cannot afford expensive wool fabrics.

To correct wrong impressions concerning the use of remanufactured wool, and also to protect consumers against unscrupulous practices, there is Wool Products Labeling Act. This act, provides that every article of wool clothing must be labeled according to the type of wool used in its manufacture. The label must state: (1) the amount of wool fiber in the fabric, (2) the percentage by weight of new, or virgin, wool fibers, (3) the percentages of recycled fibers in the fabric, (4) the percentage of each fiber other than wool, if such fibers constitute 5 percent or more of the total, (5) the aggregate of other fibers, and (6) the nonfibrous loading, filling, or adulterating substance.

New definitions of the types of wool fibers used in labeled garments were established by this act. Note that the law does not require labeling as to the type of sheep or the type of fleece from which the wool has come. The information on the labels is therefore of only limited value to the consumer.

Wool

The simple term "wool," according to government standards, must always mean new wool that has not been made up in any form of wool product. New wool comes directly from a fleece. It has never been previously spun, woven, felted, or worn.

The term "virgin wool" is now, used by the textile industry to designate new wool from a sheep's fleece, but the term is too all-inclusive to serve as a criterion of quality. Although the term testifies to the fact that virgin wool does not contain recycled wool fibers, it can be used to identify the less desirable fibers of a fleece as well as a specially fine quality of wool. Virgin wool may also include pulled or dead wool, which may be of definitely inferior stock. One should not consider that a fabric labeled "100 percent new wool" is necessarily more serviceable than one containing any of the recycled wool fibers, for there are many different grades of new wool. It is important to remember that a high grade of recycled wool makes a more serviceable fabric than one having a low grade of new wool.

Two other terms widely used on labels are "pure wool" and "wool blend," both registered certification marks of the Wool Bureau, Inc. (See Figures 4.3.)

Recycled Wool

Recycled wool is fiber that has been reclaimed and remanufactured from used or unused wool materials. The unused materials may come from combings and scraps of wool obtained during the manufacturing processes, from sample swatches, or from pieces of all-wool cloth from apparel manufacturing. The used wool is fiber salvaged from all kinds of used consumers' goods.

MANUFACTURING PROCESSES

Preparation

Fleeces vary from 6 to 18 pounds (3- 8 kg) in weight, average about 8 pounds (3.5 kg) each, and ultimately provide about 3 pounds (1. 5 kg) of scoured wool. Since wool is sold according to the lowest grades in the fleece, it is often trimmed of the poorer quality edges, rolled up, tied, and packed in sacks weighing about 225 to 350 pounds (100- 160 kg). The trimmed skirtings are baled separately. In Australia, the fleece is separated at the time of shearing according to its quality. Superior wool comes from the sides and shoulders, where it grows longer, finer, and softer, and is treated as one fleece; wool from the head, chest, belly, and shanks is treated as a second fleece (see Figure 4.3).

Domestic wool reaches the mill in loosely packed bags; imported wool comes in tightly compressed bales. Each fleece contains different grades, or sorts, of wool, and the raw stock must be carefully graded and segregated according to length, diameter, and quality of the fiber. The raw wool or newly sheared fleece is called grease wool because it contains the natural oil of the sheep. When grease wool is washed, it loses from 20 to 80 percent of its original weight. The grease, known as yolk, is widely used in the pharmaceutical and cosmetic industries for lanolin compounds because it can be absorbed by the human skin.

Sorting and Grading. Wool sorting is done by skilled workers who are expert in distinguishing qualities by touch and sight. As many as twenty separate grades of wool may be obtained from one fleece if the sorting is especially rigid. Each grade is determined by type, length, fineness, elasticity, and strength.

The standard for wool grading is based upon the quality of wool produced by the Merino sheep because it yields the finest-quality wool in terms of diameter, scales, and crimp. For example, first-quality wool is identified as fine and is equivalent to the quality of wool that could be obtained from a full- to three-quarter-blood Merino sheep; second quality is equivalent to the kind of wool that could be obtained from a halfblood Merino. The poorest qualities are identified as *common* and *braid;* they are coarse, have little crimp, relatively few scales, and are somewhat hairlike in appearance.

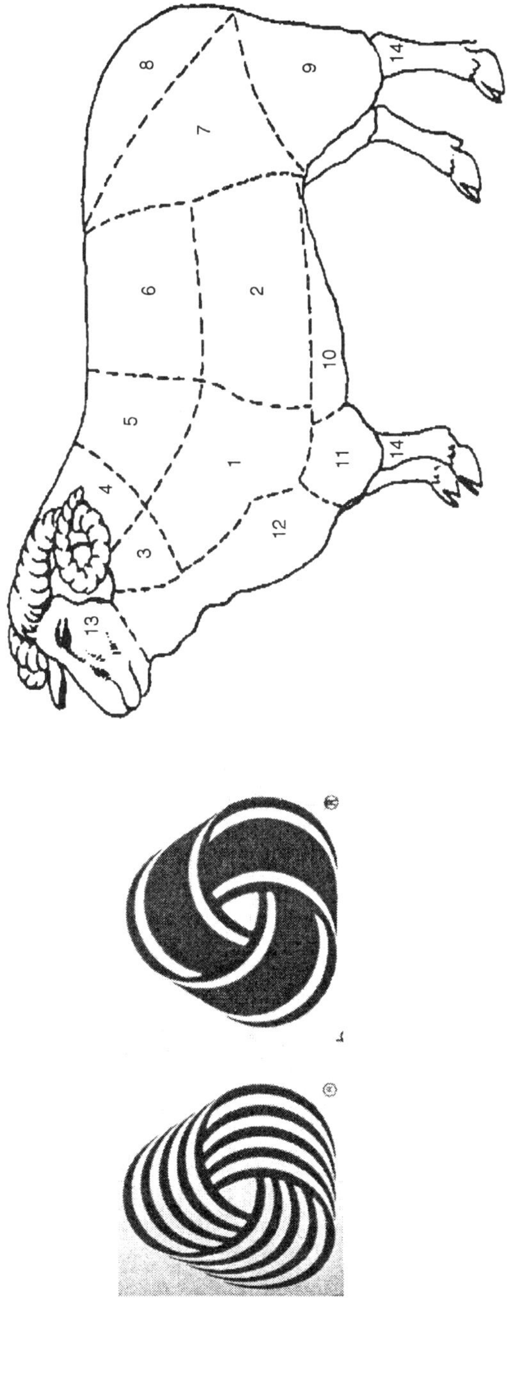

Fig.-4.3.

The grading system on the world market is based upon the British numbering system, which relates the fineness, or diameter, of the wool fiber to the kind of combed, or worsted, yarn that could be spun from I pound of scoured wool. For example, the first in quality would be that wool which is fine enough for and capable of being spun from 1 pound of fiber into the highest wool yarn counts of 80s, 70s, and 64s. The second in quality is fine enough to be capable of being spun into yarn counts of 62s, 60s, and 58s. The poorest grade is that wool which is capable of being spun into yarn counts of only 40s and 30s.

Garnetting. Recycled wool fibers are obtained by separately reducing the unused and used materials to a fibrous mass by a picking and shredding process called *garnetting.* The fibers are then put through a dilute solution of sulphuric or hydrochloric acid, which destroys any vegetable fibers that may be contained in the rawstock. This process is known as *carbonizing,* and the resultant wool fibers are called *extracts.* The new staple ranges from 6-40 mm lengths.

The quality and cost of recycled wool fibers depend on the original stock from which they were obtained. A good grade of recycled wool may cost 5 times as much as a poor grade of virgin wool.

Scouring. The next step in preparing raw wool for manufacturing is a thorouigh washing in an alkaline solution, this process is known as *scouring.* The scourilig machines contain warm water, soap, mild solution of soda ash or other alkali; they are equipped with automatic rakes, which stir the wool. Rollers between the vats squeeze out the water. If the raw wool is not sufficiently clear of vegetable substance after scouring, it is put through the carbonizing bath of dilute sulphuric acid or hydrochloric acid to burn out the foreign matter.

For some consumers' goods, the term naphthalated wool" is used, which means that the grease and dirt found in the fleece when originally sheared from the sheep's back have been removed by a series of naphtha baths followed by clear water to remove the naphtha. When wool has been thus treated by a cleansing agent, dyestuff penetrates better. For some purposes, wool is degreased by extracting the grease with a solvent, such as perchlorethylene. Excess solvent is evaporated off and recovered, and the wool is ready for further processing. This method is used both on stock and piece goods.

Drying. Wool is not allowed to become absolute dry. Usually, about 12 to 16 percent of the moisture is left in the wool to condition it for subsequent handling.

Oiling. As wool is unmanageable after scouring, the fiber is usually treated with various oils including animal, vegetable & mineral, or a blend of these to keep it from becoming brittle and to lubricate it for the spinning operation.

Dyeing

If the wool is to be dyed in the raw stock, it ts dyed at this stage. Some wool fabrics are piece-dyed, some are yarn or skein-dyed, and some are top-dyed.

Blending

Wool of different grades may be blended or mixed together at this point. It is not uncommon for taglocks and inferior grades of wool to be mixed with the better grades. The use of a mixture with a coarser grade of fiber is a legitimate practice if the purpose is to make a hardier product and a less expensive one, provided the label on the finished goods indicates a true description of the raw inaterials used. Subsequent to wool grade blending, other fibers may be blended with the wool .

Carding

The carding process introduces the classifications of woolen yarns & worsted yarns . Manufacturing processes from this point on depend on whether the wool fiber is to be made into a woolen or worsted product.

In the manufacture of woolen yarns, the essential purpose of carding is to disentangle the fibers by passing the wool fibers between rollers covered with thousands of fine wire teeth. Incidentally, this action also removes some dirt and foreign matter from the fibers. As the wool fibers are brushed and disentangled by these wires, they tend to lie parallel, which would make woolen yarns too smooth. Since woolen yarns should be somewhat rough or fuzzy, it is not desirable to have the fibers too parallel. By use of an oscillating device, one thin film, or silver, of wool is placed diagonally and overlapping another sliver to give a crisscross effect to the fibers. This permits the fibers to be disentangled and somewhat parallel and at the sarne time provides a fuzzy surface to the yarn. After this process, the woolen slivers go directly to the spinning operation

In the manufacture of worsted yarus, the essential purpose of carding is also to disentangle the fibers by passing the wool fibers between rollers covered with fine wire teeth. Since worsted yarns, however, should be smooth, the fibers are made to lie as parallel as this process will permit. Following this operation, the wool goes to the gilling and combing; processes.

Gilling and Combing

The carded wool, which is to be made into worsted is put through gilling and combing operations. The gilling process removes the shorter staple and straightens the fibers. This process is continued in the combing operation, which removes the shorter fibers of 1- to 4-inch (25-100mm) lengths (called combing noils), places the longer fibers (called tops) as parallel as possible, and further cleans the fibers by removing any remaining loose impurities.

The short-staple noils are not necessarily of poor quality. Combing noils may well be of good quality, depending on the original source of the wool. They may be used as filler for other types of wool fabrics; however, such fibers must be classified recycled wool.

The long-staple tops, which are over 4 inches (100 mm) in length, excel in color, feel, and strength. They are used in the production of such worsted fabrics as serge, whipcord, gabardine and covert.

Drawing

Drawing is an advanced operation whichl doubles and redoubles slivers of wool fibers. The process draws, drafts, twists, and winds the stock, making the slivers more compact and thinning them into slubbers. Drawing is done only to worsted yarns.

Roving

This is the final stage before spinning. Roving is actually a light twisting operation to hold the thin slubbers intact.

Spinning

In the spinning operation, the wool roving is drawn out and twisted into yarn. Woolen yarns are chiefly spun on the mule spinning machine. Worsted yarns are spun on any kind of spinning machine -mule, ring, cap, or flyer. The two principle systems of spinning worsted yarns are the English system and the French system.

In the English system (Bradford), the fiber is oiled before combing, and a tight twist is inserted. This produces smoother and finer yarns. The more tightly twisted yarn makes a stronger, more enduring fabric. In the French system, no oil is used. The yarn is given no twist; it is fuzzier, and therefore suitable for soft worsted yarns.

Wool yarns are also spun on the Selfil system developed in Australia whereby manmade filament fibers are wrapped around a core of wool staple The differences between woolen and worsted yarns are as follows:

Woolen Yarn	*Worsted Yarn*
Short staple	Long staple
Carded only	Carded and combed
Slack twisted	Tightly twisted
Weaker	Stronger
Bulkier	Finer, smoother, Even fibres
Softer	Harder

Yarn Count

The fineness or thickness of wool yarns is based on different systems for woolen and worsted. One pound of worsted yarn yielding 560 yards is identified as Ne 1. Ply yarns are numbered according to the number of the single varn from which they are spun. Thus, 2/60s worsted means two-ply yarns of Ne 60 singles, twisted together.

Warping

The yarn that leaves the spinning frame is not of sufficient length to serve as warp yarn on the loom. It is first wound on bobbins or spools and placed on a large rack or frame called a *creel.* As in the warping operation ,the warp yarns on the bobbins or spools are evenly wound on the warp beam. They may be immersed in a solution of starch, gum, or similar compound to make them smooth and strong for weaving. In the production of better-quality wool fabrics, a hard-twisted two-ply yarn is frequently used for the warp yarn, as the plied construction gives greater strength.

Weaving Woolen Fabrics

The fuzzy woolen yarns obtained in the carding process are made into woolen fabrics by using the plain weave, or sometimes the twill. The weave pattern is not always discernible because woolen fabrics often have a napped surface. The thread count of woolens is usually less than that of worsteds because the construction is not so compact.

Woolen fabrics are soft, fuzzy, and thick; they are warmer than worsted, but not as durable. Napping gives woolens a soft surface, which acts as a protection against objectionable luster. But napping can conceal poor construction and the quality of the yarns used; therefore, woolens can be more easily adulterated than worsteds. The napped surface tends to catch and hold dirt, but stains can be easily removed. If poorer yarns have been used in woolens, the fabric is less expensive than worsted. Woolens are desirable for sportswear, jackets, sweaters, skirts, blanket and similar general use.

Weaving Worsted Fabrics

The worsted yarns, which have been specially carded and combed, are woven into fine worsted fabrics with distinctive patterns, chiefly by means of the twill weave. The plain weave is infrequently used. The thread count of worsteds is higher than that of woolens because the finer yarn permits closer construction.

Worsted fabrics are firm, smooth or rough, and wiry or harsh. They are more durable than woolens and more resistant to dirt. They wrinkle less and hold creases and shape, but they become shiny with use.

Worsted fabrics are costlier than Woolens. They are appropriate for tailored and dressy purposes, for spring and summer coats and suits, and for tropical suits. They are suitable for business wear.

Inspecting and Correcting Flaws

Prior to various wet- and dry-finishing processes, wool fabrics are *perched,* or examined, for defects, which are marked with chalk. Some flaws are corrected by burling with a kind of tweezers (called *burling* irons) to remove loose threads and push knots to the back of the cloth and by *specking* to remove specks, burrs, and other foreign matter. Mending and sewing may be required to correct minor catches and similar defects

FINISHING WOOL FABRICS

Wool fabrics are given a variety of finishes similar to those applied to cotton and linen. But the nature of wool is such that certain other finishing processes are used to obtain a compact, firm body and hand.

Fulling

After the weaving process, woolen and Worsted gray goods are placed in warm, soapy water and are Pounded and twisted to make the wool fibers interlock. This application of heat, moisture, and pressure, followed by a cold rinse, is called *fulling* (also *felting* or *milling).* Sometimes, chemicals are used to help moisten, soften, and lubricate the fibers so that matting will occur.

Fulling produces a desired shrinkage and gives the fabric additional thickness and a firmer, fuller texture. The longer the fulling operation, the greater the shrinkage, with consequent increase in fabric strength. The fulling process and other finishing operations for woolens and worsteds yield flock, extremely short staple ranging from 3- 20 mm lengths. Flock is felted into the poorer grades of woolens to add weight. It is also blended with other raw wool stocks. Other waste material reclaimed from fulling is termed mungo. This is the lowest grade of waste. It is used for blending and is combined with yarn for low grade wool fabrics.

Crabbing

To set the cloth and the yarn twist permanently, wool fabric is passed over several cylinders that rotate in hot water and is then immersed quickly in cold water. The cloth is held firmly and tightly to avoid wrinkling. Repetition of the treatment with increased pressure results in setting the cloth and the finish.

Decating or Decatizing

Decating or decatizing is a shrinking treatment that is sometimes used instead of London shrinking. Decating, however, is faster and gives reasonable protection against further shrinking. There are two decating techniques, and the one that is used depends upon the luster desired in the finished fabric.

Dry Decating. If the luster is to be set, the fabric is wound under tension on a perforated roller that is then placed in a preheated boiler equipped with a vacuum system. Steam is first forced from the inside of the roller through the layers of fabric for two to three minutes; then the process is reversed. The fabric is then removed and cooled by air.

Wet Decating. If the luster is to be increased, the fabric, wound under tension on a perforated roller, is placed in hot water at 140 to 212 degree F (60- 100 degree C) that is first forced through the roller and fabric and then reversed. The hotter the water or steam used, the more effective the process will be. The cloth is then removed, cooled with cold water or cold air, and dried.

London Shrinking

This is a superior preshrinking treatment given to better-quality wool fabrics. It is a cold-water process by which the cloth is interleaved with wet blankets, dried slowly for twenty-four hours, and then set under 3500 pounds of pressure per square inch (24,000 kPa).

Additional Finishing Processes

Wool fabrics are also given the following finishing processes:

Name of Finish	Purpose
Mothproofing	for durability
Napping or gigging	to raise a fuzzy surface
Piece dyeing	to impart color to the wool fabric
Pressing	improving appearance and giving final shape to the cloth
Permanent press	for ease of care and shape retention
Shearing	cutting and shaving for a uniform surface
Shrinkproofing	for stability
Singeing and steaming	for hard finish of worsted fabrics
Steaming, sponging	removing excess glaze
Tentering	for desired uniform width
Water repellency	for all-weather wear

UNFINISHED WORSTEDS

Unfinished worsteds have the durability and tailored appearance characteristic of worsted fabrics and the comfort, greater warmth, and freedom from luster characteristic of woolens.

The soft texture of unfinished worsteds is due to additional manufacturing processes, such as fulling, brushing, or napping. Since they require more processing, the term "unfinished" gives a wrong impression.

The napped surface in the unfinished worsted gives softness of texture, serves the functional purposes of napped fabrics, and gives the beauty found in woolens. In addition, the fabric possesses the durability of worsteds. With continued wear, however, the nap rubs off, and these areas show an objectionable luster or shine. Such consumers' goods can be renapped by a cleaning establishment, but this is generally avoided since the renapping can weaken the cloth. One can enjoy longer serviceability by selecting an unfinished worsted in a light color. Light colors, such as gray, do not show luster as readily as the darker shades.

WOOL FABRICS EVALUATION

It is apparent that the quality and characteristics of wool fabrics are dependent upon the kind of sheep, its physical condition, the part of the sheep from which the wool is taken, and the manufacturing and finishing processes applied to the fabrics. While it might appear that these factors present a complicated problem in discerning preferred wool fabrics, there is much information and evidence available to the consumer to help in making satisfactory selections.

While it is not required that the labels on wool fabrics mention the type of sheep wool, fabrics made of Merino wool, frequently identified by label and in advertisements because they are prefered for their softness, warmth, resilience, fineness. It should be noted, however. that there are trademarks that are similar but not identical in spelling to Merino; such fabrics do not necessarily contain Merino wool.

Another wool fabric that may be readily identified is the Harris Tweed. The wool is obtained from Blackface, the predominant breed, and Cheviot sheep, as well as some crossbreeds which are raised principally for meat on the Outer Hebrides Islands. They produce a quality of wool that is coarse but strong and particularly well suited for durable tweeds. The wool is spun into yarn by machine in mills in Harris and Lewis and then delivered to freelance weavers who comprise the Harris Tweed Association. They weave the fabrics for the mills according to the requested length and pattern on their hand looms in their own sheds adjoining their cottages. The fabrics must be woven of at least 18 warps and 18 wefts per square inch (7.1 threads/cm^2). These tweeds are preferred for their quality of construction, durability, and exclusive designs. These fabrics are identified by the Association's Orb symbol printed every three yards (2.8 in) along the selvage and the registered number of the particular bolt of cloth (Figure 4.4)

However, the availability of Harris Tweed has been reduced as the number of members has diminished and those remaining refuse to accede to the mills' requests for a change to production on mechanized looms which can produce wider widths at faster speeds, thereby making the fabrics more available for a greater market including such items as upholstery.

Listing the amounts of new and recycled wools is also helpful. The presence of recycled wool in a fabric does not necessarily condemn it so long as the finished product is properly labeled and the consumer understands the limitations as well as the advantages of such wool fabrics. A fabric made of new or virgin wool may be of inferior quality if it is made of inferior grades or of extremely short staple. The yarns should be examined for fineness and crimp of fiber, as these factors have a direct relationship to the quality of wool.

Fig.-4.4. Genuine Harris Tweed is always identified by a label such as this containing the registered number and the association symbol.

Strength. As wool is the weakest of the natural textile fibers, some wool fabrics may be made more durable by the use of selected grades of recycled wool, although durability is gained at the expense of texture and resiliency. To determine whether temporary body (without strength) has been given by the use of flock, brush and whip the fabric vigorously. Then examine the surface and selvages for powdery particles, which are the sign of short staple. Also examine the structure of the fabric to determine whether it has been weakened by excessive napping.

Wool fabric is strengthened by the use of ply yarns. A hard-twisted two-ply yarn may be regarded as an assurance of durability. Tightly twisted single yarns also make a strong fabric.

Elasticity. Depending upon the quality of wool, the fiber may be stretched from 25 to 30 percent of its natural length before breaking. This characteristic reduces the danger of tearing under tension and contributes to free body movements. To preserve this natural elasticity, Wool garments should be hung properly after wearing and allowed to relax sufficiently to regain their shape (see Figure 4.5) .

Wool and wool blend fabrics have been given mechanical (crimp) and chemical (thermofixation) treatments to increase their elasticity and provide better two-way stretch. The chemical treatments have also resulted in improved shape retention.

Resilience. Because wool fiber has a high degree of resilience, wool fabric wrinkles less than some others; wrinkles disappear when the garment or fabric is steamed. Good wool is very soft and resilient; poor wool is harsh. When buying a wool fabric, grasp a handful to determine its quality. If the fabric retains the wrinkles and feels stiff, this may indicate an inferior grade of recycled wool.

Drapability. Wool's excellent draping quality is aided by its pliability, elasticity, and resiliency.

Heat Conductivity. As wool fibers are non conductors of heat, they permit the body to retain its normal temperature. Wool garments are excellent for winter clothing and are protective on damp days throughout the year. The scales on the surface of a fiber and the crimp in the fiber create little pockets of air that serve as insulative barriers and give the garment greater warmth. Low-twist yarns will also contribute to the warmth of the garment. Lightweight wool of sheer construction can be comfortable for summer wear in suitable garment styling because of its thermostatic quality.

Absorbency. Initially, wool tends to be water-repellent. One can observe that droplets of water on the surface of wool fabrics are readily brushed

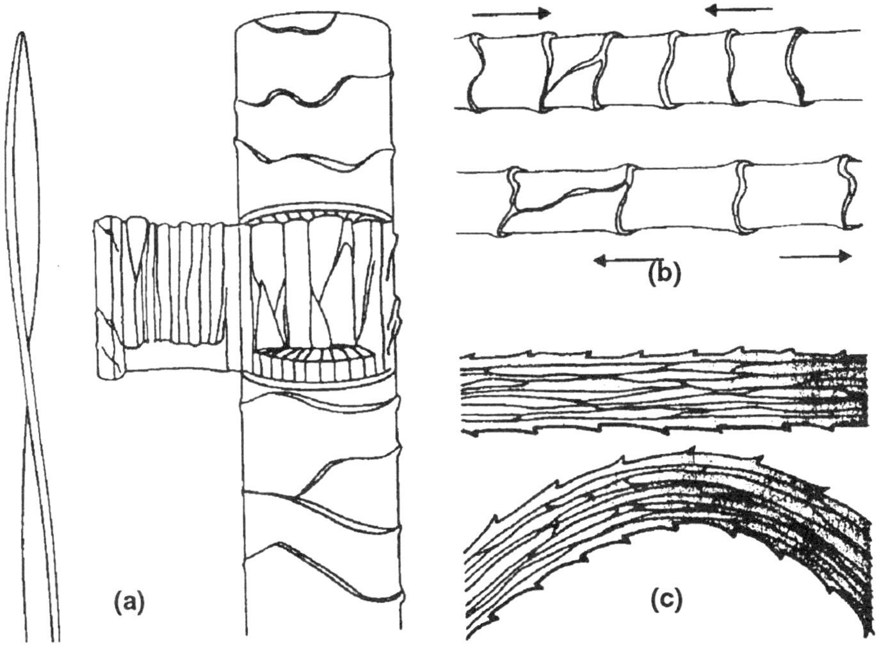

Fig.-4.5. (a) Model of a magnified wool fiber that has been partially opened to show the inner structure. The epidermal overlapping scales of the fiber cover numerous cortical spindle-shaped cells, a reproduction of which is shown at the left of the fiber model. The fiber's structure provides its elasticity, resilience, warmth, and felting properties. (b) Elasticity is facilitated by the surface scales sliding back and forth over each other. The inner cells also slide among each other in a similar manner. (c) This diagram of a wool fiber split length-wise depicts how the inner cells slide in and out of position allowing repeated bending without breaking (or creasing), thus providing resilience.

off. However, once the moisture seeps between the scales of the fiber, the fiber's high degree of capillarity will result in ready absorption. Wool can absorb about 20 percent of its weight in water without feeling damp; consequently, wool fabrics tend to feel comfortable rather than clammy or chilly. Wool also dries slowly.

Cleanliness and Washability. Dirt tends to adhere to wool fabric. Unless thoroughly cleaned, wool retains odors. Wool requires frequent dry cleaning, or laundering if the fabric is washable. Extreme care is required in laundering. Wool is softened by moisture and heat, and shrinking and felting occur when the fabric is washed. Since wool temporarily loses about 25 percent of its strength when wet, wool fabrics should never be pulled or wrung while wet. They should be lifted and squeezed.

To control the possibility of shrinking or stretching when laundering a wool sweater or a similar garment, wash it in cold water with all appropriate detergent. To dry the garment, roll it in a towel, squeeze gently to remove as much moisture as possible, then spread it out to its original shape on a towel or heavy cardboard.

Reaction to Bleaches. The household bleaches that contain sodium hypochlorite or other chlorine compounds are harmful to wool. However, a bleach containing hydrogen peroxide or sodium perborate can be safely used.

Shrinkage. Shrinkage is greater in Woolens than in Worsteds, but all fabrics made of wool are subject to shrinkage, depending upon the preshrinking treatmeiit . If the fabrics are dry-cleaned, the shrinkage will be less. Chlo*rinated wools* are wools that have been subjected to shrinkproofing, but this treatnient reduces the strength of the fabric,

Effect of Heat. Wool becomes harsh at 212 degree F (100 degree C) and begins to decompose at slightly higher temperatures. It will scorch at 400 degree F (204 degree C) and will eventually char. However, it is not easily combustible-it will smolder but not flame when fire is removed. Wool has a plastic quality in that it can be pressed and shaped at steam temperatures, whether in fabric, as for slacks and jackets, or in felt, as for hats.

Effect of Light. Wool is weakened by prolonged exposure to sunlight.

Resistance to Mildew. Wool is not ordinarily susceptible to mildew, but if left in a damp condition, mildew develops.

Resistance to Insects. Wool fabrics are especially vulnerable to the larvae of moths and such other insects as carpet beetles.

Reaction to Alkalies. Wool is quickly, damaged by strong alkalies. It is imperative to use a mild soap or detergent when laundering wool fabrics.

Reaction to Acids. Although wool is damaged by hot sulphuric acid, it is not affected by other acids, even when heated. Thisis property permits wool to be carbonized without damage.

Affinity for Dyes. Because of their high affinity for dyes, wool fabrics dye well and evenly. The use of chrome dyes assures fastness of color. A variety of other dyes may be effectively used

Resistance to Perspiration. Wool is weakened by alkali perspiration. Garments should be dry cleaned or washed with care to avoid deterioration and odor. Perspiration, generally, will cause discoloration.

WOOL BLENDS

Wool and Cotton

Wool is blended with cotton in various ratios. The properties of the yarns and fabrics will be affected by the proportion of the fibers blended. Wool contributes warmth, resilience, abrasion resistance, and drapability. Cotton adds strength and reduces the cost of the yarn and fabric. Both fibers are absorbent and can be blended to make a comfortable, durable fabric with a nice hand.

Wool and Linen

Wool is sometimes blended with linen. Such a blend is stronger and cooler than a pure wool fabric, but is more resilient and drapable than a pure linen fabric.

HAIR

Hair fibers that have qualities of wool are obtained from certain kinds of animals throughout the world. The hair of these animals has been so adapted by nature for the climate in which they live that the cloth produced from the fiber gives warmth with light weight. Some of these animals are used primarily as burden carriers; others are bred for their fleeces, which produce the most expensive fibers in the textile industry.

These hair fibers are used alone or are combined with sheep's wool for construction into fabrics whose cost varies according to the amount and quality of the blend.

CAMEL HAIR

Camel hair is a fine hair that is known to the consumer chiefly in the form of high-quality coat fabrics. This textile fiber is obtained from the two humped Bactrian camel, which is native to all parts of Asia .The climate of the desert countries, where the camel is used as a burden carrier and as a means of transportation, is exceedingly hot during the day and extremely cold at night. This constant change has produced a protective hair covering that insulates the body in both heat and cold; it is also naturally water-repellent. In the spring, the year's growth of hair, which hangs from the camel in matted strands and tufts, falls off in clumps to make room for the new growth. Masses of hair that are shed throughout the year are also accumulated. The camel is sometimes plucked to obtain the down or underhair.

Camel hair fabrics are ideal for comfort, particularly when used for overcoating, as they are especially warm but light in weight. Camel hair is characterized by strength, luster, and smoothness. The best quality is expensive when used alone. It is often mixed with wool, thus raising the quality of the wool fabric by adding the fine qualities of camel hair. The price of a mixed cloth is naturally much less than that of a fabric that is 100 percent camel hair.

In the textile industry, camel hair is divided into three grades. Grade I is the soft and silky light-tan underhair found close to the skin of the camel. This is short staple, or noil, of from 30-90 mm, but it is also the choicest quality. Formerly, it was the only true camel hair used in the manufacture of apparel. In wool, noils represent the less valuable short staple; in the hair fibers, the short fibers are the prized product and are the only ones used in high-grade hair fabrics.

Grade 2 is the intermediate growth, consisting of short hairs and partly of coarse outer hairs, ranging from 40- 125 mm in length. Grade 3 consists entirely of coarse outer hairs measuring up to 15 inches (380 mm) in length and varying in color from brownish black to reddish brown. This grade has no value for apparel manufacture; it is suitable only for cordage and for low-quality rugs.

MOHAIR

Mohair is the hair of the Angora goat, native to the province of Angora, Turkey .This species of goat is now raised in South Africa and the United

States, principally in Oregon, California, and Texas. Imported mohair is long staple, 9 to 12 inches (230- 300 mm) long, and represents a full year's growth. The domestic goat is shorn twice a year, yielding a shorter staple, from 8 to 10 inches (200-250 mm). Imported mohair can be spun to a fineness of Ne 60 in yarn count. The highest count possible for domestic fiber is Ne 40. The domestic fiber has a great amount of coarse, stiff hair, known as *kemp,* which does not process readily or allow thorough penetration of dye.

Mohair is a smooth, strong, and resilient fiber. It does not attract or hold dirt particles. It absorbs dye evenly and permanently. Its fine silklike luster permits interesting decorative effects. Mohair fiber is more uniform in diameter than wool fiber. Under the microscope, mohair shows almost no scales; its indistinct scales do not project from the shaft, as is characteristic of wool fiber. Mohair, therefore, does not shrink or felt as readily as wool.

When mohair is used in pile fabrics, the naturally strong fiber combined with the strength of the pile weave makes an especially durable and serviceable fabric. Mohair fabrics are wrinkle-resistant and do not mat readily because of the natural resiliency of the fiber. The fabric can also be made mothproof. Because mohair is very resilient and is stronger than wool or the other hair fibers, it is used to great advantage in better grades of upholstery and drapery materials and in summer suitings.

CASHMERE

The Cashmere goat is native to the Himalaya Mountain region of Kashmir in India, Mongolia, and China. The fleece of this goat has long, straight, coarse outer hair of little value; however, the small quantity, of underhair, or down, is made into luxuriously soft woollike yarns with a characteristic highly napped finish.

Cashmere is used for such garments as sweaters, sports jackets, and overcoats. It is desirable because it is soft, lighter in weight than wool, and quite warm; however, because it is a soft, delicate fiber, fabrics produced from cashmere are not as durable as wool.

LLAMA

The llama is allied to the camel in species, having many, of the characteristics of that animal, but being about one-third in size.The llama is the traditional burden carrier in the higher parts of the Andes Mountains in South America. Its hair fiber is generally coarse and brownish in color and is valued because it may be mixed with the hair of the alpaca, an animal of the same species that is raised for its fleece alone. Some noils are obtained from the undercoat of the llama.

When llama is part of a blend of fibers, it gives exquisite natural colors. Llama mixtures have a characteristic high insulative property with little weight and are used for high-quality coat fabrics, as they embody the essential qualities of wrinkle resistance, color fastness, and extreme durability.

ALPACA

In the higher regions of the Andes, 14,000 feet (4250 m) above sea level, is found another fleece bearer, the alpaca, a domesticated animal that resembles the llama and is related to the camel .The fiber is valued for its silky beauty as well as for its strength. The hair of the alpaca is stronger than ordinary sheep's wool, is water-repellent, and has a high insulative quality. The staple is relatively long, ranging from 6 to 11 inches (150 -280 mm); yet it is as delicate, soft, and lustrous as the finest silk.

Alpaca consists of two varieties of fiber: soft, wool-like hair, and stiff beard, or outer hair. Of the many colors obtainable, ranging from white to brown and black, the reddish brown variety is considered the most valuable.

A more highly selected type of alpaca is the suri-a superbreed just as the Merino is the highest type of sheep. The fiber of the suri is sought by manufacturers of outer apparel because the staple is longer, silkier, and finer, and has curl throughout its length.

VICUNA

The rare animal whose fiber makes world's most costly and most exquisite cloth, surpassing all others in fineness and beauty, is found in area of the Andes Mountains, at altitudes between 16,000 and 19,000 feet (4875-5800 m). The vicuna, one of the wildest of animals, is less than 3 feet (90 cm) high and weighs 75 to 100 pounds (35-45 kg)). A single animal yields only 1/4 pound (100 g) of hair; thus forty animals are required to provide enough hair for the average coat. To preserve the species , the vicuna is now under the protection. The fiber of the vicuna is the softest and most delicate of the known animal fibers; yet it is strong for its weight, is resilient, and has a marked degree of elasticity and surface cohesion. It is the most expensive fiber used in suitings and overcoat fabrics of natural tan to orange-brown.

GUANACO

The guanaco, native to southern Argentina where it is both wild and domesticated, is related to the llama and alpaca. The fiber is extremely soft and silky. It is also light, resilient, and warm, and the color is a honey beige. Because of these characteristics and its limited availability, it is expensive. It generally is blended with wool, frequently lamb's wool, so as not to mask the fiber's soft texture.

ANGORA

The Angora rabbit produces long, fine,silky white hair that is clipped or combed 3 to 4 months. The finest angora comes from France, Italy, and Japan. The fiber's smooth, silky texture makes it difficult to spin, and the fibers tend to slip out of the yarn and shed from the fabric; nevertheless, the fiber is desired for its texture, warmth, light weight, and pure white color, although it is sometimes dyed in pastel shades. Angora rabbit hair is used primarily for items such as sweaters,mittens, baby clothes, and millinery.

QIVIUT

One of the softest hair fibers, which makes very warm yet light fabrics, is the underhair of the musk ox, called *qiviut*

MINOR HAIR FIBERS

There are several hair fibers that are used for specialized purposes and for a limited extent. These are:

- *Cow hair* obtairied from the hides of slaughtered cows. It is used for felts and coarse rugs and cushions.
- *Horsehair* obtained from horses' manes and tails. It is used as a shape retainer in suits and coats and for stuffing in mattresses and upholstery.
- *Rabbit hair* obtained from the commen rabbit. It is used for felt in hats.
- *Down* and *feathers* obtained from geese and ducks. Thev are used for stuffing for pillows, comforters, quilted outerwear, and upholstery.

4) SILK

Silk is the very fine strand of fiber that is a solidified *protein* secretion produced by certain caterpillars to encase themselves in the form of cocoons.

HISTORY OF SILK

The possibility of making cloth from the filament that the silkworm spins into a cocoon was first discovered in China about 2600 B.C. Legend tells us that a cocoon accidentally dropped into a cup of tea that a Chinese princess was having in her garden. The hot liquid softened and loosened the fiber, which the princess pulled and drew away from the cocoon as a continuous strand.

SILK-PRODUCING COUNTRIES

When farmers in the Asiatic countries first raised silkworms, the many diseased worms and defective cocoons resulted in poor grades of finished goods. The farmers were raising silkworms only as an additional means of support. Japan was the first country producing silk in large quantities to use scientific methods in cultivating the silkworm on farms as well as in factories. Japan has therefore always ranked highest in the production of fine silk, although satisfactory types are made in other silk-producing countries-China, India, Italy, Spain, France, Austria, Iran, Turkey, Greece, Syria, Bulgaria, and Brazil.

CULTIVATION OF COCOONS

Since the discovery, so many years ago, that the fiber, or filament, composing the cocoon of the silkworm can be unwound and constructed into a beautiful and durable fabric, silkworms have been bred for the sole purpose of producing raw silk. The production of cocoons for their filament is called *sericulture*

The life cycle of silkworm;

1. The egg, which develops into the larva, or caterpillar- the silkworm
2. The silkworm, which spins its cocoon for protection, to permit development into the pupa, or chrysalis
3. The chrysalis, which emerges from the cocoon as the moth
4. The moth, of which the female lays eggs, so continuing the life cycle

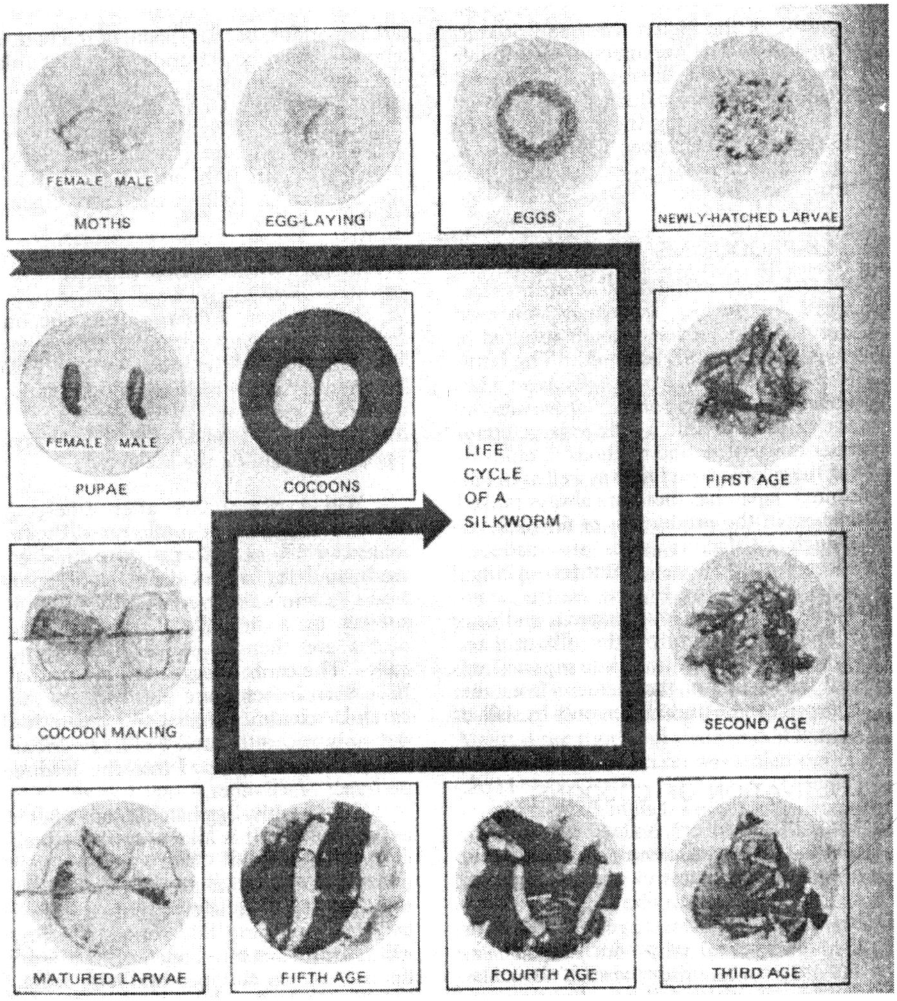

Fig.-4.6 Nature's production of silk fiber.

Within three days after emerging from the cocoons, the moths mate, the female lays 350 to 400 eggs on numbered cards, and the moths die.

Of importance to the silk industry is the small opening under the caterpillar's jaws, called the *spinneret.* The silkworm begins to secrete a proteinlike substance through its spinneret, and with a bending motion . The silkworm is hidden from view within twenty-four hours; in three days, the cocoon is completed. It is about the size and shape of a peanut shell. The filament is in the form of a double strand of *fibroin,* which is held together by a gummy substance called *sericin,* or silk *gum.* The liquid substance hardens, on exposure to the air. If left undisturbed, the chrysalis inside the cocoon develops into a moth within two weeks. To emerge, the moth must break through the top of the cocoon by secreting an alkaline liquid that dissolves the filament. As this cutting through damages the cocoon so that the filament cannot be unwound in one long thread, the life cycle is terminated at this point by a process known as *stoving,* or *stifling.* The cocoons are heated to suffocate the chrysalis, but the delicate silk filament is not harmed

FILATURE OPERATIONS

The cocoons that are raised by silk farmers are delivered to a factory, called a *filature*

Sorting Cocoons

The cocoons are sorted according to color, size, shape, and texture, as all these affect the final quality of the silk . Cocoons may range from white or yellow to grayish, depending on the source and the type of food consumed during the worm stage. Cocoons from China are white; Japanese cocoons are creamy white and yellow; Italian cocoons are yellow.

Softening the Sericin

After the cocoons have been sorted, they are put through a series of hot and cold immersions, as the sericin must be softened to permit the unwinding of the filament as one continuous thread. Raw silk consists of about 80 percent fibroin and 20 percent sericin.

Reeling the Filament

The process of unwinding the filament from the cocoon is called *reeling.* The care and skill used in the reeling operation prevent defects in the raw silk. As the filament of a single cocoon is too fine for commercial use, three to ten strands are usually reeled at a time to produce the desired diameter of raw silk thread. The cocoons float in water, bobbing up and down, as the filaments are drawn upward through porcelain eyelets and are rapidly wound on wheels or drums while the operator watches to detect flaws. As the reeling of the filament from each cocoon nears completion, operators attach a new filament to the moving thread. Skilled operators have an uncanny ability to blend the filaments, while always retaining the same diameter of the rapidly moving silk strand. The sericin acts as an adhesive. It aids in holding the several filaments together while they are combined to form the single thread.

The usable length of the reeled filament is from 1000 to 2000 feet (300 -600 m), approximately a quarter of a mile long. The remaining part of the filament is used as valuable raw material for the manufacture of spun silk.

The term "reeled silk" is applied to the raw silk strand that is formed by combining several filaments from separate cocoons. The diameter of the silk fiber is so fine that an estimated 3000 cocoons are required to make a yard (1 m) of silk fabric. The silk filaments are reeled into skeins, which are packed in small bundles called *books.*

MANUFACTURE OF SILK YARNS

From the filature, the books of reeled silk are put through the following manufacturing processes.

Thrown Silk

Reeled silk is transformed into silk yarn also called silk thread-by a process known as *throwing. Silk* throwing is analogous to the spinning process that manufactures cotton, linen, or wool fibers into yarn. Unlike those fibers, the manufacture of silk yarn does not include the processes for producing a continuous yarn by carding, combing, and drawing out. The raw silk skeins are sorted according to size, color, and length or quantity, then soaked in warm water with soap or oil. This softening of the sericin aids in handling the thread. After mechanical drying, the skeins are placed on light reels from which the silk is wound on bobbins.

During this winding operation, single strands may be given any desired amount of twist. If two or more yarns are to be doubled, they are twisted again in the same direction or in a reverse direction, depending on the kind of thread to be made. To equalize the diameter, the yarn is run through rollers. The thread is then inspected and packaged and is ready for shipment to manufacturers for construction into fabric.

Kinds of Thrown Silk Yarns. Several kinds of silk yarns, or threads, are used in the manufacture of silk goods.

Singles. Usually, three to eight strands of silk filaments are twisted together in one direction to form a yarn called a *single.* Loose-twist singles, having two or three twists per inch (about 1 twist/cm), are used primarily for the filling yarns in many silk fabrics. Hard-twist singles, having a much greater number of twists per inch, are,used in the sheer fabrics (see Fig 4.6a).

Tram. Tram is used only as a filling yarn. Usually, two to four untwisted singles are combined with only a slight twist of about three to five turns per inch (1 -2/cm). The number of turns may be increased for especially heavy silk fabrics. Tram is rarely twisted more than five turns to the inch (2/cm), except in such fabrics as radium and taffeta, which use a special hard-twisted tram of about 30 turns per inch (12/ cm (see Figure4.6b)

Voile. This yarn is used for such sheer crepes as voile. It is composed of three untwisted singles combined with 35 to 40, S turns per inch (14-16/cm) (see Fig 4.6c).

Georgette or Crepe de Chine. This yarn is composed of two untwisted singles combined with a very hard S or Z twist of seventy to seventy-five turns per inch (28–30/cm). The result is a very fine, strong, elastic yarn used for warp yarns and for such sheer fabrics georgette or crepe de chine (see Figure 4.6d .)

Organzine. Organzine is used primarily for warp yarns. It is composed of two or more singles, each of which has sixteen Z turns per inch (6/ cm). These singles are then combined by twisting them around each other in the opposite S twist, twelve to twenty turns per inch (5-8/cm), which causes them to interlock more tightly, resulting firmer, stronger yarn (see Fig 4.6e)

Grenadine. This yarn is composed of three to five singles, each given a twist of about thirty-six Z turns per inch (14/cm), then combined by being twisted around each other in the opposite S direction, twenty-five to thirty-five turns per inch (10- 14/cm). Although these yarns have a high twist, they are nevertheless fine and are used for such sheer fabrics as organdy and grenadine (see Figure 4.6 f)

Two by Two (Grenadine Type). Each of two pairs of untwisted singles is twisted about thirty-six Z turns per inch (14/cm), then twisted around the other twenty-five to thirty-five turns (10- 14/cm) in the S direction. These yarns are consequently much like the grenadine yarns but are heavier. Their weight, body, and high twist make them desirable for crepe fab rics (see Figure 4.6g)

Compensene S. This yarn is each of two pairs of untwisted singles. One pair is twisted together forty to fortyfive S turns per inch (16- 18/cm); the other is twisted the same number of Z turns per inch. These twisted pairs are then twisted around each other five S turns per inch (2/cm). The opposing directions of these twists prevent kinking but give elasticity. These yarns are often used for knitted fabrics (see Figure 4.6h)

Crepe. Some crepe fabrics are made of crepe yarns. These yarns are composed of each of two pairs of untwisted singles. One pair is twisted sixty to eighty-five turns per inch (24-34/cm) in the S direction; the other is twisted the same number of turns per inch (cm) in the Z direction. They are then twisted around each other two and one-half to five S turns per inch (1-2/cm) (see Figure 4.6i).

Yarn Count ofThrown Silk. The size or the yarn count of silk threads is based on system known as *den*ier represents a weight of 0.05 gram and the standard length of a raw silk skein is 450 meters. An increase in weight of a standard length indicates an increase in diameter and, therefore, denier. A 450meter skein weighing 0.05 gram would be of a thread of one denier, a skein of 0. 50 gram would be of a thread of 10 denier, and so forth. Another way of expressing the weight is in grams per 9000 meters.

Degumming of Thrown Silk. Thrown silk yarns still contain some sericin that must be removcd in another soap bath to bring out the natural luster and the soft feel of the silk. As much as 25 percent of the weight is lost by the degumming process. When the gum has been removed, the silk fiber or fabric is a creamy white color, beautifully lustrous, and soft.

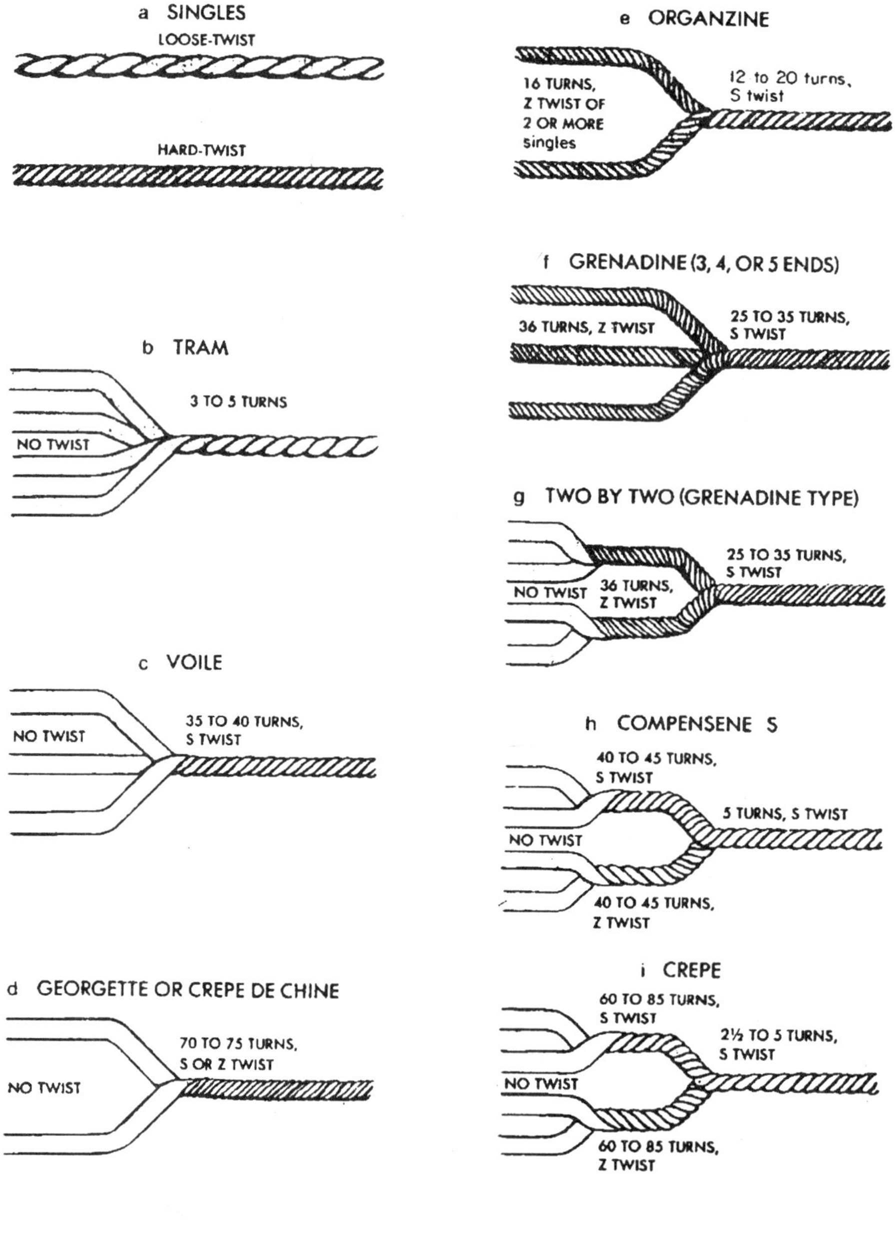

Fig.-4.7. Types of thrown silk yarn. "Turns" means turns per inch.

Degumming may take place after the silk yarn is thrown in order to prepare it for yarn dyeing or it may be done in any finishing process after the fabric is woven.

Spun Silk

Short lengths of inferior silk filaments obtained from waste material are not used in producing reeled silk. After the short lengths have been carded and combed, they are spun together much as linen, or wool yarns are spun. **Spun silk** yarns are soft, but they are less lustrous than reeled silk and are not as strong or elastic. Spun silk fabric tends to fuzzy after wearing because the made of short staple.

There are several sources of staple silk:

1) Pierced cocoons, the result of breeding moths that have emerged from their cocoons;

2) Double cocoons, the result of two cocoons having been spun by two silkworms too close together

3) Floss, brushed from cocoons before reeling;

4) Frison, the coarse and uneven silk fiber at the beginning and end of each cocoon;

5) Scrap, the machine waste left from reeling, throwing, and the like.

Spun silk is less expensive than reeled silk. Although spun silk has less strength and elasticity because of the shorter staple used, it possesses all the general characteristics of reeled silk. Spun silk is used for shantung and pile fabrics; for dress trimmings, linings, elastic webbing, and sewing silk; for wash silks, velvets, umbrella fabrics, and insulative materials.

The waste derived from the processing of spun silk yarn is also used. Such fiber be labeled as ***waste silk, silk waste, noil silk,*** or ***silk noil.*** For obvious reasons, the last two designations are most frequently used. Silk noil may be reprocessed into spun yarn and woven into textured fabrics for draperies, upholstery, and sportswear. These fabrics are dull, rough, have a cottonlike appearance, but are generally more resilient.

Yarn Count of Spun Silk. The method of determining the size of spun silk yarn is similar to that used for cotton yarn. In cotton, the term

"60/2s" signifies a two-ply yarn consisting of two single strands twisted together, each having a yarn count of 60 (9.8 tex), resulting in the equivalent thickness of a 30s (19.7 tex).

In spun silk, a two-ply yarn is indicated by the figures "60s/2." Although this term appears to be the same as the cotton term, it does not mean the same. In spun silk, 60s/2 means that two yarns, each of a yarn count of 120 (4.9 tex), have been twisted together to produce a ply yarn that has a count of 60 (9.8 tex).

FINISHING SILK FABRICS

As with other textiles, silk fabrics may be given a variety of finishes. There is one finish, though, that is unique to silk. It is weighting.

Weighting

The amount of weight that silk loses in the degumming process is an appreciable factor in manufacturing costs because the manufacturer buys silk by weight. As is customary in any business, the price of the finished product must offset this loss; therefore, silk has always been an expensive fabric. The weighting of silk fabric with metallic substances to make up for the weight lost by degumming is an accepted practice in the silk industry. This procedure lowers the cost of silk to the consumer.

Weighted silk is less compactly woven than unweighted silk and less silk is used in the construction of the cloth. In other words, weighting rather than compact construction can give firmness and body to a silk fabric. Weighting is done during the dyeing process. To weight colored silks, stannic chloride is used, followed by treatment with sodium phosphate. Black silks are weighted with metallic mordants, such as iron salt and logwood.

A small amount of metallic weighting, correctly applied to a fabric that is well woven to hold the weighting, is not considered injurious. In addition to lowering the cost, it is claimed that weighting gives silk crispness, luster, and firmer body and feel. When weighted silk is pleated, the crease is retained. Weighted silk, however, loses the natural elasticity of the silk fiber and is subject to deterioration when exposed to sunlight, perspiration, and dry cleaning. When the fabric is not properly constructed, threads shift. If the fabric is not woven suffciently wide to allow for natural shrinkage, there is an unsatisfactory amount of shrinkage.

Taffeta is a commonly used fabric that is usually heavily weighted, because today there is little demand for pure-dye taffeta. Weighted taffeta is apt to crack and split at the places subjected to the strain of wear and folded for a length of time. (Rayon and acetate taffeta do not contain any metallic weighting.)

Pure-Dye Silk

As silk is weighted during the dyeing process, the term "pure-dye silk" indicates that weighting was not added at that time. Pure-dye silk is defined as a fabric made exclusively of silk fibers containing "no metallic weighting whatsoever."

Strength

Silk is strongest natural fibre. The smoothness of the silk filament yarns reduces the problem of wear from abrasion. The inherent strength of silk along with its fine diameter and lightness has made it a highly desirable fiber for sheer yet durable fabrics. The strength of silk fabric is also affected, of course, by its construction as well as its finish.

Spun silk yarn, though strong, is weaker than thrown silk filament yarns. The quality of spun silk depends upon the source of the staple. Douppioni and pierced-cocoon silk are generally stronger than the other silk staple, which tend to be less uniform.

Elasticity. While silk is an elastic fiber, its elasticity varies, as may be expected of a natural fiber. Silk fiber may be stretched from 1/7 to 1/5 its original length before breaking. It returns to its original size gradually and loses little of its elasticity. This characteristic means less binding and sagging, thus contributing to the wearer's comfort. It should be kept in mind that the elasticity of the yarn and the fabric is affected by the kind of yarn used (thrown or spun), the construction of the fabric, and the finish that it is given.

Resilience. Silk fabrics retain their shape and resist wrinkling rather well. This is particularly true of the fabrics rnade from pure-dye silk and from wild silk. Fabrics that contain a large percentage of weighting or are made from short-staple spun silk have less resilience.

Drapability. Silk has a pliability and suppleness that, aided by its elasticity and resilience, give it excellent drapability.

Heat Conductivity. Like wool, silk is a **protein** fiber; therefore, it is also a non-conductor of heat. Because silk prevents body heat from radiating outward, it is desirable for winter apparel, including scarves. Thin silk fabrics are also comfortably warm when used for lingerie, pajamas, robes, and linings. The warmth giving quality is lessened by weighting because the metallic content causes the fabric to become a conductor of heat.

A question often raised is why silk is used for summer fabrics when it is a nonconductor of heat. The answer is that silk, being fine and strong, may be made into very fine yarns and woven into very sheer fabrics. This permits the body heat and the air to pass freely through the open construction of such cloth.

Absorbency. The good absorptive property of silk also contributes to its comfort in a warmer atmosphere. Silk fiber can generally absorb about 11 percent of its weight in moisture, but the range vary from 10 percent to as much as 30 percent. This property is also a major factor in silk's ability to be printed and dyed easily.

Cleanliness and Washability. Silk is a hygienic material because its smooth surface does not attract dirt. When dirt does gather, it is given up readily by washing or drycleaning. Care should be exercised in laundering silk-always use a mild soap, Wringing or strong agitation in the washing machine should be avoided, as silk weakens slightly when wet.

All silks water-spot easily, but subsequent washing or dry cleaning will restore the appearance of the fabric, unless it has a special finish. Taffeta, for example, may be given a finish that could be permanently stained by water. Dry cleaning is preferable for weighted silks, but wildsilk and spun-silk fabrics may be washed.

Reaction to Bleaches. Strong bleaches containing sodium hypochlorite will deteriorate silk. A mild bleach of hydrogen peroxide or sodium perborate may be used with normal caution.

Shrinkage. Because of the straightness of the filament, smooth-surfaced silk fabrics have only a normal shrinkage, which is easily restored by ironing. Crepe effects shrink considerably in washing, but careful ironing with a moderately hot iron will restore the fabric to its original size.

Effect of Heat. Silk is somewhat sensitive to heat. It will begin to decompose at 330 degree F (165 degree C); therefore, it should be ironed while damp with a warm iron.

Effect of Light. Continuous exposure to light weakens silk faster than either cotton or wool. Raw silk is more resistant to light than degummed silk, and weighted silk has the least light resistance. Silk drapery and upholstery, fabrics should be protected from direct exposure to the light.

Resistance to Mildew. Silk will not mildew unless left for some time in a damp state or under the extreme conditions of tropical dampness.

Resistance to Insects. Silk may be attacked by the larvae of clothes moths or carpet beetles, and it may be destroyed when blended with wool which is attacked by these insects.

Reaction to Alkalies. Silk is not as sensitive as wool is to alkalies, but it can be damaged if the concentration and the temperature are high enough. Use a mild soap or detergent in lukewarm water when laundering.

Reaction to Acids. Concentrated mineral acids will dissolve silk faster than wool. Organic acids do not harm silk.

Affinity for Dyes. Silk has a very good affinity for dyes. It readily absorbs basic, acid, and direct dyes. Prints on silk are taken so well that the color on the back of the fabric often differs only slightly from the face.

Dyed silk is colorfast under most conditions, but its resistance to light is unsatisfactory. The resistance of weighted silk is particularly poor; therefore, silk is not recommended for window curtains. Pure-dye silks may be redyed by the consumer, provided a suitable commercial dye is used and the directions on the contaner are followed.

Resistance to Perspiration. Silk fabrics are damaged by perspiration. The silk itself deteriorates, and the color is affected, causing staining. Garments worn next to the skin should be washed or otherwise cleaned after each wearing.

SILK BLENDS

Silk is blended with many fibers. When it is to be blended with any of the natural fibers, silk noil is used. This makes blending and spinning possible because all of the fibers are of staple length. The resultant properties depend upon the ratio of the fibers blended.

Silk and Cotton

When silk is blended with cotton, silk contributes a soft, smooth hand, lightness of weight with strength, resilience, comfort, and good color possibilities. Cotton provides body and lower cost.

Silk and Linen

Silk is not regularly blended with linen. Such a blend frequently includes other fibers as well. Silk and linen both provide strength and absorbency. Silk reduces weight and adds good hand. Linen provides body. Both add prestige.

Silk and Wool

Silk and wool are usually blended on a worsted system, producing a fine, strong yarn. The fabrics may have a soft sheen. They are lightweight, resilient, durable, and drape well. Silk/wool blends are used for such apparel as suits, particularly summer weights.

5 PROPERTIES OF MAN MADE FIBRES

A) NYLON

The word "nylon" is a generic term that designates group of related chemical compounds classified as *poly amides.* Nylon is a long-chain synthetic polyamide in which less than 85 percent of the amide linkages are attached to two aromatic rings.

METHODS OF MANUFACTURE

Nylon is actually a group of related chemical compounds. It is composed of hydrogen, nitrogen, oxygen, and carbon in controlled proportions and structural arrangments. Variations can result in types of nylon plastics, such as combs, brushes, and gears. We are here concerned with the production of nylon yarn. Since the two types of nylon that predominate the market are nylon 6,6 and nylon 6, we shall consider their basic methods of production. (See Figure 5.1)

By a series of chemical steps beginning with such raw materials as coal, petroleum, or such cereal byproducts as oat hulls or corncobs, two chemicals called *hexamethylene diamine* and *adipic acid* are made. These are combined to form nylon salt. Then, since the nylon salt is to be shipped to the spinning mill, it is dissolved in water for easy handling. At the spinning mill, it is heated in large evaporators until a concentrated solution is obtained. The concentrated nylon salt solution is then transferred to an autoclave, which is like a huge pressure cooker. The heat combines the molecules of the two chemicals into giant chainlike ones, called *linear superpolymers.* This process gives nylon a molecular structure somewhat like wool and silk and is also the source of nylon's strength and elasticity.

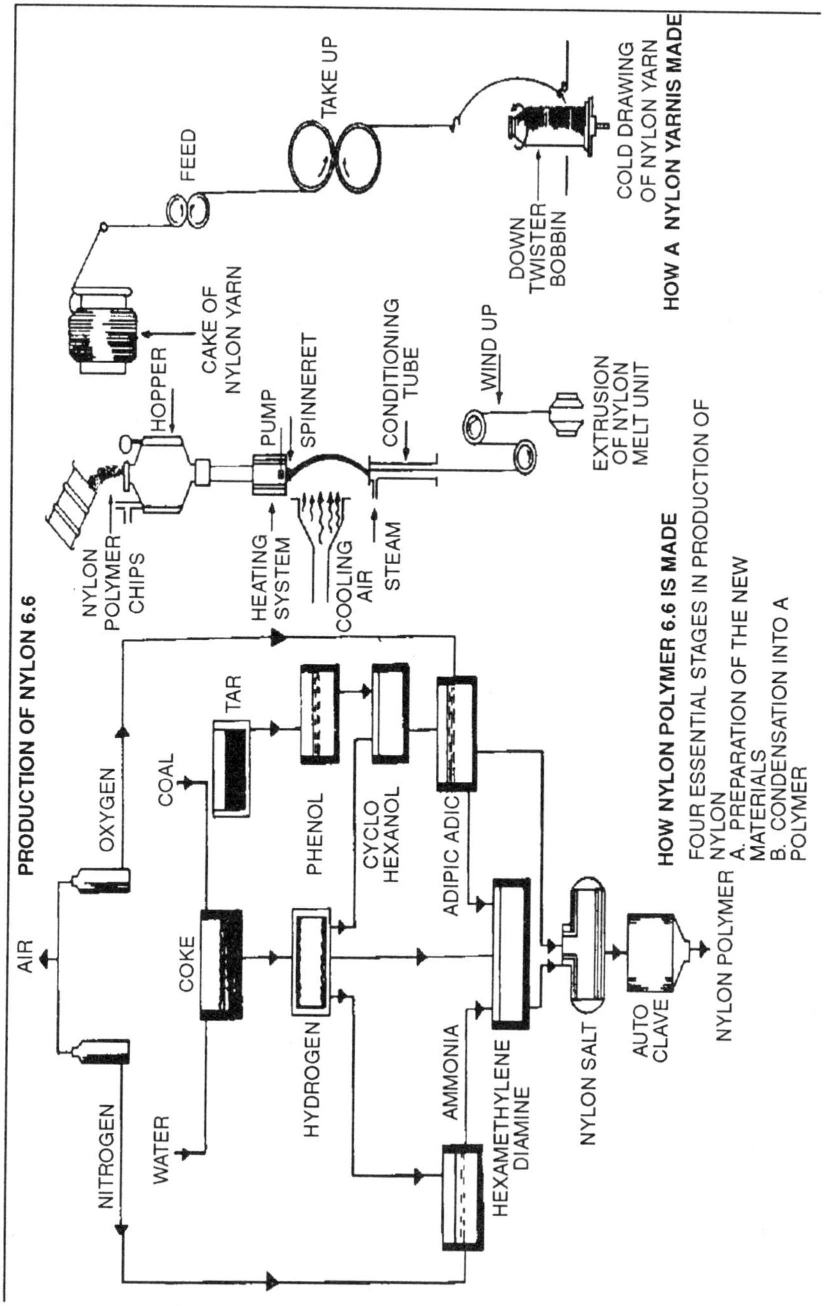

Fig.-5.1. nylon 6,6 production

The linear superpolmer is then allowed to flow out of a slot in the autoclave onto a slowly revolving casting wheel. As the ribbons of molten nylon resin are deposited on the wheel, they are sprayed with cold water, which hardens them to milky white opaque ribbons. The ribbons are removed from the casting wheel to a chipper, which transforms them into flakes

Nylon 6 Synthesis

Beginning with coal, a series of chemical steps produces another complicated chemical called *cyclohexanone-oxime,* which converts to a substance called caprolactum when it is treated with sulphuric acid. Polymerization of the molten caprolacturn is begun by gently heating it in a steam-jacketed stainless steel vessel as it is constantly mixed. It is then filtered and pumped to a polymerization kettle where, under carefully controlled steam heat and pressure, the caprolactum is stabilized as a superpolymer. The molten nylon 6 is converted to chips

Spinning the Fiber

Nylon fiber can be made in several ways. The most important of these methods is the *melt process* that, depending upon the denier (or decitex) of the filament desired, generally uses either the grid or extruder spinning technique. In grid spinning, nylon flakes from several autoclaves are blended and poured into the hopper of the spinning machine to insure uniformity in the final nylon yarn. Through a valve in the bottom of the hopper, the nylon flakes fall onto a hot grid, which melts them. The molten nylon is pumped through a sand filter to the spinneret, a disk about the size of a silver dollar. The spinneret has one or more holes, depending on the purpose for which the yarn is to be made. As the filaments come out of the spinneret and hit the air, they solidify. After they cool, the filaments converge, pass through a conditioner where they are moistened sufficiently to make them adhere together, and are given a few turns per inch (centimeter) to form a single thread and facilitate further handling.

Extruder spinning is primarily used for heavier yarns. The chips flow by graviity into a device that forces them by screw action through heated zones. The combined action of the heat and screw pressure melts the chips. The molten liquid is subsequently processed in the same manner as described for grid-spun yarn.

Variations in the ultimate appearance of the nylon filaments may be accomplished. It is possible to obtain a bright, lustrous nylon that can be used for satin or a semidull or dull nylon for curtains. Nylon may be delustered by a process similar to delustering rayon and acetate. The delusterants are titanium oxide, barium sulfate, zinc oxide, or zinc sulfate. When any of these chemical compounds are mixed with the polyamide solution, they will cause the nylon to be delustered. Although nylon is naturally white, the whiteness can be increased by adding an optical whitener to the molten polymer.

The nylon filaments are usually spun from round holes and have a round cross section; such fibers are smooth and slippery. The appearance and texture of the nylon filament can be altered by adjusting the shape of the holes of the spinneret. Nylon filaments may be spun to have a trilobal cross section. Antron, a nylon 6,6 fiber, and Enkaloft, a nylon 6 fiber, are of this form. They have a unique luster, a dry, pleasing hand, greater opacity, and can be printed with a sharper definition and clarity. Antron III nylon 6,6 and Enkalure 11 nylon 6 are forms of soil-hiding nylon fibers. Although they will hide soil, they will nevertheless get dirty. Their somewhat elongated trilobal very smooth surfaces highly reflect light in such a way that sheen overcomes the darkened (dirty) areas. These yarns are crimped for appropriate applications, such as carpets.

Nylon multifilaments, such as Antron III and Erikalure II can also be produced so that they develop a permanent crimp. Crepeset is a 20-denier monofilament nylon 6 fiber that is perrnanently, crimped. The fiber is extremely well suited for producing crepe fabrics that do not require a high twist. Such fabrics not only have a crepe appearance but, in addition, have a soft, luxurious texture not usually, associated with crepes.

Nylon filaments, such as Ultron may be produced as epitropics or *conductive* epitropics. They contain minute particles of carbon powder embedded in their surfaces, thereby providing the abilltv to conduct electricity. Excellent antistatic properties can thus be produced in multifilament yarn with an extremely small amount of the carbon particles in a relatively few filaments of such yarn.

High-tenacity nylon has been developed for tires, seat belts, cordage, and industrial fabrics. There are several types produced for such specific purposes.

Drawing the Fiber

Up to this point, the chemical structure of the filaments is about the same as the flakes from which they were made. The filaments are opaque, have poor pliability, and are not very strong because of the random arrangement of the linear superpolymer molecules. This can be changed, however, by stretching, or cold drawing, the filaments from two to seven times their original length. The amount of stretching is dependent on the diameter, elasticity, and strength desired. As the filaments are stretched, they become **more** and more transparent. The polyamide molecules straighten out, become parallelized, and are brought very close together. Up to a point, the nylon becomes stronger, more elastic, more flexible, and more pliable.

This elongation by cold-drawing, which is permanent, is accomplished by unwinding the yarn from one godet, or wheel, and winding it onto another godet that is rotating much faster. The speed of the second wheel determines the amount of cold-drawing; that is, if the nylon filament is to be stretched four times its original length, it is unwound from one godet and wound on another at a speed that will subject it to a fourfold stretch during the operation.

The yarn from the second godet is wrapped on a cylindrical tube called a pirn. A small amount of twist is normally inserted in the yarn as it is wound on the pirn so as to keep the filaments together and aid in the future processing of the yarn

In conjunction with the drawing process, the nylon filaments may be textured. Draw-texturing at the production stage places this important process under the control of the fiber producer and eliminates the additional subsequent step of texturizing by the yarn producers.

TYPES OF NYLON YARN

The diameter of the individual nylon filaments is determined by the rate of delivery from the pump to the spinneret, by the number of holes in the spinneret, and by the rate at which the yarn is drawn away from the spinneret. The denier, or size, of the yarn before drawing is determined by the diameter and number of filaments in the yarn. The size of the yarn after drawing is determined by its original diameter and the amount of cold-drawing. If it is drawn three times its original length, the stretched yarn will be one-third of its original diameter. The individual filaments produced usually range from 1 to 15 denier (1-17 dtex).

Monofilament Yarns

Though single-filament, or monofilament, yarns of 7 denier (8 dtex) are produced, 12-denier (13 dtex), 15-denier (17 dtex), or heavier yarns are more often manufactured. The monofilament yarns are used for hosiery and for industrial filters. These yarns are very fine and have little or no twist. Consequently, they are relatively weak nylon yarns. Heavier and stronger monofilament yarns are also produced for various purposes.

In 1963 Du Pont introduced a new type of nylon monofilament yarn for hosiery under the trademark of Cantrece. it is a bicomponent fiber created by extruding nylon 6,6 and 6,10 solutions from a single spinneret to form the filaments adhering as one. It is a self-crimping yarn. Upon exposure to steam heat, Cantrece nylon develops a helical, or corkscrew, shape as a result of the different effects of the heat on the components of the fiber. The amount of crimp is dependent upon the temperature and rate of heating. The crimp provides greater resilience and superior fit as well as fit retention and comfort. The improved fit characteristic is said to increase the life of the hose, since there is less strain on the yarn.

Multifilament Yarns

Multifilament yarns are made in both standard and high-tenacity forms. The number of filaments in each yarn varies according to the purpose of the yarn. The yarns generally range in denier from 20 to 210 (22-233 dtex). Multifilament yarns are stronger than monofilament yarns because of the numerous filaments. The strength can be further increased by the amount of twist given to the yarns.

Stretch Yarns

Nylon filaments can be processed to have a crimp or coiled characteristic. This gives yarns made of such nylon filaments the ability to be greatly stretched (like a spring) and come back to shape when the tension is released. These yarns are produced under several trademarks, of which one of the better known is Helanca.

Textured Yarns

Nylon filaments can also be processed to have a looped characteristic. Crimp-textured nylon is bulk continuous filament nylon. It is given a permanent crimp by the producer. Thrown yarns of these filaments have a texture and hand similar to yarns made of a staple fiber, such as cotton, but retain all the other characteristics of filament yarns. One of the best known of these textured yarns is Taslan, which is used for sport shirts and similar apparel. Some textured filament yarns have a curly appearance that imparts a resilient, springy effect called loft. Examples of these are Cumuloft and Enkaloft, which are used for rugs

Spun Yarns

Nylon filaments may be cut about 1 to 5 inches (25- 125 mm) in staple length. The individual filaments range in denier from 1.5 to 15 (1.7- 17 dtex). The staple is usually crimped and spun on a cotton system. These yarns are fuzzy and soft. They have lower tensile strength but greater abrasion resistance. They are not so elastic as the filament yarns and take longer to dry.

FINISHING NYLON FABRICS

Nylon fabrics can be given various finishes:

Name of Finish	Purpose
Antistatic finish	for reduction of electrostatic buildup
Embossing	for pattern or design
Heat setting	for permanent shape
Moireing	for shimmer effect
Molding	for shaping fabrics
Nylonizing	for increased absorbency
Water repellency	for added protection against water

An outstanding feature of nylon is that it is thermoplastic; consequently, a nylon fabric or garment can be heat-set by subjecting it to a high degree of heat while being held in a particular shape. After being heat-set, the fabric or garment will always retain its shape, creases, or pleats, and require little or no ironing. Washing, dry cleaning, or wear will not cause loss of shape. Properly done, heat-setting prevents nylon fabrics from shrinking.

Since nylon is thermoplastic, the application of a hot embossing roller will cause the nylon to melt in conformity with the ernbossing pattern. This results in a permanent finish that cannot be removed by wearing, washing, or dry cleaning. The same principle applies to nylon moire. As with thermoplastic acetate, nylon moire is permanent.

Because nylon is thermoplastic, fabrics made of nylon may also be *thermoformable,* which means that they can be molded into shapes by the application of pressure and heat. The fabrics may have a woven, knitted, or lace construction that has been only partially drawn in the manufacturing process. When such a fabric is preheated and then pressed in a heated mold, the drawing operation is, in effect, completed and the fabric is heat-set to the desired permanent shape. Examples of such products are hats, brassieres, and swimsuits.

Raised designs may also be created on nylon fabrics by printing the background area with phenol, which causes the treated nylon to shrink and the untreated areas to pucker.

Nylon is not very absorbent, which is a disadvantage for shirts and lingerie. To overcome this, nylon fabrics may be treated by a process known as Nylonizing. The technique utilizes nylon 8, which is more absorbent than other forms of nylon.

Nylon fabrics may also be treated with a water-repellent finish, which makes them ideal for rainwear and for shower curtains.

EVALUATING NYLON FABRICS

Because nylon fabrics are produced in such a wide variety, they can be made to appear similar to cotton batiste and plisse to the texture of linen, to Jersey for sweaters, and to silk, rayon, or acetate shantun and velvet. Nylon has superseded wool for rugs and carpets. The properties of these fabrics depend on the type of nylon, the cross section of fiber, whether the fabric is made of multifilament or spun yarn and how the fabric is constructed.

Strength. Nylon is produced in both regular and high-tenacity strengths. Al though one of the lightest textile fibers, it is also one of the strongest. It is surpassed in strength only by aramid and glass. Its strength competes with high-tenacity viscose rayon as well as with polyester fibers.

The strength of nylon will not deteriorate with age. These advantages make nylon desirable for sheer hosiery, curtains, blouses, dress fabrics, upholster and carpets. Nylon not only has great tensile strength with light weight, it is also tough and pliable. Nylon has the highest resistance to abrasion of any fiber.

Elasticity. Nylon is one of the most elastic fibers that exists today, though it does not have the exceptional elastic quality of spandex fibers. After being stretched nylon has a strong natural tendency to return to its original shape. Like any other textile, nylon has its own limit of elasticity. If stretched too much, it will not completely recover its shape. In addition, the type of yarn and the construction of the fabric may contribute to the behavior of the garment. For exampled spun nylon is not so elastic as filament nylon. Knitted spun nylon fabrics, used in sweaters, will sag more easily than knitted filament nylon fabric, such as those used in tricot.

Of course, such stretch nylon yarns as helanca and Agilon have exceptional elasticity. These yarns have given rise to a wide variety of stretch garments that retain their shape and comfortably conform to the contours of the body.

Resilience. Nylon has excellent resilience. Nylon fabrics retain their smooth appearance, and wrinkles from the usual daily activities fall out readily. Pile fabrics, such as velvets and carpets, keep a neat uncrushed appearance.

Drapability. Fabrics of nylon filament yarn have excellent draping qualities .Lightweight sheers may have a flowing quality, medium-weight dress fabrics can drape very nicely, and heavier-weight Jacquards also drape well.

Heat Conductivity. Nylon fabrics may or may not conduct heat well. The warmth or coolness of a nylon garment depends on the weave of the fabric and on the type of yarn used. The smoothness, roundness, and fineness of nylon filaments permit the manufacture of very smooth, very fine yarns, which can be packed very closely when weaving the fabric. If nylon fabric is woven compactly, it will not be porous. The tight construction will not permit air to circulate through the fabric, and the heat and rnoisture of the body will not readily pass through it but will build up between the fabric and the body; so, the wearer will feel very warm. Such fabrics are good for winter apparel, such as windbreakers, but are not suitable for summer garments.

On the other hand, these fine nylon filament yarns may be woven into extremely thin, lightweight, sheer fabrics. These materials are very porous and permit the circulation of air. Consequently, they are cool and can be used for summer blouses and curtains.

Spun nylon yarn will produce warm fabrics. These yarns are composed of thousands of short, crimped fibers twisted together, which provide millions of tiny dead-air spaces that act as insulators. This insulation makes spun nylon fabrics warm.

Absorbency. Nylon does not absorb much moisture. Fabrics made of nylon filament yarns will not readily wet through the material-most of the water remains on the surface and runs off the smooth fabric, which therefore dries quickly. Such fabrics are useful for raincoats and shower curtains. Spun nylon fabrics, however, will not dry quickly. Droplets of water tend to cling to the sides of the thousands of staple fibers, clogging the air spaces and relatively increasing the drying time for spun nylon fabrics. Nylon's low absorbency has a disadvantage in that the fabric feels clammy and uncomfortable in warm , humid weather. (Nylon 4 and nylon 8 varieties have moisture-absorption properties similar to cotton. However, due to other factors, little is produced.) Sometimes a hydrophlic (water-attracting) or a Nylonizing finish is used on nylon 6 or 6,6 fabrics.

Cleanliness and Washability. Because of nylon's smooth surface, dirt and stains often come clean merely by using a damp cloth. If the yarn has an antistatic component in it or if the fabric has an antistatic finish, then dirt particles are less likely to be attracted and cling, and the garment will stay cleaner longer. Otherwise an antistatic additive could be used in the washing or in the drying machine. To wash nylon garments by hand or washing machine, use lukewarrn water at about 100 degree F (38 degree C) and a detergent or soap with a water softener.

White nylon fabrics should always be separated from colored fabrics before washing because the nylon will pick up color and develop a dingy gray appearance that is extremely difficult to remove. Garments should be thoroughly rinsed to obtain thorough removal of soil particles and drip-dried to obtain maximum freedom from wrinkling.

Nylon filament fabrics dry very quickly. They need little or no ironing because the garments are usually heat set to retain their shape, pleats, or creases.

Spun nylon has a tendency to pill, or form balls, on the surface of the fabric. To minimize this, such fabrics should not be rubbed. They should be washed gently, preferably by hand. Brushing with a soft brush will reduce the pilling.

Effect of Bleaches. With proper care, nylon fabrics retain their whiteness and should not need bleaching. However, if the nylon does become yellow or gray due to either the finish on the fabric or the absorption of color from other fabrics washed in the same water, a good, common household bleach may be used with reasonable care.

Shrinkage. Nylon has good dimensional stability and retains its shape after being wet.

Effect of Heat. Like acetate, nylon will melt if the iron is too hot; therefore, the iron should be set at the proper heat level. Special care must be taken with fabrics made of nylon 6 because it has a lower melting point at 420 degree F (216 degree C) than nylon 6,6 at 480 degree F (250degree C)

Effect of Light. Bright nylon is more resistant to the effects of sunlight than most other fibers. Dull nylon will deteriorate a little more quickly than bright nylon; however, even dull nylon has good resistance to light.

Resistance to Mildew. Mildew has absolutely no effect on nylon. Mildew may form on nylon, but it will not weaken fabric.

Resistance to Insects. Moths and other insects will not attack nylon because it nas no attraction for them.

Reaction to Alkalies. Nylon is substantially inert to alkalies.

Reaction to Acids. Nylon is decomposed by cold concentrated solutions of such mineral acids as hydrochloric, sulfuric, and nitric acids. A boiling dilute 5 percent solution of hydrochloric acid will destroy nylon.

Affinity for Dyes. Nylon 6 has greater affinity for dyes than nylon 6,6 and can be more easily dyed with a wider range of dyes. Both types of nylon retain their color and have good resistance to fading. Nylon 4 has excellent dyeability.

Resistance to Perspiration. Nylon fabrics are resistant to perspiration. The color, however, may be affected.

NYLON FIBER BLENDS

The consumer uses many textile products that do not possess all the properties that may be desired in a fiber. For example, one may prefer a coat with sufficient warmth but less weight; cool, light summer clothes that would not lose their fresh, clean appearance on hot sticky days; fabrics that would wash readily, dry quickly, and not lose their shape. Textile designers and engineers are producing new fabrics to meet such needs. These combine or blend two or more fibers to give the desired properties to the fabrics. We can consider here blends of nylon with other fibers thus far discussed.

Nylon and Cotton

When properly combined with cotton, nylon adds strength, which allows the development of unusually fine textures no possible to obtain from cotton alone. Nylon provides smoothness, silkiness, and dirt rejection. It also reduces the weight of the fabric and increases its wrinkle re sistance. The cotton gives softness and moisture absorption. This combination permits the weaving of fabrics that are soft, supple, and extremely serviceable If the combination is not properly bal anced, the cotton may shrink, causing the fabric to pucker. Also, the nylon fiber may cut the cotton fibers. A blend of a least 17 percent high-tenacity nylon staple with cotton can make a very durable fabric.

Nylon and Wool

The proper combination of nylon and wool will produce a lighter-weight fabric with greater durability. Such a fabric will retain the hand, drape, body, absorbency, and warmth of wool as well as the elasticity, resilience, and shape retention of nylon. The properties of the fabric wil be in direct proportion to the amount used of each of the two fibers. A blend of 10 to 15 percent nylon and the remainder wool is considered satisfactory.

Nylon and Silk

In this combination, the silk improves the **hand and provides moisture absorption.** The nylon improves the stability or shape retention, as well as the elasticity and strength.

Nylon and Rayon

In this blend, the nylon gives wrinkle resistance and strength. The rayon gives suppleness, drape, and moisture absorption. Such a combination makes possible a fine-quality fabric of extremely light weight. As with cotton, if the combination is not properly balanced, the rayon may shrink, causing the fabric to pucker. Also, an improper blend of nylon and rayon may result in the nylon fibers cutting the rayon fibers. Like cotton, rayon staple blended with high-tenacity nylon staple can produce fabrics with 70 percent longer wear than all-rayon fabrics if the nylon is blended in a proportion of at least 17 percent. This blend is desirable for garments classed wash and wear.

Nylon and Acetate

The acetate in such a blend provides a luxurious hand and the nylon gives light weight and strength. As with cotton or rayon, improper blending may result in the nylon cutting the acetate fiber, and in some fabrics puckering may occur. Also, neither nylon nor acetate absorbs much moisture. Such fabrics may feel clammy and uncomfortable in warm and humid atmospheres.

Nylon and Triacetate

A blend of 15 percent nylon and 85 percent- triacetate in gabardines for shirts, slacks, and fabrics for outerwear is a satisfactory combination. The nylon provides strength to give good durability. Fabrics of this blend hold their creases and pleats and shape well. They can be laundered easily and need little or no ironing. Garments made of such a blend are among those classed as wash and wear type.

B) POLYESTER

Polyester fibers are long-chain polymers produced from elements derived from coal, air, water, and petroleum. These fibers are chemically composed of at least 85 percent by weight of an ester of a substituted aromatic carboxylic acid, including but not restricted to substituted terephthalate units and para substituted hydroxybenzoate units.

METHODS OF MANUFACTURE

Generally, each company produces only one variety of polyester, though there are likely to be modifications under specific trademarks. For example Dacron a bright, high-tenacity PET polyester fiber.

It is interesting to note that the same polyester used to produce a PET fiber is also made in thin, transparent film form. It is marketed under the trademark Mylar and used as a protective coating over metallic yarns, such as Lurex. Mylar is also used for magnetic tape for recording purposes.

PET Polyester

The process of manufacture of PET polyester fiber is similar to that of nylon, but the chemicals used are different .The principal raw material is ethylene obtained from petroleum. The ethylene is oxidized to produce a glycol monomer dihydric alcohol that is then combined with another monomer, terephthalic acid, in an autoclave at a high temperature in a vacuum. Polymerization takes place with the aid of catalysts. The clear, colorless, molten polyester then flows from a slot in the vessel onto a casting wheel and forms into a ribbon as it cools to a porcelainlike hardness. The polymer is then cut into very small chips, dried to remove all traces of moisture, and blended for uniformity in preparation for spinning into yarn.

PCDT Polyester

The original PCDT polyester fiber is Kodel. This form of polyester is made by condensing terephthalic acid with 1,4-cyclohexane-dimethanol to form the tongue twister, poly- 1,4-cyclohexylene-dimethylene terephthalate; hence, the convenient abbreviation PCDT polyester. As for PET polyester, PCDT is processed for melt spinning.

Spinning the Fiber

The molten polymer is rigorously maintained in an airtight condition, as oxygen will affect its stability. The spinning technique is similar to that used for nylon fibres. The viscous melt is extruded through a spinneret, and the filaments are subsequently drawn into the desired polyester fiber. Variations in the. production proecss depend upon the desired end results.

The holes, of the spinneret may be round or modified to be trilobal, pentalobal, hexalobal, or octalobal shapes to achieve specific effects, Such as greater cover and opacity, enhancement or suppression of luster, wicking, comfort, and hand. Thc fibers may be produced hollow to give a large diameter with light weight and provide greater cushioning and insulative properties. Crimp may be developed to achieve crepe effects.

Drawing the Fiber

Upon extrusion from the spinneret, the polyester filament does not have all the desired characteristics because of the random arrangement of the super polymer molecules. The fibers are therefore drawn, or elongated, with the aid of godet wheels, in the same manner as nylon fibers are drawn. The temperature conditions and the extent to which the fibers are drawn depend upon the properties desired. The polyester fibers are usually drawn to 5 times their original length (Which results in a fiber diameter that is one-fifth the original size upon extrusion from the spinneret). If higher-tenacity fiber is to be produced, the filaments are drawn to a greater extent, as this increases the linear molecular orientation of the fiber. As they emerge from the drawing process and meet cold air, the filaments solidify.

Generally, the PET polyester filaments are drawn hot because this procedure produces more uniform fibers. However, when heavier diameters are desired, the monofilaments may be drawn at room ternperture because the poor heat conductivity of the fiber results in irregularities in thick filaments that are drawn hot. PCDT polyester fibers are drawn at a higher temperature because of their higher melting point.

During the drawing process, the fibers may be textured. Draw-texturing saves steps, time, and production costs, and it gives the fiber producer greater quality control over the finished fiber. On the other hand, the fibers may be partially drawn, or oriented Such POY production reduces investment costs for the producers and increases the flexibility and productivity of the tcxturizers.

TYPES OF POLYESTER YARN

The diameter of the polyester yarn is determined by (1) the rate of extrusion of the filaments from the spinneret, (2) the number of spinneret holes and therefore the number of filaments, and (3) the rate of drawing of the filaments. The yarns come in a wide range of diameters and staple lengths. The yarns are produced, basically as monofilament, multifilament, and spun.

Filament Yarns

Filament yarns are produced of PET polyester. They are made in monofilament and multi filament forms. The direction and amount of twist are determined by the desired end use. The variety of characteristics of the yarns is also predetermined.

Bright, regular tenacity polyester yarn is one popular type. It has good light resistance, as well as stretch and sag resistance. It can be used for sheer, lightweight fabrics, such as tulle, voile, and organdy, and is very suitable for curtains. Another very popular type is the regular tenacity, semidull yarn. It is used for a wide variety of apparel, including dresses and lingerie. A duller version is used for shirts and blouses.

Another type produced is a semidull polyester containing an additive that gives it all affinity for basic dyes, thereby giving the yarn greater versatility for use in fabrics that can be cross-dyed. Sometimes the PET polyester is treated with all optical brightener so that the fabric made of this type of yarn will have a permanent White character. To impart more drapability, softer hand, and greater luster, the yarn may be made of filaments that are trilateral, or trilobal. Polyester yarns, which are resistant to various chemicals, seawater, and microorganisms, are made of a bright, high-tenacity fiber for such industrial uses as conveyor belts, ropes, netting, and sails. High-tenacity polyester filament yarns are available for tyre cord.

Textured Yarns

Textured polyester yarns are produced of PET multifilaments. They are given a texturizing either in conjunction with the drawing process or subsequently as part of the throwing and texturizing process in producing the finished yarns.e.g. Taslan polyester fiber

Spun Yarns

Spun yarns are made of staple or of cut, crimped tow of either PET or PCDT polyester fiber (see Figure 5.2)

The staple is produced in a wide range of deniers and lengths according to the desired end uses. The staple may be bright, semidull, or dull. The fiber may be polished to reduce the crimp and increase the luster. It may be regular, mid, or high-tenacity. It may be round or trilateral for increased sheen. The staple may be spun directly, into yarn or blended with other staple, such as cotton, wool, or rayon, and then spun into yarn.

The type of fiber cut into staple depends upon the ultimate end use. PCDT polyester fiber is particularly suited to staple and spun yarn purposes.

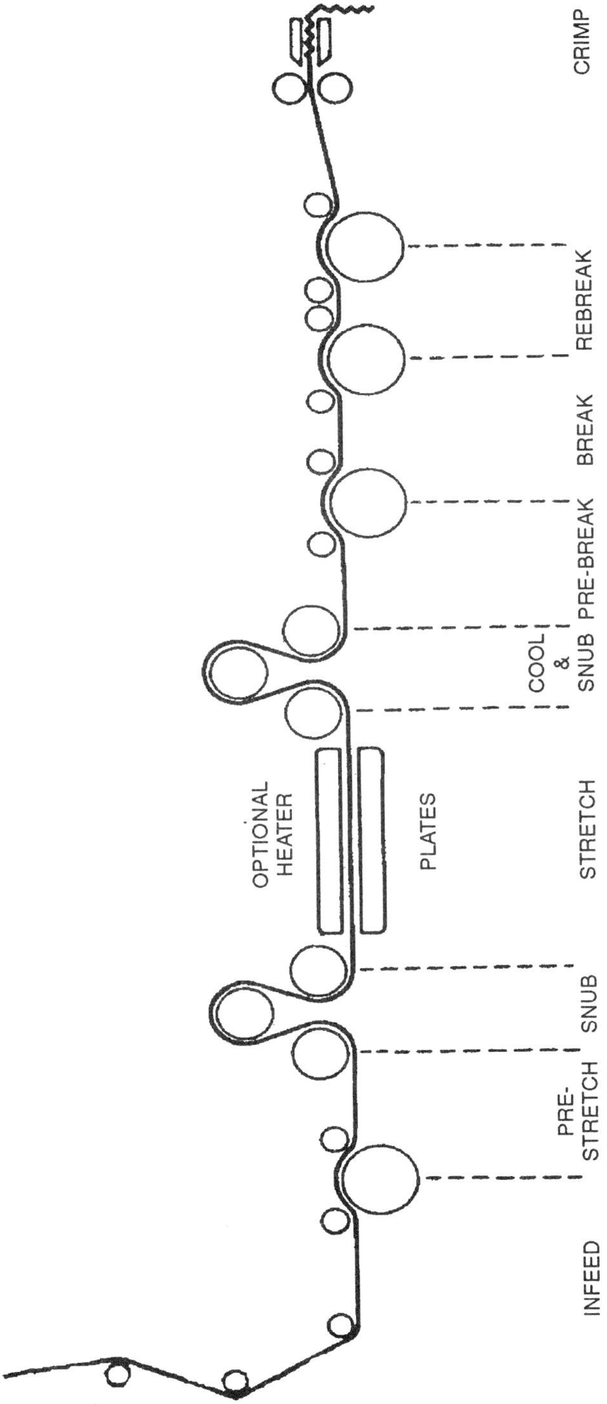

Fig.-5.2. The flow diagram spun yarn formation

It has great resilience, exceptional bulking ability, and good resistance to pilling.

Semidull, regular-tenacity polyester staple may be spun on either the cotton or wool system, depending upon the ultimate yarn desired. Finer yarns are used for summer suitings; that require both resiliency and dimensional stability to prevent puckering and change in shape during humid weather. Heavier yarns made of this staple may be used for outerwear and for knitted fabrics because of their exceptional shape retention and stretch resistance. Semidull, regular tenacity polyester may also be spun on the worsted or rayon system. These yarns are used for winter-weight and spring weight fabrics. Such fabrics include finished worsteds like sharkskin, gabardine, and Bedford cord, as well as such napped unfinished worsteds as flannel and serge. Still heavier weights may be made of bright, regular tenacity fiber and spun on a woolen or modified worsted system for pile fabrics.

Regular tenacity polyester staple containing an optical brightener may be spun into yarn for such products as men's knitted underwear. Mid-tenacity polyester is very suitable for blending with cotton and high wet-modulus rayon fibers for spun yarn for such purposes as men's shirting fabrics.

Bright, trilateral, polished staple may be spun into yarn to be used to make carpets or upholstery fabrics. Trilateral,polished, basic-dyeable staple is also available for such purposes as upholstery fabrics.

A variety of staple polyesters called conductive epitropics has also been developed. These polyesters contain tiny particles of carbon powder embedded in the surface of the fiber. The carbon particles give the fiber the ability to conduct electricity, which provides antistatic protection. Remarkably small quantities of the fiber are needed to be blended with nonepitropic fibers to provide excellent antistatic effects. It is also expected that epitropic fibers will be developed for other purposes, such as heat conductivity.

A variety of high-tenacity polyester staple is available for spun yarns required for sewing threads, belts, ropes, fire hoses, and various other industrial purposes.

Polyester staple is also produced for fiberfill, rather than yarn. It is lightweight and has excellent resilience and loft, which provides comfort and insulation. These properties are enhanced when the fiber is produced in hollow form. Since it is also nonallergenic, it is used for pillows, quilting, skiwear, and sleeping bags

FINISHING POLYESTER FABRICS

Several finishes can be given to polyester fabrics to increase their usefulness. Among the most important are:

Name of Finish	Purpose
Antistatic finish	for reduction of electrostatic build-up
Calendering	for smoothness and reduced pilling
Compressive shrinking	for increased shrink resistance
Embossing	for design and luster
Heat setting and stabilizing	for permanent shape retention, wrinkle resistance, and improved hand
Shearing	for smooth, even pile or nap
Singeing	for improved hand and reduced pilling
Water and soil repellency	for comfort and ease of care

Fabrics made of PET polyester yarn should be given compressive shrinking and heat setting to obtain dimensional stability to subsequent finishing processes and washing. This is particularly important for polyester blends with cotton and rayon. Fabrics made of polyester spun yarn can be effectively stabilized in normal dyeing and finishing operations. PCDT polyester fabrics need not be initially heat-set because they are inherently stable. Both forms of polyester fabrics can be permanently pressed since they are thermoplastic and hold their shape exceedingly well. Blends of polyester and wool may be fulled, crabbed, and decated to improve compactness and dimensional stability.

Stabilized fabrics made of either polyester filament yarn or spun yarn have excellent wrinkle resistance and recovery from wrinkling. Essentially permanent creases can be pressed into them at low to medium temperature of about 275 degree F (135 degree C) and remain sharp after washing. Such creases can be ironed out if desired. This means that such garments as suits made of polyester staple will hold their shape and press in abnormally damp weather and even when wet. After heat setting, the polyester fabric may be given a controlled caustic soda treatment to improve its hand and drape by passing it in a relaxed state through the alkali bath, which dissolves away a small amount of the fiber surface and sets the yarn crimp of the weave construction.

Singeing has been found to be an effective method for reducing the pilling of spun fabrics. While Some typ es of polyester yarns are inherently pill-resistant, singeing does yield a firmer hand.

Careful control of the speed of the fabric movement and the height of the flame is maintained merely to remove fuzz and yet prevent melting of the fibers in the fabric, which will cause loss in fabric strength.

Calendering also improves the pilling resistance by flattening the fiber ends and smoothing thesurface. It also provides increased luster and better covering power by reducing the size of the fabric pores.

Fabrics made entirely of polyester filaments yarns can be pre shrunk in finishing as much as 20 %. Consequently, such fabrics will not shrink to any significant extent thereafter. It is therefore also possible to produce cloth with very little porosity. Since polyester is hydrophobic and therefore will not absorb much moisture, polyester fabrics serve excellently for such purposes as raincoats.

EVALUATING POLYESTER

FABRICS

Strength. As a group, polyester fibers may be characterized as relatively strong fibers. The PET polyesters are, in general, stronger than the PCDT polyesters.

Fabrics of regular tenacity PET polyester filament yarns are very strong and durable. The high-tenacity PET polyester filament yarns used for tyres and industrial purposes are extremely strong; some types are the strongest of all textiles except glass, aramid, and certain highly specialized, exotic fibers not commonly used for consumer products. The staple fibers also vary in strength depending on the type of fiber. In general, PET polyester staple ranges from high-tenacity, which is stronger than nylon staple, to regular tenacity, which is about equal to or slightly weaker than nylon staple.

The abrasion resistance of polyester fiber is exceptionally good, being exceeded only by nylon among all of the commonly used fibers. However, the abrasion resistance of low-pilling types, including those of PCDT polyester is of a lower order that is generally similar to wool.

The strength, abrasion resistance, and stability of polyester make it very suitable for sewing thread. Such thread will not shrink and cause the fabric to pucker and it has adequate elasticity to yield to tension without resulting in loss of garment shape. The thread may be spun of polyester staple or core-spun of polyester filament core surrounded by cotton staple, to be selected for use as fabric composition and garment construction may require.

In summary, the tensile strength and abrasion resistance of polyester fiber are very good, and the fiber will provide relatively good service. PET polyester is superior in this regard to PCDT Kodel 200 series polyester.

Elasticity. Polyester fibers do not have a high degree of elasticity, although PCDT polyester is more elastic than PET polyester. In general, polyester fiber is characterized as having a high degree of stretch resistance, which means that polyester fabrics are not likely to stretch out of shape too easily. This property makes polyester suited for knitted garments; sagging and stretching that would ordinarily occur are reduced. Fabrics of polyester fiber have good dimensional stability.

Resilience. Polyester fiber has a high degree of resilience. PCDT polyester more resilient than PET polyester. Not only does a polyester fabric resist wrinkling when dry, it also resists wrinkling when wet. For example, a suit of polyester will keep its pressed appearance after many wearings, even after exposure to rain or moist, humid weather. And heatset polyester fiber is suitably resilient for use in carpets.

Drapability. Fabrics of polyester filament yarn have satisfactory draping qualities. The trilobal filament type is more supple and imparts better drapability. Staple polyester can produce spun yarn that is more flexible and softer, thereby imparting the draping quality. Drapability of fabrics of blended polyester staple will depend upon the type and proportion of blend in the yarn as well as the fabric construction.

Heat Conductivity. Fabrics of polyester fiber are better conductors of heat than fabrics made of acrylic fibers The basic polyester filament fiber is round. This results in a smoother yarn woven into fabrics with fewer air spaces and less insulation. When the filaments are textured, there is an increase in loft and therefore some amount of insulation. Polyester staple fiber is crimped and this does provide greater insulation in the yarns and fabrics. But a fabric of polyester spun yarn would not be as warm as a fabric made of the acrylics, silk, or wool; it would be warmer than if made of cotton, linen, or rayon. One of the reasons for the apparent greater warmth of polyester is its low absorbency. However, polyester crimped fiberfill or hollow staple variants can provide bulk and insulative properties.

Absorbency. Polyester is one of the least absorbent fibers. This low absorbency has two important advantages. Polyester fabrics will dry very rapidly since almost all the moisture will lie on the surface rather than penetrate the yarns. Fabrics of polyester fiber are therefore well suited for water-repellent purposes, such as rainwear. Furthermore, this low absorbency means that polyester fabrics will not stain easily. Many substances that would stain other fabrics lie on the surface and call be wiped or washed off easily. (One limitation, though, is polyester's affinity for oil, which stains and is extremely difficult to remove,)

Fabrics of low absorbency generally have the disadvantage of being uncomfortable in humid weather because they will not absorb perspiration or atmospheric moisture. As a result, all absorbent fiber such as cotton is often blended with the polyester staple.

Cleanliness** and **Washability. Since polyester fibers generally are smooth and have a very low absorbency, many stains lie on the surface and can easily be washed by hand or machine. Strong soaps are not needed. However, oil stains are more stubborn and under certain circumstances cannot be entirely removed. Some polyester fibers, such as Spectran, have built-in superior stain release and less redeposition of soil during laundering.

Fabrics of polyester filament yarn dry very quickly. Those of spun yarn dry comparatively rapidly if wrung out well. There is essentially no water shrinkage of polyester fabrics; therefore, shirts, blouses, and even slacks made entirely of polyester (including the sewing thread) may be safely laundered.

When ironing polyester fabrics, it is best to use low to medium heat. Excessive heat will cause polyester to melt. Actually, little ironing is needed even after long wear or after being completely wet, because garments made of polyester hold their shape and creases after being heat-set. Furthermore, the wrinkle resistance of polyester is extremely good.

Fabrics of spun polyester yarn that have a tendency to pill should be washed gently and brushed with a soft brush while drying in order to disentangle the fiber ends and straighten them out.

Effect of Bleaches. Fabrics of polyester may be safely bleached because polyester has good resistance to deterioration by household bleaches. If the polyester has an optical brightener, no bleaching is necessary.

Shrinkage. Polyester fabrics shrink as much as 20 percent during wet-finishing operations and they are generally heat-set in later treatments, Consequently, finished polyester woven and knitted fabrics will not shrink. They have excellent dimensional stability.

Fabrics of polyester blends should be properly treated for permanent press so as, to prevent the nonpolyester component from shrinking. Also, garments should be sewn with polyester thread to avoid puckering.

Effect of Heat. Depending upon the type, polyester will get sticky at 440 to 468 degree F (227- 242 degree C). Therefore, if ironing is needed, it should be done at lower temperatures such as those used for ironing rayon. At temperatures in the range of 480 to 554 degree F (249- 290 degree C), polyester will melt and flame but will self-extinguish when heat or flame is removed unless the fabric has a finish which burns or supports combustion. Since sparks, burning cigarette ashes, and the like will easily melt holes in polyester fabrics, appropriate care should be exercised. However, flame-retardant variants are available

Effect of Light. Polyester has good resistance to degradation by sunlight. Fabrics of polyester are therefore well suited for outdoor use. Over a prolonged period of exposure to direct sunlight, however, there will be a gradual deterioration of the polyester fiber. When exposed to sunlight behind glass, polyester shows a considerable increase in resistance to sunlight; it has a marked superiority over most other fibers under these conditions and is therefore very well suited for curtains.

Resistance to Mildew. Polyester fabrics are absolutely resistant to mildew. They will not be stained or weakened. Should mildew form on the fabric, it would be due to the finish; but mildew should readily wash off the fabric without any deterioration to it. However, there may be some discoloration.

Resistance to Insects. Polyester is unaffected by moths, carpet beetles, silverfish, or other insects.

Reaction to Alkalies. At room temperature, polyester has good resistance to weak alkalies and fair resistance to strong alkalies. This resistance is reduced with increased temperature. At boiling temperatures, it has poor resistance to weak alkalies and dissolves in strong alkalies.

Reaction to Acids. Depending upon the type, polyester has excellent-to-good resistance to mineral and organic acids. Highly concentrated solutions of a mineral acid, such as sulphuric acid, at relatively high temperatures will result in degradation.

Affinity for Dyes. Polyesters can be dyed with appropriate disperse, azoic, and developed dyes at high temperatures, producing a good range of shades that have good-to-excellent washfastness and fair to-good lightfastness. Some polyesters are modified to take basic (cationic) dyes. Solvent dispersion-dye techniques using ammonia or hydrocarbon solvents, such as perchlorethylene, may enhance dye reactions. Pigment colors have a tendency to crock and rub off.

Resistance to Perspiration. Polyester has no significant loss of strength from continued contact with either acid or alkaline perspiration.

POLYESTER FIBER BLENDS

Polyester and Cotton

For satisfactory wash and wear purposes, fabrics for rainwear, tailored clothing, dress shirts, and sport shirts usually have a blend of at least 65 percent polyester with the cotton. Polyester will provide wrinkle resistance and shape retention. Cotton will provide absorbency and consequent comfort. However, unless properly constructed and properly cared for, a fabric of a polyester and cotton blend may pucker and lose its shape if the cotton should shrink or if cotton thread is used in sewing. Polyester and cotton blends are well suited for fabrics to be given a permanent press resin finish. The polyester not only contributes its own inherent shape-retentive qualities but also retains its strength, thereby reducing the total potential strength loss from resin finishing that an all-cotton fabric would have.

Where greater absorbency and softer hand are desired, a 50/50 blend is preferable, but there will be a corresponding strength loss of as much as 20 percent as well as a slight loss in resilience. A 50/50 blend of polyester and cotton is also satisfactory for effective permanent press finishes.

On the other hand , blends of as much as 80/20 of polyester and cotton, respectively, will have a somewhat stiffer, slicker hand. Strength, wrinkle resistance, and shape retention will be increased but absorbency will be reduced.

Polyester and Wool

In combination with wool, polyester provides outstanding wrinkle resistance and crease retention, so that wet or dry, the shape retention is improved according to the proportions used. The greater abrasion resistance of polyester also provides longer wear. The wool contributes good draping quality and elasticity. The wool also reduces the hazard of melted holes due to burning tobacco. The greater the proportion of wool, the less pilling there is likely to be.

Blends of polyester and wool generally range from 65 percent polyester and 35 percent wool to 60/40, 55/45, and 50/50, respectively. For lightweight, shape-retentive summer suiting, 65 percent polyester and 35 percent wool is a satisfactory blend. For optimum benefits of both fibers, a 60/40 blend of polyester and wool. respectively, appears to be generally for medium worsteds. A blend of 55 cent polyester and 45 percent wool is suitable for year-round garments. Where greater warmth is desired, a 50/50 blend for woolens is preferable.

Polyester and Rayon

In a blend with viscose rayon, polyester gives greater resiliency, shape retention, and durability. Viscose rayon provides absorbency and variety of color and texture. For satisfactory wash and wear service, a blend of at least 55 percent polyester with the rayon is desirable. Variations with other rayon variants are possible. For example, a 50/50 blend of polyester and a viscose rayon variant like the hollow Fibro HSO will provide greater absorbency, body, and drape than a similar blend of polyester with either regular viscose or cotton.

A blend of 65 percent polyester and 35 percent high wet-modulus rayon provides a strong, durable, and serviceable fabric. The fabric has a good hand and drapes well. The rayon again provides the absorbency that polyester lacks.

Polyester and Triacetate

Since both fibers are thermoplastic, fabrics made of polyester and triacetate will have excellent shape retention and provide good wash and wear service. But they will have low absorbency and are likely to feel clammy in humid weather. Polyester is important because it adds strength to the blend, since triacetate is a weak fiber. The fabric will pill unless it is made of PCDT Kodel 200 polyester, a PET reduced pilling variant, and/or finecount yarn.

A suitable blend of 50/50 is satisfactory. However, this blend produces a yarn weaker than a similar blend of polyester and any cellulosic fiber.

Polyester and Nylon

Nylon contributes strength and abrasion resistance. Polyester contributes outstanding wrinkle resistance. Such a combination offers stability, easy laundering, quick drying, and resistance to damage from mildew and insects. The fabric will be clammy to the skin, however, in warm, humid weather. Since both fibers are thermoplastic and neither is very absorbent, any combination in the blend will provide good wash and wear characteristics. Care should be taken to avoid pilling of fabrics with this type of blend.

3) ACRYLIC

Basically, acrylic is a type of plastic. An acrylic fiber is "any long-chain synthetic polymer composed of at least 85 percent by weight of acrylonitrile units."

ORLON ACRYLIC

METHOD OF MANUFACTURE

The manufacture of Orlon acrylic resin is the result of complicated chemical synthesis (Figure 5.3),.

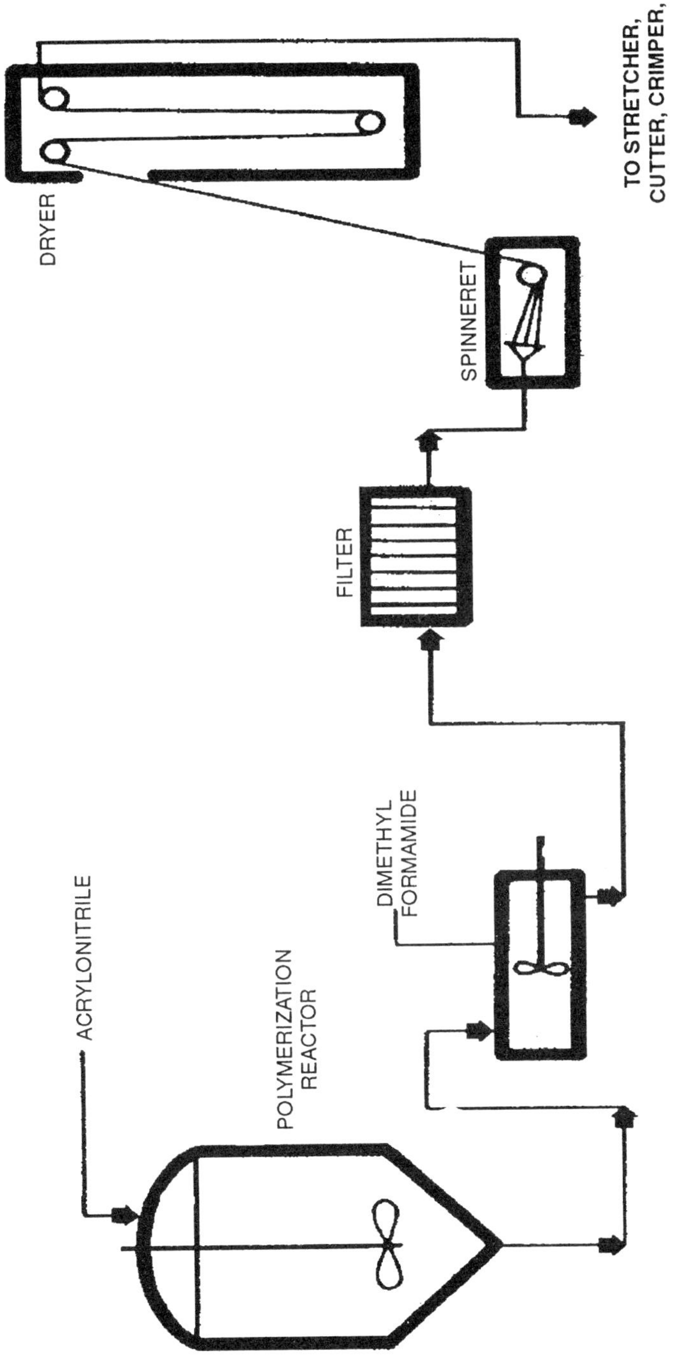

Fig.-5.3. Flow chart of the manufacturing process of Orlon acrylic fiber

Acrylonitrile may be made from acetylene or from ethylene both are petroleum derivatives. When the ethylene is treated with hypochlorous acid, a chlorohydrin is formed. The chlorohydrin is reacted with sodium hydroxide to form ethylene oxide. Hydrocyanic acid is added to the ethylene oxide,producing cyanoalcohol which is dehydrated to yield acrylonitrile. The acrylonitrile is then polymerized into poly acrylonitrile resin, a long-chain linear polymer. The polyacrylonitrile is dissolved in a suitable solvent, such as dimethylformamide and extruded through a spinneret. By adding a delusterant, such as the one used for nylon, Orlon is, made semidull. After coagulation, the filaments are oriented and stabilized by stretching.

Variations in the basic process that have been developed to meet specific needs change the fiber both in appearance and in certain properties

FORMS AND TYPES OF ORLON ACRYLIC YARNS

After orientation and stabilization, the Orlon filaments are shipped as tow or cut into staple lengths for spinning into yarn. The fibers are identified according to type and have particular characteristics suitable for particular purposes. These varieties provide Orlon fibers with considerable flexibility in application to serve numerous consumer uses.

Type 21 is designed for use in bulky knits and in hand-knitting yarns. It is a bicomponent acrylic fiber with a reversible, permanent crimp. The components, each having different shrinkage potential, are extruded together and adhere as one fiber. When treated with heat and moisture in later finishing processes, one component shrinks more than the other and causes a permanent random-spiral crimp. The crimp enhances the loft, bulk, and covering power of the yarn, giving it a warm, soft, pleasing hand. The elasticity and resilience of the yarn are also considerably increased while still retaining the inherent crease-retentive property of the fiber. The crimp may be described as reversible-that is, the fiber has the ability of decreasing its crimp, thus elongating the fiber when wet and recovering its spiral crimp when dry. This unique characteristic provides excellent retention of its built-in elasticity in knitted fabrics after repeated laundering.

Spun Yarn

The Orlon acrylic tow ranges from 2 to 10 denier (2.2-11.1 dtex). The tow is usually processed through the Pacific Converter, Seydel Stretch Breaker, the Turbo Stapler or through the Turbo Poly Breaker .The cut staple ranges from 1. 5 to 5 inches, depending on the type of yarn to be made. The staple is crimped and spun on a cotton or wool system into fuzzy yarns. The more twist in the yarn, the finer, smoother, and harder the yarn will be. The less twist in the yarn, the thicker and softer the yarn will be. Spun yarns of Orlon with a low twist have the hand of cashmere. Soft spun Orlon yarns, however, are fuzzy and have a tendency to pill, or form little balls on the fabric surface.

As indicated above, Orlon fibers are produced in a variety of homofil and bicomponent forms to serve particular objectives. The yarns produced from them may be sold under any one of several Du Pont certification marks of consurner serviceability appropriate to the use for which the yarn was made.

Ardina *is* the certification mark for group of coarse-count worsted spun yarns, made of 50 to 100 percent of Orlon Type 21 bicomponent fiber with reversible permanent crimp for bulk, that have the visual and textural appearances associate with high quality wool yarns for such out erwear as sweater coats and jackets, capes and accessories.

Civona *is* the certification mark for worsted spun yarns blended of 60 to 75 per cent of Orlon Type 21 bicomponent fibe with another Orlon acrylic fiber of fine denier to produce a yarn having super fine, Merino-like hand.

Sayelle *is* the certification mark for spun yarns of 100 percent Orlon 'Type 21 bi component fiber that has medium bulk.

Nomelle *is* the certification mark for spun yarn of 100 percent homofil Orlon Type 43 fiber that has a soft, luxurious cashmerelike hand.

Wintuk represents a variety of made from combinations of certain Orlon bicomponent and homofil fibers, that have loft and bounce with textures ranging from that of lamb's wool to mature shetland Wool.

Tri-Lustra *is* made of 100 percent fine diameter trilobal Orlon or of blends with fine wool, that has a soft sheen.

Vernille *is* made of either 100 percent Orlon or of Orlon blended with Dacroll polyester for velvety, chenille yarns.

High-Bulk Yarn

Orlon acrylic crimped staple may be spun into quite thick, soft, spongy yarns called high-bulk yarns. Such yarns produce warm, lightweight fabrics with a luxurious hand. Sometimes Orlon crimped staple may be blended with other fibers, resulting in greater stretch as well as high bulk in the yarn.

FINISHING FABRICS OF ORLON ACRYLIC

Several finishes can be given to Orlon fabrics to increase their usefulness. Among the most important are:

Name of Finish	Purpose
Antistatic finish	for reduction of electrostatic buildup
Heat setting	for permanent shape
Water repellency	for better protection against water

An outstanding feature of Orlon is that a fabric or garment made of it can be given a permanent shape by being subjected to a high degree of heat. If properly heat-set, the fabric will retain its shape as well as its creases or pleats. Nor will washing, dry cleaning, or wearing cause the garment to lose its shape.

Orlon is not a particularly absorbent textile. To make it less absobent, it may be treated with a water repellent, such as Syl-Mer or Zelan. This process makes the fabric suitable for such garments as rainwear.

EVALUATING FABRICS OF ORLON ACRYLIC

The properties of fabrics made of Orlon depend on the type of fiber used as well as how the material is woven, knitted, or finished. The several types of Orlon provide for flexibility in application due to differences in their properties. Therefore, fabric and garment performance should be evaluated in terms of these particular characteristics as well as general properties common to all Orlon acrylic fibers.

Strength. Orlon fiber is of moderate strength, but it is the weakest of the acrylic fibers. Compared with the natural fibers, it is weaker than all with the exception of wool. Since Orlon is used primarily as a replacement for wool, its greater strength is an advantage. The abrasion resistance of Orlon is good and compares favorably with that of wool.

Elasticity. Like the other acrylics, Orlon has little stretch. The low stretchability makes it useful for knitted wear, since it is not likely to stretch unduly. Most of the stretch that does exist is due to the mechanical crimp put into the fiber. The additional random-spiral crimp of some types of Orlon provides good extensibility without straining the fiber, thus providing freedom of movement without developing sag.

Resilience. Orlon fiber has very good resilience and therefore will not wrinkle easily. Fabrics of Orlon staple are not as lively in springing out from a creased position as polyester or wool, but they are still good in this respect. High resilience makes Orlon desirable for men's slacks and suits as well as for women's dresses.

Drapability. The drapability of Orlon varies with the type of fiber. Generally speaking, it provides satisfactory draping qualities .

Heat Conductivity. Like all acrylics, Orlon does not conduct heat rapidly; therefore, fabrics of Orlon can be warm. The fiber has a dog-bone cross section, which provides overlapping and bulk (with little weight). As a result, fabrics of Orlon staple have about 20 percent greater insulating power per ounce (28 g) of fiber than wool fabrics. Since an ounce of Orlon fabric is thicker than an ounce of wool fabric, it is possible to obtain an Orlon fabric that, while being as thick and as warm as wool, is about 20 percent lighter in weight. The warmth of the yarns can be increased by bulking through the use of special types of Orlon and by blending with the high-shrinkage type Orlon.

Absorbency. Orlon, like the other acrylics, has low absorbency. Nevertheless, fabrics made of Orlon staple will take on quite a bit of water on account of the staple's adsorbency: the tendency for water droplets to cling to the surface of the individual fibers. Since these water droplets get into the air spaces between the fibers and evaporate slowly, fabrics of Orlon spun yarn dry slowly, although not as slowly as wool fabrics.

This low adsorbency gives the fabric the advantage of resisting stains. Many substances that are ordinarily absorbed by other fibers merely remain on the surface of fabrics made of Orlon yarns and can be easily removed by wiping, washing, or dry cleaning.

Cleanliness and Washability. These fabrics do not soil or stain easily, and washing or dry cleaning quickly renews their freshness. A mild detergent should, however, be used in laundering since strong detergents will damage them. If desired, any ordinary cleaning fluid and household bleach may be safely used.

Soft, bulky Orlon yarns will pill. To reduce this tendency, such garments as sweaters should be laundered while turned inside out, with as little rubbing as possible. After rinsing through mild suds and then lukewarm water, squeeze out the water, turn the garment right side out, spread it on a towel, and gently brush it with a very soft brush while drying. The tendency of Orlon to pill is reduced when it is blended with most other fibers, Tightly spun yarns of Orlon will not pill readily because they are harder, smoother, and not too fuzzy.

Sweaters of some types of Orlon require special attention. They can be washed in a machine or by hand with equally satisfactory results. White sweaters should be washed with only white articles to avoid developing a dingy appearance caused by pickup of dye particles, colored sweaters can be laundered with other colored garments. Neither white nor colored sweaters should be washed in the same load with lint-shedding fabrics.. Sweaters trimmed with sequins or other delicate materials should be washed by hand and air-dried. Of course, such sweaters can also be dry-cleaned.

Effect of Bleaches. Fabrics of Orlon yarn may be safely bleached with any of the household bleaches.

Shrinkage. The discussion regarding the various types of Orlon fiber shows that some will shrink in processing and that this characteristic is utilized in obtaining desired effects, such as high-bulk yarns and pile fabrics. However, once the finished product reaches the consumer, it may be expected to have excellent dimensional stability since the Orlon fiber will have practically no further shrinkage.

Effect of Heat. Orlon fiber gets tacky at 455 degree F (235 degree C) which is slightly above that of nylon. At higher temperatures, it will melt.

Fabrics of Orlon should be ironed with a moderately warm iron; in fact, they may be ironed while dry. Old creases may be removed, and new ones added. Since fabrics of Orlon yarn may be heat set, it is often unnecessary to press them, but some ironing may be desired to smooth the cloth.

Effect of Light. Orlon has resistance to light. Its extreme resistance to such degradation makes it especially useful for fabrics that will be exposed to sunlight for an extended period of time.

Resistance to Mildew. Mildew may form on the surface, but it will have no effect on fabric of Orlon yarn. It may be easily wiped off.

Resistance to Insects. Orlon is unaffected by moths or their larvae or by carpet beetles.

Reaction to Alkalies. Orlon has fair-to good resistance to weak alkalies and to. strong alkalies at room temperature.

Reaction to Acids. Orlon has good-to excellent resistance to strong mineral acids as well as organic acids.

Affinity for Dyes. Some types of Orlon fibers are specific to acid dyes and some to basic dyes, which can provide interesting cross-dyed effects. Other types of Orlon can be dyed in a wide range of colors and hues with cationic, disperse, naphthol, and selected vat dyes. The colors have satisfactory fastness to washing and light.

Resistance to Perspiration. All indications are that fabrics of Orlon yarn are not readily deteriorated by perspiration, but the color may be affected.

ORLON ACRYLIC FIBER BLENDS

Orlon has many desirable properties that may be imparted to fabrics containing other fibers as well, depending on the relative amount of each fiber used.

Orlon Acrylic and Cotton

In combination with cotton, Orlon adds light weight and body. The cotton contributes strength and absorbency. The fabric is wrinkle-resistant, retains its shape well, and provides easy care. A blend of 80 percent or more of Orlon with cotton will provide the general characteristics of a wash-and-wear fabric, such as is used for sport shirts.

Orlon Acrylic and Wool

One of the outstanding characteristics of Orlon is its bulk, so that when the staple is blended with wool, the resulting fabric is lightweight and yet warm. It also has a soft hand but there may be some pilling. Fabrics of this combination have very good crease retention and wrinkle recovery. These blends are washable. Where there is a good proportion of Orlon, the fabrics seldom need pressing. A good blend for a wash and wear tailored garment should have 60 percent or more

Orlon with the wool, though too much acrylic makes the fabrics too bulky. Such a blend will also be stronger than an all wool fabric.

Orlon Acrylic and Silk

Orlon and silk provide interesting crossdyed and textured effects. Such blends have outstanding hand and excellent stability. In addition to the good appearance, the combination gives long wear. Orlon contributes easy-care qualities and shape retention; the silk contributes absorbency and strength. The fabric is very resilient and may be warm, depending on its weight.

Orlon Acrylic and Rayon

To the versatility of rayon, Orlon adds wrinkle resistance and stability. New and unusual surface and dye effects, including cross-dyes, are possible. It provides a dry, warm, and soft hand. A wash and wear blend should have at least 70 percent Orlon with the rayon.

Orlon acrylic blended with high wet modulus rayon provides a stronger fabric with the same general properties as that of a blend with regular rayon. A blend could therefore have a lower proportion of Orlon fiber.

Orlon Acrylic and Acetate

Orlon and acetate together in a fabric provide a soft, luxurious feel and excellent drapability. It also has excellent shape retention and good resilience. The fabric' launders easily with mild soap and warm water, dries rapidly, and is easy to iron. Orion provides greater resistance to sunlight. Neither Orlon nor acetate is particularly absorbent, which presents a disadvantage in warm, humid weather. Such blends will be warm and clammy.

Orlon Acrylic and Nylon

The strength and abrasion resistance of nylon combined with the luxurious hand and covering power of Orlon produce attractive, warm, strong fabrics. Similar qualities of Orlon and nylon, such as wrinkle resistance, crease retention, and easy care, are increased when these fibers are combined. Such fabrics will not be very absorbent.

Orlon Acrylic and Polyester

Orlon improves the hand of a fabric when combined with a polyester fiber, giving better body comfort and warmth. The polyester fiber contributes even greater wrinkle resistance, especially under humid conditions. A 50/50 blend will provide good wash and wear characteristics. Such a fabric will generally wear well because of the strength of the polyester fibers and the good abrasion resistance of Orlon; however, it is likely to pill if care is not exercised.

COMPARISON OF ACRYLIC FIBERS

The above table is a comparison between the main available acrylic fibresi.e. orlon , acrilan, creslan, zefran and is a summary composite based on information supplied by the producers of these fibers and on evaluations of the performance of the acrylic fibers.

COMPARISON OF PROPERTIES OF THE ACRYLIC FIBERS

PROPERTY	ORLON	ACRILAN	CRESLAN	ZEFRAN
Strenth	Fair	Fair	Fair to good	Good
Abrasion resistance	Fair	Fair to good	Fair	Good
Elasticity	Low; good extensibility for Sayelle	Low	Low	Low
Resilience	Very good	Very Good	Excellent	Excellent
Absorbency	Little	Little	Little	Little
Laundering care	Varies;requires care, use mild soap or detergent; may pill	Launders readily; some pilling may occur	Easy care with mild soap; relatively pill-resistant	Easy care with mild soap; fair resistance to pilling
Ironing temperature	Moderately warm	Moderately warm	Moderately warm	Moderately warm
Shrinkage	Virtually none	Virtually none	Virtually none	Virtually none
Household bleaches	All safe	All safe	Requires sodium, chlorite; some types have built-in whiteness	All safe

(Contd......Table) ***COMPARISON OF PROPERTIES OF THE ACRYLIC FIBERS***

PROPERTY	*ORLON*	*ACRILAN*	*CRESLAN*	*ZEFRAN*
Resistance to light	Good	Excellent	Excellent	Good
Resistance to mildew	wholly resistant	wholly resistant	Wholly resistant	Wholly resistant
Reaction to alkalies	Fair to good resistance to weak alkalies and to strong alkalies at room temperature	Fair to good resistance to weak alkalies, moderate resistance to cold strong solutions	Fair to good resistance to weak alkalines, moderate resistance to strong alkalies at room temperature	Dyeable : Good resistance to weak alkalies; pre-colored; fair resistance
Reaction to acids	Good to excellent	Good to excellent	Generally good ; tendency to bleach	Dyeable; generally good; precolored; excellent
Resistance to perspiration	Good	Good	Good	Good
Colorfastness	Good	Good; excellent for solution-dyed types	Good	Good; excellent to precolored

6 IDENTIFICATION OF TEXTILES

Ready recognition and identification of fiber content in fabrics has become extremely difficult even for knowledgeable and experienced merchants because of the growing variety of types of fibers, the blending techniques in yarn and fabric construction, and the finishes that affect the appearance and hand of the fabrics. Therefore, certain laboratory tests are used for identification and verification.

The consumer has the greatest handicap in identifying fiber content of fabrics. Should the identification and/or care labels be mutilated or lost from a textile product, one may not know the composition of the fabric and therefore not know what to expect of it. Because one is usually not in a position to make a laboratory analysis, reliance must be placed upon certain non technical tests.

THE NONTECHNICAL TESTS

There are several methods that do not require any special equipment for identifying textile fibers. Although these methods have certain limitations, they are useful because they are simple to perform and, under certain circumstances, provide ready identification.

Feeling Test

The feeling test requires perception if it is to be of any value. Skilled perception is acquired only after handling many different fabrics over a period of time. To understand what is meant by *feeling* a fabric, place your finger on a sample of wool. The heat generated by the finger remains in the area because wool is a nonconductor of heat. Consequently, wool fabric feels warm to the touch. If your finger is placed on a sample composed of the vegetable fibers-that is, cotton, linen, or even rayon-the heat of the finger passes off because such fibers are conductors of heat. These fabrics, therefore, feel cool to the touch. Limitations of this test become apparent when examining and comparing fabrics of different fiber contents.

Burning Test

To recognize the composition of fabrics by the burning test, the sample of fiber, yarn, or fabric should be moved slowly toward a small flame and the reaction to the heat carefully observed. One end of the sample should then be put directly into the flame to determine its burning rate and characteristics. After it is removed from the flame, the burning characteristics should continue to be observed and the burning odor noted. After the sample has cooled, the ash should be examined for characteristics such as amount,form, hardness, and color (see Table 1)

If both, the lengthwise and the crosswise yarns in a fabric are known to be of the same substance, the sample may be tested as a whole. More than one kind of yarn, however, is sometimes used in a fabric. When the presence of different yarns is suspected, the lengthwise yarns should be separated from the crosswise yarns and each set should be tested separately.

When it is believed that more than one fiber has been blended into a single yarn, the yarn should be untwisted and, with the aid of the magnifying glass and tweezers, the individual fibers separated. However, if biconstituent fibers are used, this is not possible.

One should also be alert to the possibility that finishing agents may have used on the fabrics. These finishes change the burning characteristics of sample.

Special varieties of manmade fibers have also been developed. They are flame retardant and therefore cannot be adequately tested for identification by burning.

Cotton. Cotton yarn blazes quickly when it comes in contact with the flame because the cellulose ingredient is highly flammable. The ash is light and feathery and has a vegetable odor similar to that of burned paper; mercerized cotton produces a black ash. Because cotton is highly flammable, do not use cotton where its proximity to flame becomes a fire hazard, unless it is treated with a fire retardant finish.

TABLE-1 : BURNING TEST

NATURAL FIBERS

Fiber	Approaching Flame	In Flame	Removed From Flame	Odor	Ash
COTTON	Scorches : ignites readily	Burns quickly yellow flame	Contunues to burn rapidly;	Buring paper	Light, feathery, grayish;black ash denotes mercerized cotton
LINEN	Scorches; ignites easily	Yellow flame burns slower than cotton if yarns are heavier	continues to burn	Burning paper	Feathery, gray ash
WOOL	Smolders	Small, slow flickering flame; sizzles and curls	Ceases flaming	Like burning feathers or hair	Crisp dark ash ; irregular shape; crushes easily
SILK (pure dye)	Smolders	Burns; melts slowly; sputters	Supports combustion with difficulty; ceases flaming	Like burning feathers or hair, but less pronounced than wool	Round, crisp, shiny black beads; easily crushed
SILK (weighted)	Smolders	Burns with a glow	Burned part becomes briefly incandescent; then chars	Like burning feathers or hair	Screenlike skeleton of original sample

TABLE-1 : BURNING TEST *(Continued)*

MANMADE

Fiber	Approaching Flame	In Flame	Removed From Flame	Odor	Ash
RAYONS Viscose High Wet-modulus	Scorches : ignites quickly	Burns quickly: yellow flame	Continues to burns; no after-glow	Burning paper	light, grey, feathery
ACETATE	Fuses away from flame; turns black	Flames quckly; fabric puckers, sputters, melts, drips like burning tar	Continues to burn and melt	Like vinegar	Brittle, hard, irregular black ash, difficult to crush

MANMADE FIBERS

Fiber	Approaching Flame	In Flame	Removed From Flame	Odor	Ash
TRIAC-ETATE	Fuses away from flame; turns black	Flames quickly; fabric, puckers, sputters, melts, drips like burning tar	Continues to burn and melt	Like vinegar	Brittle, hard, irregular black ash, difficult to crush
NYLON	Fuses and shrinks away from flame	Burns slowly with melting	Flame diminishes and tends to die out	Some what pungent	Hard, round tough, gray bead
ARAMID Nomex	Shrinks away from flame	Puckers and chars over 700°F (371°C)	Self-extinguishing`	None	Hard, black bead

TABLE-1 : BURNING TEST *(Continued)*

MANMADE

Fiber	Approaching Flame	In Flame	Removed From Flame	Odor	Ash
POLY-ESTERS	Fuses and shrinks away from flame	Burns slowly with melting	Burns with difficulty	Slightly sweetish	Hard, round brittle, black bead
ACRYLICS Orion	Fuses and shrinks away from flame	Flames rapidly; fabric puckers, sputters, melts	Continues to burn and melt	Faintly like burning meat	Brittle, hard, irregular, black bead
Acrilan	Fuses and shrinks away from flame	Flames rapidly and melts	Continues to burns and melt	Burning steak	Brittle, hard, irregular, black bead
Creslan	Fuses and shrinks away from flame	Flames and melts	Continues to burns and melt	Sharp sweet	Brittle, hard, irregular, black bead
Zefran	Fuses and melts	Sputters slightly; flames	Continues to burn and melt	Turmeric-like	irregular black ash that crushes easily
MOD-ACRYLICS Verel	Fuses and shrinks away from flame	Burns very, slowly with melting	Self-extinguishing	Shapr, similar to burning gunpowder	Brittle, hard, irregular, black bead
SEF	Fuses and shrinks away from flame	Burns very, slowly with melting	Self-extinguishing	Sharp sweet	Hard, irregular black bead
SPANDEX	Fuses but does not shrink away from flame	Burns with melting	Continues to burn with melting	Acrid	Soft, fluffy, black

Linen. Linen, when burned, produces an ash similar to cotton ash because both fabrics are of vegetable substance. Linen ash is also light and feathery and has the odor of burned paper. Although linen fabric burns somewhat more slowly than cotton because linen yarns are usually heavier, the pace of burning is not sufficiently different to aid in distinguishing linen from cotton.

Wool. Wool is slow to ignite, burns with a characteristic small, flickering flame, sizzles, and curls.Itcan be extinguished easily, as the fabric ceases flaming when the fire is withdrawn. Wool ash is dark and crisp, and it falls into an irregular shape that can be crushed easily. The ash has a strong animal odor resembling burning feathers or hair, which indicates the presence of an animal substance or of a fiber obtained from an animal. The characteristic odor of burned wool is due to the sulfur in it.

Silk. Pure silk also burns slowly and ceases flaming when the fire is withdrawn The ash of silk appears in the form of round, crisp, shiny black beads that, like the ash of wool, can be crushed easily with the fingers. The ash has an animal odor less pronounced than that of wool, as silk does not contain sulfur.

In manufacturing, additional body is given to silk fabrics by weighting them with metallic fillers. Weighted silk burns without showing a visible flame. The burned part becomes incandescent; it chars and gradually smolders away, leaving a coherent ash that is a screenlike skeleton of the original fabric. The odor of the ash of weighted silk is similar to that of pure silk.

Rayons. Like cotton, the rayons Ignite quickly unless they either are fire-retardant types or are given a fire-retardant finish. They burn with a bright yellow flame, sometimes more rapidly than cotton because rayons are essentially purified cellulose. The odor of burning viscose and high wet-modulus rayons is like that of burning paper, also a cellulose product. The ash disintegrates unless the fiber has been chemically dulled.

Acetate. Acetate blazes as it burns. The edge of the fabric puckers and curls as the material fuses and melts into a hard mass .Acetate sputters and drips like tar. The ash of acetate is hard and brittle, and is difficult to crush between the fingers. Because of the acetic acid used in the manufacture of acetate, the ash has an acid odor similar to that of vinegar.

Triacetate. Triacetate is similar to acetate in both its chemical composition and its reaction to heat and flame. It flames quickly and then melts into a hard mass. As triacetate burns, it drips like burning tar. The ash is hard and brittle and has an acid odor like that of vinegar.

Nylon. Nylon melts before it burns. As it burns, it shrinks from the flame and forms a hard, round bead that cannot be crushed between the fingers. While burning, it has a pungent odor.

Aramid. The aramid fibers are highly flame-resistant. At temperatures above 700degree F (371degree C) Nomex, for example, shrinks away from the flame. It puckers and chars but will self-extinguish when the flame is removed. The residue is hard.

Polyesters. The polyesters fuse and shrink from the flame. They melt and burn slowly in the flame; when they are removed, they burn with difficulty. Kodel produces a slight soot. Dacron has a slightly sweetish odor; Kodel smells faintly like burning pine tar. The ashes of polyesters are hard, round, black, and beady.

Acrylics. The acrylic fibers Orlon, Acrilan, and Creslan melt, shrink away from the flame, fuse, and burn leaving a brittle, black, irregular-shaped bead. Their rate of burning is between that of cotton and acetate. Orlon gives off an odor that faintly resembles burning flesh; Acrilan smells a little stronger, like burning steak; Creslan has a sharp, sweet odor. Zefran flames rapidly and sputters slightly. The edges Curl as the fabric blazes, leaving a black ash that can be crushed easily between the fingers. The odor is somewhat like the herb turmeric.

Modacrylics. The modacrylic fibers, Verel and SEF, will not support combustion and do not flame. They melt, shrink away from the flame, and harden into a brittle ash. Verel has a sharp odor similar to that of burning gunpowder.

Spandex. Spandex yarns are usually combined with yarns of other fibers or may be encased in a layer of other fibers. In both instances, the spandex fiber must be separated. Spandex fibers melt, fuse, and burn without shrinking away from the flame; they leave a soft, fluffy, black ash and give off an acrid odor.

Olefins. The olefins that are polypropylene also shrink, fuse, and curl away from the flame. They melt and burn slowly, giving off an odor that faintly resembles burning asphalt. They have a hard, round, light tan bead.

Glass. Glass fiber does not burn; it melts, however, at temperatures above 1500 degree F (815 degree C).

Metal. Metallic fibers do not burn. However, the film that covers the metal will melt and burn with an odor characteristic of the burning film, which may be of acetate or polyester. The residue from this film will be a brittle, beady ash.

Rubber. Rubber fiber is usually covered with another fiber that must be removed for this test. Rubber melts, shrivels away from the flame, and is self-extinguishing. It leaves a hard, irregular ash and a very disagreeable pungent odor.

imitation of Burning Test. It is apparent that many fibers have similar burning reactions that might cause doubt and occasional confusion. Nevertheless, the burning test provides a means of preliminary examination and elimination. It will separate and identify certain types or groups of fibers for technical testing when this is necessary.

THE TECHNICAL TESTS

Where laboratory equipment is available, much more reliable testing techniques may be employed. However, these require technical knowledge and skill, particularly in handling many chemicals.

Microscope Test

Identification by microscope with a magnification of at least 100 power is a reliable test that can be used to distinguish the fibers. This is particularly true of natural fibers. Manmade fibers are sometimes more difficult to identify because some are very similar in appearance, and variants can complicate matters further. Knowing what the fibers look like under the microscope will also help you understand other identification tests. Certain manufacturing and finishing processes, such as mercerizing and delustering, affect the appearance of a fiber under the microscope. Besides, a very dark-colored fabric cannot be identified under the microscope because light which is necessary for identification cannot pass through a dark substance. The dyestuff must be removed, or stripped, by the use of a bleach , which is determined by the suspected composition of the fabric. When stripping is essential and there is considerable doubt as to the composition of the fabric, chemical tests are advisable. Each of the natural fibers has its own distinctive structural shape and markings that facilitate the identification of the fiber.

Chemical Tests

In addition to the microscope, chemical tests are another technical means of identifying fibers. But chemical tests are not intended for the general consumer. Their value is demonstrated, however, by the fact that some consumer magazines and commercial firms have their own laboratories for testing fabrics.

There are two chemical testing methods that may effectively be used: stain and solvent.. Every commonly known fiber has its own distinct two-color reactions when treated with the stain. A fiber stained at the boil in the presence of dilute acetic acid will turn to a color specific only to that fiber; when that fiber is stained in the presence of a mild alkali, such as carbonate of soda, that fiber will turn to an entirely different color that is also specific only to that fiber. This double testing technique is the reason for the designation *double-barreled* stain identification. Examples of this identification include the following: acetate turns light green in acetic acid, but orange in dilute carbonate of soda; nylon stains beige in one bath, bright red in the other.

The solvent method of identification has become increasingly difficult as fibers that are chemically similar have been developed and more fibers are blended and mixed in fabrics. There is no individual solvent or chemical identification for each fiber and no single solvent procedure for separating and identifying fibers in combinations. However, testing by solvents is very effective when it is used for eliminating or cross-checking.

In order to obtain accurate results, the fabrics to be tested should be thoroughly cleaned and finishing agents should be removed. The fabric should be unraveled, yarns untwisted, and the fibers put in as loose. a form as possible.

Distinguishing Animal from Vegetable Fibers with an Alkali. As strong alkalies destroy animal substances, a 5 percent solution of lye in water (1/2 teaspoon of lye in a glass of water or 5 milliliters [ml] in 100 ml) can be used to eliminate wool and silk fibers from a sample that contains a mixture of fibers. The action of this chemical (also known as sodium hydroxide) is hastened by boiling the solution before the sampic is immersed. The wool and silk fibers will be completely dissolved. The vegetable fibers will not be affected; therefore, another test is necessary to identify those fibers.

Distinguishing Vegetable from Animal Fibers with an Acid. As dilute acids destroy vegetable fibers, a 2 percent solution of sulphuric acid may be used to distinguish vegetable from animal fibers. A drop of the solution is placed on a sample of the fabric, which is then placed between two blotters and pressed with a hot iron. The spotted area will become charred if the fabric is cotton, linen, or rayon.

Distinguishing Linen from Cotton. Before any chemical test is made to distinguish linen from cotton, all surface dressings should be removed from the samples by boiling them for a few minutes in a solution of dilute sodium hydroxide, about 1/2 percent. Then any of the following tests can be made:

Immersing cotton and linen samples in a 1 percent solution of fuchsin in alcohol produces a rose'-red color in both samples. After the samples have been washed and then immersed in ammonia, linen retains the red coloration, but cotton does not. This test is sometimes made with a 1 percent solution of magenta, a red dyestuff.

Cotton fibers are weakened more than linen fibers if samples are immersed in concentrated sulpuric acid for two minutes. After the samples are rinsed and immersed in weak ammonia, the cotton fibers dissolve, leaving the linen fibers unaffected.

When cotton and linen samples are immersed in a solution of iodine and zinc chloride, cotton is stained reddish purple and linen is stained blue to purple.

When samples are immersed in a caustic soda solution, cotton remains white and linen turns yellowish.

Distinguishing Silk from Wool. If the fibers in a sample are known to consist of silk and wool, and identification of each is desired, the use of concentrated cold hydrochloric acid will dissolve the silk and cause the wool fiber to swell.

Distinguishing Rayons from Acetate. A solution containing equal parts of concentrated sulphuric acid and iodine (crystals) may be used to distinguish each of the different fibers. When samples are immersed in this solution, a dark-blue coloration indicates viscose; a yellow coloration indicates acetate. Another test to distinguish acetate from rayon, when both types are known to be used in a fabric, is to immerse the sample in a 50 percent solution of acetic acid. The acetate dissolves; the rayons are not affected. All rayons will dissolve in a 60 percent solution of sulphuric acid or a concentrated solution of hydrochloric acid.

Distinguishing Acetate from Other Fibers. If a sample of acetate is immersed in an 80 percent solution of acetone (a chemical used in nail polish removers), the acetate fibers will dissolve but triacetate and Verel modacrylic will swell.

Distinguishing Triacetate from Other Fibers. When a specimen of fabric or a blend of fibers is immersed at room temperature for one hour in a mixture of 90 percent methylene chloride and 10 percent ethanol (or methanol), triacetate and acetate will dissolve, but other commonly used fibers will be virtually unaffected. Triacetate can be differentiated from acetate by immersing a sample of fabric or fibers in benzyl alcohol at 200 degree F (930 degree C) for one hour. Triacetate is virtually unaffected, but the acetate completely dissolves.

Distinguishing Nylon from Other Fibers. Nylon can be distinguished from acetate by attempting to dissolve it in acetone. Nylon will not dissolve in acetone. If the yarn or fabric is thought to contain wool and/or nylon, the fabric may be immersed in a boiling solution of sodium hydroxide. The nylon is insoluble in such a solution, but wool will dissolve. In fact, nylon's insolubility in boiling sodium hydroxide makes it easily distinguishable from most other fibers, The only common solvents in which nylon is soluble are concentrated formic acid, phenol, and cresol.

Distinguishing Polyester from Other Fibers. Like acetate and nylon, polyester is soluble in hot metacresol; however, unlike acetate it is not soluble in acetone, and unlike nylon it is not soluble in concentrated formic acid.

Distinguishing Acrylics from Other Fibers. Acrylic is often blended with cotton, wool, silk, rayon, acetate, nylon, and polyester. Even when not blended, acrylic may be mistaken for some of these fibers. Since acrylic fibers will dissolve in a 70 percent solution of ammonium thiocyanate at 266 degree F (130degree C) at the boil but the other fibers will not, this test may be used.

Distinguishing Modacrylics from Other Fibers. Although a modacrylic is often used alone, it may be blended with other fibers. It is easily distinguishable, however, from other fibers by chemical tests. It is highly resistant to a wide variety of inorganic acids, bases, salts, hydrocarbons,and most organic solvents.

Distinguishing Spandex from Fibers. The characteristics and appearence of spandex fibers should make them readily identifiable. However, there is sometimes some confusion with the stretch yarns, including those made from rubber. In this case, a test for spandex fiber is to heat the specimen in dimethylformamide. Spandex fiber will dissolve in the solution at 200 degree F (93 degree C).

Distinguishing Olefins from Other Fibers. Olefin fibers are soluble in metaxylene at 282degree F (139 degree C) at the boil.